PORTRAITS
Edward Shils

EDWARD SHILS

PORTRAITS
A GALLERY OF INTELLECTUALS

Edited and with an introduction by

JOSEPH EPSTEIN

THE UNIVERSITY OF CHICAGO PRESS   *Chicago & London*

EDWARD SHILS, who died in 1995, was professor of sociology and social thought at the University of Chicago, honorary fellow of Peterhouse, Cambridge, and editor of *Minerva: A Review of Science, Learning, and Policy.* Joseph Epstein is the editor of the *American Scholar.*

The University of Chicago Press, Chicago 60637
The University of Chicago Press, Ltd., London
© 1997 by The University of Chicago
All rights reserved. Published 1997
Printed in the United States of America
06 05 04 03 02 01 00 99 98 97   1 2 3 4 5

ISBN: 0-226-75336-0 (cloth)
ISBN: 0-226-75337-9 (paper)

Library of Congress Cataloging-in-Publication Data

Shils, Edward Albert, 1911–
    Portraits : a gallery of intellectuals / Edward Shils ; edited and with an introduction by Joseph Epstein.
        p.   cm.
    ISBN 0-226-75336-0 (alk. paper).—ISBN 0-226-75337-9 (pbk. : alk. paper)
        1. Intellectuals—United States—Biography.   2. Scholars—United States—Biography.   3. United States—Intellectual life—20th century.   I. Epstein, Joseph, 1937– . II. Title.
    CT3990.A2S55   1997
    920.073—dc20   96-33162
                                                            CIP

⊚ The paper used in this publication meets the minimum requirements of the American National Standard for Information Sciences—Permanence of Paper for Printed Library Materials, ANSI Z39.48-1984.

CONTENTS

MY FRIEND EDWARD

Joseph Epstein

"DO YOU KNOW any intelligent people in this city?" Saul Bellow asked me one night in 1973, not long after I had met him. Before I could reply, he said, answering his own question, "I know three: Harold Rosenberg, David Grene, and Edward Shils."

All three men, along with Bellow himself, were then members of the Committee on Social Thought at the University of Chicago. Harold Rosenberg, then also the art critic for *The New Yorker*, invented the useful phrase "a herd of independent minds." David Grene, who has a reputation for being a spirited teacher, is the translator of Herodotus and the great Athenian playwrights. I didn't know much about Edward Shils—although I had read his essays in *Encounter*—except that he was a social scientist, and, when I was an undergraduate at the University of Chicago, he was known for being a very formidable figure, distinctly not a man to fool with. I only subsequently learned that he had had the decisive hand in designing what for me were the best courses I had taken at that school, the courses in the College called Social Science II and History. I was, then, already in debt to Edward Shils without knowing it. Over the following years, from 1973 until his death on January 23, 1995, this debt would grow beyond reckoning.

Perhaps because his prose was chaste, even severe, I pictured Edward Shils as tall, slender, a bit gaunt. I couldn't have been more wrong. When Saul Bellow showed up at my apartment with Edward one night, I discovered a man of five foot eight, portly (though with no flabbiness or anything soft about him), a paucity of rather wispy grayish hair, and the florid coloring that suggested the potential pugnacity of a former redhead. He carried, but didn't really use, a walking stick, and he wore a tweedy getup of various shades of brown with a green wool tie and an Irish hat. I took him, correctly, to be a man of good taste for whom personal vanity had a low priority. I watched his eyes roam across my living room, checking the books in my glassed-in bookcases, the prints on my walls, the plants on my windowsills. Clearly, he was, as Henry James says one must always try to be, a man on whom nothing was lost.

We dined at a Korean restaurant on Clark Street, and Edward interrogated me, calling me Mr. Epstein. He wanted to know what I was writing and for whom. He asked what I was teaching (I had begun to teach at Northwestern University that year). He inquired about what I happened to be reading at the moment. When I told him that I was reading Alison Lurie's novel *The War Between the Tates*, he tersely replied, "A book, I take it, about academic screwing." I wouldn't have thought to formulate it quite that way, but of course that is exactly what the book is about. He obviously hadn't read it, but somewhere along the way he had read another Alison Lurie novel, and, such was his ability to extrapolate, he didn't need to read any more of them. Later in the evening I described someone as a political scientist. "With the scientist understood," he inserted, before deftly conveying a bit of pork and rice to his mouth on his chopsticks, "as in Christian Scientist."

I met Edward Shils around the time that his and Saul Bellow's friendship was under great, and complicated, strain, and, for a while, I found myself in the middle, friends to them both. They had been quite close—Bellow's biographer James Atlas has told me that Edward made substantial editorial suggestions that much improved *Mr. Sammler's Planet,* my own favorite among Bellow's novels. The morning after Bellow introduced us, I told him over the phone how remarkable I found Edward. Bellow replied that Edward was his "alter super-ego." Edward would have preferred the word *conscience,* for when I knew him he never took Freud all that seriously. I subsequently learned that he performed the function of conscience for a number of people—many students along with some professors—and indeed for entire institutions. It is an invaluable service, but not one that everybody finds congenial or that pays handsome dividends to the person willing to take it up. As Saul Bellow and Edward pulled further apart, Edward and I became closer. For me, this was an immense piece of good fortune. My friendship with Edward, it didn't take me long to realize, was to be the crucial intellectual event of my life. Although by the time I had met him I was thirty-six years old—he was then sixty-three—and had already published a book and perhaps sixty or seventy articles and reviews in magazines, not long after meeting him my writing began to change; it could scarcely have been otherwise, for so, under the influence of Edward's presence, had my view of the world. He had released something in me that made life seem richer and writing about it consequently more joyous. As a writer, I began to see the world as simultaneously more complex and more amusing; to feel a fine surge in confidence; to be concerned scarcely at all about anyone's good opinion—except Edward's.

A small number of people called him Ed, but it was generally a mistake to do so. He himself did not go to first names easily, and to diminutives never. I was always Joseph to him, he Edward to me. I am not sure how I was able to break through to address him by his first name, or why he early chose to call me by mine, though I am glad that this happened. He had students, acquaintances, really quite dear friends of several decades whom he continued to call Mr. or Mrs. or Miss; they usually called him Professor Shils. It was part of his formality; and Edward's formality was a reminder that the word *formality* has its root in the word *formidable.*

Edward never went out of the house without a suit or sport coat, necktie, hat, and walking stick. (The ones he carried were thick and dark, knotty and gnarled, sturdy not elegant appurtenances.) He spoke with a mid-Atlantic accent—he had been teaching half the year in England, first at the London School of Economics, then at Cambridge, since just after World War II—often with a pronunciation system of his own devising. For example, a columnist in Chicago named Kupcinet, who pronounces his name exactly as it is spelled, Edward always called Kupchinesque. When

I told him that the man himself pronounced it *cup-si-net*, Edward said that it was a Hungarian name and that the columnist, ignorant fellow, simply didn't know how to pronounce his own name. Kupchinesque, in our conversation, it remained.

As someone known as his friend, I was often asked the most rudimentary questions about Edward. Is he English? people would ask. Is he Jewish? When the man who wrote Edward's obituary for the *Times* of London, a Cambridge don who I believe knew Edward longer than I, called me for information, he said: "He came from railroad money, didn't he?" Railroad money! Edward would have had a good chortle about that.

Edward's parents were Eastern European Jewish immigrants who settled first in Springfield, Massachusetts, then in Philadelphia, where Edward, the younger of two sons, grew up roaming the streets and reading his way through the public library. Edward's father was a cigar maker—Samuel Gompers, the first president of the American Federation of Labor, was head of the cigar makers' union. Edward looked like his mother, who, though her schooling had been limited, was a serious reader, especially of Russian and European novels. The Judaic element in the household could not have been strong; fetching oysters home for dinner was one of Edward's delightful memories of a Philadelphia boyhood.

He spoke Yiddish, which he loved for its subtlety and philosophical and comical possibilities. He added to my own Yiddish vocabulary, bringing to it words that I now find myself using with great frequency, among them *hegdisch* (for serious mess), *tiness* (for grievance), *cacapitze* (for altogether trivial stuff). Sometimes he would speak in Yiddish aphorisms; sometimes he would insert the ornately precise—and often quite new to me—word.

"Joseph," he said, pointing to three thuggish-looking youths standing on the opposite corner as we emerged one gray winter afternoon from Bishop's chili parlor on Chicago's light-industrial near West Side, "note those three *schlumgazim*."

"I'm afraid I need a subtitle for that word, Edward," I said.

"*Schlumgazim*," he readily replied, "are highwaymen who, after stealing your purse, out of sheer malice also slice off your testicles."

Edward honored his Jewishness without observing it. In the

same way, he loved America, with all its philistinism and coarseness, and he once cited it to me, approvingly, as "the country of the second chance." He reveled in the country's ethnic variety, its inventiveness, its mad energy. He loved the sort of American who could build his own house. He admired Americans when they showed they would not be buffaloed by ideas put into play by academics or intellectuals (he was himself, in many of his writings, the world's leading observer of intellectuals, in both their strengths and foibles). He knew how vast our country is, how full of surprises: that it contains people hipped on grammar from Tyler, Texas, people who read through the Loeb Classics in Santa Rosa, California, and people in other unlikely places who demonstrate heroism, a winning bullheadedness, or radical common sense.

I bring up Edward's love of America because he did not seem particularly American—in fact, as he once told me, he had deliberately set out to make himself European. He had done this, my guess is, early in life, out of his regard for the older, denser culture of Europe. At the University of Pennsylvania, where he was an undergraduate, he majored in French literature. The German social theorists—Georg Simmel, Ferdinand Tönnies, and above all Max Weber—later imbued him with a love for Continental thought and for the German language.

Not long before he died, Edward suggested that I take six months off to live in France, where I might improve my own French accent. It seemed a strange suggestion to make to a man in his late fifties who was juggling three jobs (teaching, writing, and editing). Only later did Edward make plain that behind the suggestion was his wish for me to internationalize myself—as he had internationalized himself.

His success in this endeavor, I should say, was complete. His reading, his diet, his manner of dress, much of his thought had become thoroughly Europeanized. But he had become a European of the kind that, as T. S. Eliot said, Henry James had become: a man, that is, of European spirit who belonged to no particular European country. Edward accomplished what Henry James did not—nor did T. S. Eliot, who turned himself into an Englishman—which was to keep the American in himself altogether alive. What was especially impressive about Edward was that he commanded deep, even intimate knowledge of several national cultures without ever losing touch with his own.

In almost every country in Europe, Edward had a wide acquaintanceship and a few close friendships: Franco Venturi and Arnaldo Momigliano in Italy, Raymond Aron and others in France, innumerable scholars in Germany, practically everyone of intellectual importance in England from R. H. Tawney through Audrey Richards to H. R. Trevor-Roper. (Had he taken up permanent residence in England and become a citizen, he would, I suspect, long ago have been Sir Edward.) In the last seven or eight years of his life, Edward attended conferences at Castel Gandolfo, the summer residence of the Pope. Edward much admired the Pope for his intelligence and character, and there is reason to believe that his admiration was reciprocated, my guess is on the selfsame grounds.

Early in our friendship, and long before he began attending the conferences at Castel Gandolfo, Edward reported a dream to me that he had had the night before. In the dream he had been made a cardinal. It was quite wonderful, he said. He wore the red hat and robes of a cardinal, and he was permitted to roam the inner recesses of the Vatican, searching its archives in complete freedom. "And you know, Joseph," he said, "no one asked that I believe any of the Church's doctrine." He paused, then added, "Jacques Maritain arranged the whole thing."

Edward lived in India for an extended period between 1956 and 1957, and he visited the country every year thereafter until 1967. It was Edward who introduced me to the splendid books of Nirad C. Chaudhuri (author of *The Autobiography of an Unknown Indian* and other works) and to the novels of R. K. Narayan. Narayan mentions Edward more than once in his book about America, and, on the only occasion we met, gentle man that he is, Narayan's eyes glowed with pleasure when I told him I was a friend of Edward Shils. Owing to his curiosity and imagination, Edward was able to become not merely immensely knowledgeable about but quite at home in any culture.

Although Edward earned his living as a social scientist, he had read more literature than I, a literary man, ever expect to read. I never mentioned a writer, no matter how minor, whose work he had not read and whose measure he had not taken. He was a great reader of novels. He read Dickens over and over again. He regularly re-read Balzac. He adored Willa Cather. We once had a swell talk about who was smarter, Proust or James. Our conclusion was that James was deeper but that, in seeking out a restaurant or anything touching on practical matters, Proust would have been the more valuable man. Edward was much taken with George Eliot and thought her particularly fine on the Jewish family in *Daniel Deronda*. Shakespeare he felt was simply beyond discussion—and so we never discussed him. He taught a course on T. S. Eliot and was very respectful of his ideas about tradition, a subject to which, in his own writings, Edward was delicately attuned. Above all novelists, he admired, I believe, Joseph Conrad. He was impressed not alone with the great Pole's penetration but with his theme of fidelity. Fidelity, in the Conradian sense of duty before all else, was the ideal by which Edward himself tried to live. He owned Jacob Epstein's powerful bust of Joseph Conrad and kept it, along with a bust of Max Weber, in the living room of his Chicago apartment.

Edward's reading of the great writers of all languages was part of his grounding and his greatness as a social scientist. If Freud said he learned all he knew from poets, so perhaps ought social scientists to learn from novelists, though I suspect very few modern social scientists do. (Edward, his former student, the distinguished Israeli sociologist S. N. Eisenstadt recently told me, came to social science through literature, not the other way round.) He also felt it his duty to stay *au courant* with contemporary culture, however empty and irritating he found much of it. Edward did not own a television set and never turned on his radio. (In an essay for *The American Scholar*, he once referred to the latter as "the wireless," a word I persuaded him to change.) During the years I knew him, he went only rarely to the movies, though he had gone much more when he was younger. As a boy he had been a baseball fan, and he had a complete knowledge of the sport up to the year 1930, when he lost interest.

Edward kept in touch with contemporary culture by reading the *New York Times*—whose ideological waffling never ceased either to inflame or to amuse him—and the large number of magazines that I saved for him. As I would drag a plastic supermarket bag or two filled with these magazines into his apartment, he could be depended on to say something on the order of: "Joseph, you are my dear friend, and it is always a great pleasure to see you, but when I look upon these wretched magazines you bring along, I realize that even the best of friendships has its cost." Once the catalogue of a southern university press was atop these magazines. "Oh, good," he said, "filled, I am sure, with announcements of biographies of Shoeless Jim Hopkins and other great southern politicians."

I was regularly astonished at how much Edward was able to get out of the magazines I brought him. Some magazines he read just to keep himself abreast, as he said, of what the dogs were up to. He enjoyed my referring to the *Chronicle of Higher Education*, a dreary journal that reports on university life, as *Pravda*, by which I meant that, like the Russian paper under the Communists, everything, to hear the *Chronicle* tell it, was going just splendidly. Edward was too sensible to read much of what I brought him all the way through. But by efficient skimming, gleaning, reading first and last paragraphs, he always caught the chief point and quickly penetrated through the smoke of intellectual obfuscation to find the deep illogic or empty complaint at the heart of the writer's composition.

As a scholar and social philosopher, Edward taught Hegel and Hobbes, Tocqueville and Weber, and he wrote papers on nationalism and civil society, on the primordial and the traditional. But as an intellectual he was interested in the popularization of ideas. Although he didn't write often for the intellectual magazines, except for *The American Scholar* and in earlier years for *Encounter*, he liked to keep a hand in. He always knew who the passing figures were, and he was able astutely to gauge their quality. Of Camille Paglia, for example, he commented, "She is more intelligent than her beliefs." Not long after I first met Edward, he called Christopher Lasch "a good graduate student whose unconcentrated anger would never allow him to become much more than that." By way of placing someone at his own university, he said, "I fear he believes Richard Rorty is a deep thinker." I once heard him upbraid his son for taking a course at Northwestern University in which one of the books on the syllabus was David

Halberstam's *The Best and the Brightest*. "That," said Edward, "is a book one reads in an airport." Hannah Arendt, Allan Bloom, Susan Sontag, the Frankfurt School, the New York intellectuals, Michel Foucault—in the matter of contemporary intellectuals and academic savants, Edward knew whom *not* to get excited about. He could be deadly in his deflationary remarks. I enjoyed these stiletto thrusts greatly, not only because they were done with great economy and insight—of a troublemaking don at Cambridge, he once said to me that his speciality was inserting bullets in other men's guns—but because they had superior perspective behind them. The three large intellectual influences on his own life were the economist Frank Knight and the sociologist Robert Park, both of whom he encountered as a young man at the University of Chicago, and Max Weber, against whose work, I believe, Edward measured his own writing. Good though he knew it was, he nonetheless found, by this measure, his own writing wanting.

Among contemporary writers and scholars, Edward much admired V. S. Naipaul, Arnaldo Momigliano, Philip Larkin, Peter Brown, Owen Chadwick, Franco Venturi, Barbara Pym, E. H. Gombrich, and Elie Kedourie. He greatly respected Aleksandr Solzhenitsyn, Sidney Hook, and Hilton Kramer for their tenacity in doing battle with liars. He was death on intellectual fraudulence. But he attacked it less through his writings, which are not notable for personal attack, than in conversation. About a famous, still-living American sociologist who in his style and manner made pretense to being upper-class, Edward once remarked to me: "I'll say this about X. At least he never takes undue advantage of being Jewish." He one day told me that a New York intellectual had announced to him that, in Israeli politics, he was of the war party. "Yes," said Edward, with a nod and the peculiar set he could give to his jaw. "Israel will go to war and he'll go to the party."

Edward not only spoke his mind but could be very confrontational. At a dinner party, I once introduced him to the English journalist Henry Fairlie. "Mr. Fairlie, good to meet you," Edward said. "You wrote some brilliant things in the 1950s. [It was then, I should explain, the late 1970s.] Now, I understand you have become a socialist. Please explain yourself." Fairlie said that what had brought about his conversion was hearing Michael Harrington lecture in Chicago. "Michael Harrington in Chicago," said Edward, without smile or pause, "surely a case of worst comes to worst." Fairlie, pretty well lubricated by alcohol, went off, feeling no pain.

Edward could also be immensely courteous, holding back his true opinions, when he was fond of people in whose company he found himself. But in other surroundings he would say precisely what he thought. Since he held no received opinions whatsoever, this could often be dangerous. Someone at a party might express admiration for a particular novelist, which might cause Edward to ask that person—a married man or woman—if he or she then approved of adultery, since the novelist in question clearly did. Many of the icons of our day never came close to finding a place in his pantheon. He believed I. F. Stone's Stalinism shouldn't have been so quickly forgotten. He didn't consider Isaiah Berlin great, but merely charming, a man who often wanted courage because he was intellectually hostage to certain Oxford dons. The only contemporary American social scientists he spoke about with respect were James Q. Wilson and Edward Banfield, who he thought had retained the fundamental common sense that contemporary social science seemed able to remove from most of its adherents. Such outspokenness made Edward many enemies, for his wittily wounding darts not only hit but frequently got back to their targets.

Edward founded, and for more than twenty-five years edited, the magazine *Minerva,* a review devoted to science, higher education, and policy. (He was also, along with his friend Leo Szilard, one of the founders of the *Bulletin of the Atomic Scientists.*) To say Edward edited *Minerva* is, however, to indulge in euphemism. He really wrote most of it, often under the names of living contributors, for his own high standards forced him into heavily editing if not actually rewriting the manuscripts he had accepted for publication.

I have seen some of his letters to *Minerva* contributors. One—which I do not have before me—was to a young left-wing woman in Canada, to whom Edward wrote that he was much impressed with the research in the article she had sent him. Then he added (I am paraphrasing from memory): "It is only the opinions

expressed in the article that I despise. If you would agree to remove these opinions, I shall be pleased to publish your article. If
you feel the article still in need of opinions, I shall of course be
only too glad to supply my own." He told another contributor that
he would agree to publish his article if he would remove its barba-
rous academic jargon. The man wrote back to say that he wouldn't
at all mind removing the jargon, which was, he supposed, really a
matter of taste. This caused Edward to shoot back a note saying,
"Yes, it is only a matter of taste—good versus bad taste." "I take
the leather whip to my contributors," he once said to me, "but it
doesn't seem to matter. They have steel bottoms."

I appear to be Boswelling my friend Edward, but perhaps this
is not inappropriate, because he often seemed to me very Johnson-
ian. Edward himself loved Samuel Johnson. He admired Johnson's
gravity, a word that Edward himself frequently used to explain his
regard for certain writers. Marguerite Yourcenar was one such
writer. Theodore Dreiser was another. In Edward's view, Dreiser
was a much greater writer than E. M. Forster, whom Edward knew
when both were fellows at King's College, because his writing had
greater gravity.

An engraving of Sir Joshua Reynolds's portrait of Johnson
faced Edward's desk in his apartment in Chicago. Edward shared
with Johnson that unteachable intellectual quality known as authority, a quality that in both men derived from their moral cen-
teredness. Both knew where they stood, and the mere fact of their
standing where they did made the ground beneath them firm. Like
Johnson, Edward came into his authority young. In his book *The
Torment of Secrecy*, written when he was in his middle forties,
availing himself of this authority, he could persuade by the power
of undeniable assertion.

Edward's apartment, on the ninth floor of a neo-Tudor sky-
scraper on Stony Island Avenue, had none of the squalor of Johnson's various abodes. Across from Jackson Park, in sight of the Museum of Science and Industry, with a spectacular view of Lake
Michigan, it was roughly five blocks from his office in the Social
Sciences Building at the University of Chicago. Its floors were covered with Oriental carpets, about which he knew a good deal; its
walls, just about all of them, were lined with books, about which

he knew everything. Eight-foot-high bookcases extending along the length of both sides of the front hall were the first things that struck one on entering this apartment. The living room was similarly lined with bookcases. The books were organized by subject matter: political philosophy in the hall; religion, European and ancient history in the living room. Reference works—the *OED*, the *Britannica* (eleventh edition), the *DNB*, and various specialized dictionaries—were in a bookcase opposite his desk and in a revolving bookcase alongside the desk. The dining-room table was generally at least half-covered with manuscripts, correspondence, and bills, which he tended to pay with a rhythm all his own.

Another hallway, this one leading to his bedroom, held books on India and things Asian. His bedroom was the place for literature. Here one found handsome sets of the great writers: Hazlitt, his beloved Dickens, Balzac, many French writers in Pleiade editions, all the Russians. By his bedside were the Christian mystics and wisdom writers. Social science was in the guest bedroom; a second desk and office (once meant to be a maid's room) contained books on higher education. Closets harbored back issues of *Horizon* and other journals. The kitchen and two of the three bathrooms were the only rooms devoid of bookcases, though the bathroom in which he bathed always had eight or ten books and a few magazines at the back ledge of the tub for him to read while soaking.

All the furniture was carefully chosen for its subdued elegance and feeling for tradition. In the living room, along with the Jacob Epstein bust of Conrad and the bust of Max Weber, was a self-portrait by Epstein; the few feet of wall space in this room not covered by bookcases were dominated by Piranesi prints. The coat closet in the hall contained two red fezzes, one for Edward and the other for his son, Adam, obtained in Egypt when Adam was a child of seven or eight. Another closet farther down the hall was set up as a wine cellar of sorts, with bottles of champagne, Jack Daniels, and various quite good wines; cigar boxes were on an enclosed shelf atop still more books.

The kitchen was set up for a serious cook, which Edward was. A vast quantity of spices, teas, superior knives, and other rather elaborate kitchen technology lined the walls; a worktable was in the center of the room. Edward was a gourmand, someone who not only likes delicacies but plenty of them. Apart from books, Edward's other extravagance was for what Wallace Stevens, in a letter, called "fancy groceries." Unlike Stevens, Edward could fabricate elegant dishes as well as devour them.

I always thought of his cooking—a mélange of splendid Central European dishes—as Edwardo-Hapsburg. It was immensely rich and flavorful, with no bow in the direction of odious healthy eating; the word *cholesterol* never passed his lips. He made marvelous soups (rich minestrone, thick bean and barley, dark lentil and sausage), he often began meals with smoked salmon, and he provided fine main courses, notable among them an aubergine (never, by Edward, called eggplant) dish known as "the Imam swoons": whether he swooned at the wonderful taste or at the expense of the ingredients, Edward once explained, was not clear. Meals generally ended with refreshing fresh fruit salads. Until near the very end, he never permitted help from guests, either in the kitchen or in the matter of cleaning up.

The conversation at these meals was quite as rich as the food. Subjects I recall included the work of the KGB in England; the fate of books among the beetles and in the steamy climate of India; the great bookstores of Philadelphia in the early decades of this century; mad old Trotskyists; and great scholars and their eccentricities. At table, talking about the splendors of the old British postal system, he once told about a letter from India addressed "Edward Shils, Sociologist, England" that was actually delivered to him. The last large meal in company I had at Edward's was prepared not by him but by his friend and neighbor in Cambridge, Thomas Moffett, who had retired as a butler at Peterhouse, where Edward was an honorary fellow, and who had come to Chicago to care for Edward in his illness. Everyone at that dinner told a story about crème brûlée, which was our dessert. All I could contribute was that a sympathetic reviewer of one of my books compared my prose to crème brûlée, saying it was very rich stuff, but you don't want to take too much of it in one sitting.

On the matter of food, as on that of books and friendship, Edward exercised very little restraint. I often took him shopping. Edward did not drive a car (nor did he type or use a computer) but he knew all the city's streets and the best places to buy the finest things. As a man who knew all the major cities of the world—he was always a great walker—he would gently mock Chicago for its crudity, but, clearly, he also loved the city.

We generally began north at the Paulina Market, easily the best butcher shop in the city, an establishment that would cause a vegetarian to faint, with its more than fifteen-yard-long display cases of loins and links, steaks and chops, meats smoked and cured. It is run by a third generation of German working-class men, chiefly from the surrounding neighborhood. Many of its butchers knew Edward and called him "Professor." Professor was what he was called, too, at the N & G Produce Market, where he would pick among the vegetables and fruits, always paying his bill by check, and where he had talked the owner's son out of becoming a dental technician and into staying in the family business. We would cross the street to buy olive oil and cheese. Occasionally we would have lunch, always upstairs, at the Greek Islands on Halsted, where Edward was greeted as "Perfetcher" by the sons of the original owners, whom he also knew. Sometimes we would stop on Taylor Street for an Italian ice, which we ate in the car as we watched the passing parade of young Mexicans, Italians, and blacks. On the way back south, we would stop at Bruno's, the Lithuanian bakery, where Edward would buy the weighty and coarse-textured rye bread he favored.

Edward admired few things more than shopkeepers. He was impressed by their courage in staking everything on their small businesses. A beautiful shop, locally owned, such as the Italian ceramics shop Tutti Italia that was in my own neighborhood, set him vibrating every time we entered it together. Along with making a point of telling its young owner how elegantly everything was set out, he always bought an item or two. He once told me that he judged any city by the number of interesting blocks of shops it provided. London and Paris were the hands-down winners here.

Edward also admired working men and women. He once surprised me by telling me how large the sum was that he contributed to the staff of janitors, doormen, and receiving-room clerks in his building. He had himself been pleased, many years before, at having been mistaken by another tenant in his building, an older woman, for "the city engineer." What pleased him was being taken for an honest working man of great competence, for he much valued competence wherever he came upon it. In this, as in other ways—his intellectual fearlessness as well as his physique—he resembled H. L. Mencken, who wrote: "Competence, indeed, was my chief admiration, then as now, and next to competence I put what is called being a good soldier—that is, not whining."

Edward took particular interest in Chicago's ethnic character. He enjoyed the ethnic carnival, which meant not only ethnic differences but generalizations about those differences. He was certainly not to be stopped in this mild pleasure by contemporary political correctness. (Besides, he truly judged people on their merits and so had no need to worry about being thought prejudiced.) He loved such comic ethnic distinctions as: the difference between a Hungarian and a Romanian was that both would sell you their grandmothers but the Romanian wouldn't deliver. Like Mencken again, he didn't mind calling a Krauto-American a Krauto-American. He had great regard for the Poles, Lithuanians, and other Eastern Europeans who had settled in Chicago, and he much respected the tidiness with which they kept their houses and lawns. He thought that the blacks had been sold a very sad bill of goods that allowed them to believe in their own victimhood. He was particularly hard on his own, the Jews; and on pretentious Jewish intellectuals he was hardest of all.

Edward's once great respect for intellectuals and academics had dwindled considerably after the 1960s. More and more he tended to think of academics and intellectuals as essentially quacks pushing untested ideas at no personal risk. For those true scholars—Arnaldo Momigliano, Gershom Scholem, Peter Brown, Paul Oskar Kristeller, Jacques Barzun—Edward had great regard. But for those to whom the least fraudulence adhered—names on request—he was merciless in his criticism. He frequently reverted to the Yiddish words *chachem* and *chachema*, meaning greatly learned wise man or woman, always used sarcastically, to refer to the false wise men and women of our day. His list of the false contemporary *chachemin* would put the lights out in several major universities.

He once told me that, had he the chance of beginning life again, he might choose a career in the military. I know he much enjoyed his years during World War II, when he was seconded to the British army to interrogate captured German soldiers. I, for one, am glad he was a teacher. A life in the military might not have given him the opportunity to stock his mind as richly as he was able to stock it as a university professor. The best, though still poor, analogy I can come up with for Edward's mind is that of the magician's glass, out of which the magician takes hardy swallow after hardy swallow. When the glass is set down, *mirabile dictu*, it turns out to be still full to the brim. It seemed there was nothing Edward did not know, nothing he ever forgot: until the very last, I never knew him to stumble in his memory of a name or title of a book. Vast quantities of literature, history, philosophy, anecdotes, jokes—all were neatly filed away in his mind, which also contained a mental Rolodex that began around the year 1000 B.C. with, so far as I could determine, no names missing.

I make Edward sound a walking *vade mecum*, which, true enough, in part he was. But none of this would have been of the least interest if he hadn't had a mind capable of great powers of penetration and formulation. He amply demonstrated this on serious subjects—nationalism, civil society, tradition, collective consciousness—in his books. But his conversation glittered with his rich verbal gifts; his vocabulary was, for me, a continuous delight, full of surprising twists and turns. (He was endlessly curious about the etymology of phrases and idioms.) He might call a man "an ignorant zealot," not a phrase much used in our century. Scruffy neighborhood kids playing with untied gym shoes and baseball hats on backwards he might refer to as our *jeunesse dorée*. I once described an acquaintance of ours to him as rat-faced. "Yes," said Edward, "now that you mention it, he is rather rodential." *Rodential*—who else but Edward would have thought of such a word, which sounds like an insurance company for mice.

His metaphor-making powers were dazzling. Sometimes these could take an oddly—for so urban a man—rural character, as when, in one of his books, he described congressmen as "fidgety as a hen atop a nest of woodpeckers." He used to refer to his friend Melvin Lasky, whose editing of *Encounter* he much respected and whom he frequently attempted to advise, "as a dog who knows seven languages and obeys in none." More often, his metaphors were brilliant in their ornateness. He likened the condition of his French to a set of crystal in a glass cabinet after a bombing raid on London in 1943 (which didn't stop him from reading sixteen volumes of Tocqueville's letters in fewer than three weeks).

Once, at a meeting of the Editorial Board of *The American Scholar*, on which Edward sat for eighteen years, one of the members questioned the function of the board. She wondered if it wasn't, in her words, "just window dressing." "Allow me," Edward began, "to take up Mrs. Trilling's fenestral metaphor. One has a window. One acquires a shade for it. Curtains. Perhaps a cornice. Possibly venetian blinds. Drapes may be in order. I suppose all that is window dressing. Yes, we, his Editorial Board, are, in some sense, Mr. Epstein's window to a wider outlook on the world. But you know, just because one has a window, that doesn't mean that one wants to look out of it all the time. Mr. Epstein doesn't, after all, have to refer to us, his Editorial Board, ceaselessly." That, I should say, is worthy of Henry James.

The flow of wit in Edward was unsurpassed by anyone I expect ever to meet. A rather pretentious Czech friend once told me that, in the old days, before the advent of the Communists, his father, a high bourgeois, never shaved himself. "More likely the truth is," said Edward, when I reported this to him, "his father shaved his mother." When the University of Chicago had a rather embarrassing faculty member who had years before gained tenure, Edward suggested to Robert Hutchins that the university acquire a bungalow in Gary, Indiana, and make this man dean of the University of Chicago at Gary, with no students and no responsibilities whatsoever. I called him in the midst of his preparing an elaborate dinner for an important figure at the University of Chicago, about which he commented: "I don't know why I bother. If he really cared about good food, he would surely have left his wife years ago." He once described a certain intellectual to me as "a rabid anti-Communist"; then, after a perfectly timed pause, he added, "Wait a minute—so am I."

Edward was very generous about my own attempts at wit, and he frequently improved on them. The University of Illinois at

Chicago was for many years known as Circle Campus, sometimes called Circle, and I took to calling it Vicious Circle. Edward thought this quite amusing, though he turned up the joke a full notch by referring to the school as Old Vish. In company, he was always asking me to tell my jokes, and I would learn that, behind my back, he was telling a few of them himself and was giving me credit for having invented them.

Being with Edward was endlessly amusing. Once he arranged for me to be invited to a formal dinner at the University of Chicago in honor of his friend John Sparrow, then the Warden of All Souls College, Oxford. At the time, I did not own a tuxedo, and Edward's "soup and fish," as he jokingly called his dinner clothes, were in Cambridge. I told him I would acquire two tuxedos from a place that rented them. "Very well, Joseph," he said, "but something simple, you know—no rock 'n' roll, no pimpery." When I explained to the man at the tuxedo rental shop what was wanted—two simple sets of black dinner clothes, shawl collars, shirts, and cummerbunds—he said, "No problem" and then proceeded to call his downtown office and ask for "two Tony Martins." At drinks, before the dinner itself, Edward slipped up behind me and whispered in my ear, "Joseph, comforting, is it not, to know one is wearing one's own socks."

Edward was, as I noted earlier, a man on whom nothing was lost, and the subtlety of his observations seemed to me often astonishing. "He is a man who often laughs but in between seldom smiles," he once said to me of Saul Bellow. He admired the economists of the University of Chicago, trained under Jacob Viner and Frank Knight; and he had spent more than half a century in the company of Milton Friedman and George Stigler and found both to be men of superior intelligence. But he felt that the Chicago economists, brilliant though they could be, were insufficiently impressed with the mysteries of life. It was these mysteries—the role of the primordial, the part tradition plays—that most stirred him, and he struggled with the questions that they posed till the very end of his own life. "Take me home, Joseph," he said to me, rather wearily one night as we were departing the Hong Minh restaurant on Twenty-second Street in Chicago's Chinatown. "I need to return to my desk to invent more stories about how society is organized."

Edward made it a point to introduce me to anyone he found interesting or charming. Many of these people I met at dinners he had prepared, and a vast number of them were Europeans: Leszek Kolakowski, Erica Reiner (the editor of the Assyrian dictionary at the Oriental Institute), the grandson of Theodor Mommsen, Hugh Lloyd-Jones, who was then the Regius Professor of Greek at Oxford. But on November 12, 1976, according to my journal, he invited me over to meet Arnaldo Momigliano. "One of the most charming men I have ever met," reads my journal entry of the next day. "Small, muffled in what seemed like many layers of clothes, peeping out at the world from behind glasses of plate-glass thickness, he proved a man of wit and of sweet humor and of great intellectual power; and along with all this, an absolute thesaurus of information. He is, as he remarked of himself, very much a Piedmontese. A lovely accent [it resembled Bela Lugosi playing Dracula], many fine gestures with his hands, a rumpled appearance, a penetrating mind—all combine in a personage at once formidable and adorable. Edward noted me gazing at him in admiration. We looked at each other, Edward and I, and smiled."

Arnaldo Momigliano was, in the truest sense, Edward's only peer. Arnaldo, who had been forced into exile by the Italian Fascists, found an intellectual home in England. He and Edward shared the international spirit in scholarship and in life. He was the only man who seemed to know as much as Edward, though Edward always advertised Arnaldo as knowing much more. Neither, in my presence, ever called the other by his first name. Edward referred to Arnaldo as Professor Momigliano, and Arnaldo, in the European manner, often referred to Edward as Shils.

Twice a year we traveled to *American Scholar* Editorial Board meetings as a threesome. Walking through O'Hare and LaGuardia—Edward with his walking stick, Arnaldo with his crushed Borsalino hat—I always felt that we resembled the intellectual equivalent of the Marx Brothers, with me as Zeppo, far and away the dimmest of the lot. Edward looked after Arnaldo, who was less confident of his way and who had to be frisked at airport security because he wore a pacemaker. Arnaldo had various airplane tickets, newspaper clippings, and foreign letters pinned to him or sticking out of his pockets. He always carried what looked to be roughly three pounds of keys—I do not exaggerate—to various apartments, offices, and library carrels around the world. Such a disorderly exterior, such an orderly mind.

A certain amount of Arnaldo's and Edward's conversation, having to do with such (to me) arcana as founders of Romanian folklore or classicists in the Soviet Union, floated amiably above my head. Usually, though, I found it most amusing. I remember one conversation about a student whom Edward and Arnaldo agreed was altogether too good-looking ever to become a true scholar—they were perfectly serious about this. When one of Arnaldo's best students left the University of Chicago for Princeton, both he and Edward were disappointed, and Arnaldo said, wistfully, "Ah, a Jewish boy, the Ivy League beckons, what do you expect?"

Edward had brought Arnaldo to the University of Chicago as something like a permanent visiting professor and argued for his remaining there when the administration, failing to be properly impressed with his greatness, wanted to release him at normal retirement age. Edward took personal responsibility for him. When Arnaldo's bad heart condition worsened, Edward, the Jewish grandmother in him kicking in, moved Arnaldo out of the room he occupied at the faculty club and into his own more capacious apartment. There, with an oxygen tank in his room, Arnaldo continued to see his students until he returned to England, alas, to die. Edward cooked for him and did his laundry and looked after all his needs. I recall Glen Bowersock, a dear friend of Arnaldo's, saying that he had never seen anything quite like the way Edward looked after Arnaldo—usually a lesser man might look after a greater, but here was one great man extending himself completely for another.

Had things worked out the other way round, I am fairly sure that Arnaldo would not have done the same for Edward. I say this not in the least to disparage Arnaldo but to highlight the extraordinary generosity of which Edward was capable. Through the son of a friend who had been a student at Cambridge, where Edward

kept a small house on Tennis Court Road near his college, Peterhouse, I recently learned that Edward was thought a tightwad.
This came from his sometimes taking leftover desserts home from
college lunches and serving them for dinner at his own table. At
the Greek Islands Restaurant, he used to have the waiters put the
extra lemons and unused bread into a bag that he would take
home. But these were habits of Edward's Depression-era mental-
ity—he simply hating seeing food go to waste.

At the same time that he would take home bread and lemons, he would give—not loan, *give*—a graduate student ten thousand dollars to help her finish a difficult final year of her studies.
He might give another young couple a five-thousand-dollar Christmas gift, merely because he wanted them to know he loved them.
He was immensely generous to his own son and daughter-in-law
and, had they permitted it, would have done even more for them.

Edward was even more generous with his time. He would
see students at all hours. He would take them to restaurants. He
lavished great care—and vast quantities of his green ink (Mr. Alfred's [Dunhill] Ink for Writing Instruments)—on the papers they
wrote for his classes. He was sometimes contemptuous of how
little his colleagues seemed to do by way of imposing standards
on their graduate students' dissertations. If you wrote a dissertation under Edward, you were sent to the south of England, thence
to Sumatra and back, but when you were done, you really knew
everything about your subject. Many a student must have left his
apartment, heart weighted down with a list of another thirty
tomes he would have to plough through and head spinning from
having discovered that, to take the next logical step in his studies,
he would have to learn Polish. But, if the student was fundamentally sound, he would know that what Edward had asked him to
do was right.

Edward's effect on me was inevitably to make intellectual
effort seem worthwhile. He was like a great ship captain in Conrad, not standing at the helm, but seated at his desk at all hours,
working through the problems he had set himself as a young man
and felt he had not exhausted. He was a man who was able to get
by with four or five hours of sleep. One might drop him off at ten
at night, and he would get in another three hours at his desk: mak-

ing corrections on student papers, perhaps working on the ninth draft of an essay, dictating letters, or writing lengthy testimonials for students and friends for jobs, grants, and further schooling.

A testimonial from Edward could be a dangerous thing. The problem was that Edward not only had standards, which are easy enough to possess, but he applied them, which is not so easy. He might praise a student, or a former student now in his forties or fifties, for honorableness, upstandingness, and industry but not for being deeper than Goethe, more brilliant than Stendhal, or subtler than Proust, and the absence of these qualities could be dampening in the current inflationary academic testimonial market. At the same time, a recent student of his told me that Edward had written him a brilliant many-paged testimonial showing how his, the student's, own work made him a perfect fit historically for the sociology department to which he had applied. Edward knew the history of this department, I have no doubt, better than anyone currently in it.

As Henry James could never lie about art, so Edward could never lie about intellect. His high standards caused him truly to anguish over the state into which the universities, and intellectual life generally, seemed to him to have fallen. He, who perhaps knew more about the history of scholarship than anyone living, looked about him and everywhere saw compromise, dumbing down, politicization. (Anyone who thinks that the attacks on the politicization of academic life are themselves at base political ought to look into *The Torment of Secrecy*, Edward's book of 1956, written during the heart of the congressional investigation of security in the United States, to see an example of majestic disinterested political thought in action. In the pages of that book, Edward, without underplaying the genuine menace of the Soviet Union, shows why McCarthy and other vastly opportunistic congressmen were able, through menacing work of their own, to stir up the country.) The great university traditions that he so much admired—had really devoted his life to carrying on—were everywhere, in his view, being worn away, undermined, all but sabotaged.

His anguish often turned into rage. I have been personal witness to some of his spectacular tirades on the subject of the swinish behavior of academics. Edward was one of the world's fastest talkers, and I have heard tirades of his that lasted no less than an uninterrupted half hour. This made for a vast number of well-chosen words from a master of vituperation. His anger at what he saw before him gave him the reputation of a curmudgeon, when in fact he was a man driven to the deepest sadness by the spoilage of all that he most loved in the world.

Edward's position as a strong figure who disapproved of so much that was now de rigueur in academic and intellectual life tended, even within the University of Chicago, to set him on the margin of things. He continued to teach at the university, without payment of any kind, until only two months before his death at the age of eighty-four, but his counsel was only rarely sought on any matter of important university policy, which hurt him greatly, though he never made this complaint out loud, at least not to me.

While Edward Levi was president of the University of Chicago, Edward was something akin to the cardinal he dreamed Jacques Maritain had made him. He was not a gray but a purple eminence; he was a powerful and not at all behind-the-scenes influence, whose advice was sought and very often followed. In good part it was owing to the two Edwards—Levi and Shils—that the University of Chicago did not knuckle under to student protest in the middle 1960s and was never humiliated and, subsequently, diminished by it in the way that Berkeley, Columbia, Michigan, and other universities had been.

The degradation of the great academic traditions was not something with which Edward could ever come to terms. He functioned as something of a conscience in these matters, but the truth is that people don't feel the need of such a conscience, least of all those who are flourishing quite nicely without this important, invisible organ of the spirit.

Courage has its price, though Edward would have dismissed the notion that he was ever genuinely courageous. When he gave the Jefferson Lecture in 1979, he chose as his subject the regrettable incursions of the federal government into higher education. People afterwards told him that it had taken courage to say what he thought. Not at all, he responded; it takes courage in the Soviet Union or in South Africa to say what one thinks, not in the United States.

The price of Edward's courage was loneliness. He was not only excluded from the inner councils at the University of Chicago, but he was invited out less and less. He maintained some friendships at the university, but increasingly his life was spent among students and a few friends not in positions of any power. His many English and European friendships bucked up his spirits. He used to say that, if his son and three or four friends didn't live in Chicago, he would have retired permanently to England.

Luckily for me, he never did. His friendship and wisdom meant a very great deal to me. I used to check in with him regularly on subjects about which I was writing and found him unfailingly helpful. He once told me that, without the element of personal intellectual progress, life was pretty empty, a notion especially useful for anyone who teaches and hence is tempted to repeat himself endlessly. Another time he recited for me the four intellectual possibilities: to be unoriginal but right; to be original but wrong; to be unoriginal and wrong (the most common possibility); and, rarest of all, of course, to be original and right. He always asked me what I was reading; and I could not mistake the slight disappointment in his voice when I reported reading at length a writer who he thought not really worth the time: the last such, to give an idea of Edward's standard, was Elizabeth Bishop.

If I have made Edward out to be lonely—without the large family life he would have enjoyed, with a vastly attenuated connection to the university where he had taught for more than fifty years—I don't want to make him sound tragic. His curiosity was too wide, his mind too lively for him ever to seem a broken reed. He knew how to take pleasure from the everyday delights life provided: good food, good books, good friends. "Through all my days I have never known more than momentary boredom," he once told me. With his mind, boredom was not really a possibility.

Edward never degraded the material life. Up to the very end, he remained an enthusiastic collector of books. He would go into Williams-Sonoma to buy some kitchen *tsotchke*, knowing full well he needed it, as he said, like a *loch in kop*. He claimed that acquiring new things gave one a sense of futurity, of life continuing, no matter what one's age. His own age, once he reached his middle seventies and beyond, became a standing joke with him.

"As the United States seems to have passed, as Bryce remarked, from barbarism to decadence without attaining civilization," he once told me, "so I seem to have gone from ignorance to wisdom without ever having been considered very intelligent." Once, when two former students of his from the 1930s came to visit him, men now in their seventies, he capped his report of their visit by saying to me, with his winning smile, "Nice boys."

Edward had extraordinary physical gifts. He could keep later hours, eat more and spicier food, talk longer, and get up the next day in much better fettle than I or just about anyone else I knew. His energy remained amazing until his illness. I always thought he would die in England of a heart attack. I thought I would receive a call, and a voice in a gentle English accent would tell me that Edward had died in his sleep or, better, at his desk. "I want to go with my boots on," he told me more than once. "No tubes up my nose, lashed to three IVs, strangers milling about."

What he died of was cancer: colon cancer metastasized to the liver. (He might have said, like the archbishop in Willa Cather's novel, "I shall die of having lived.") Although he was eighty-three when the cancer was discovered, he enrolled himself for the full-blast regimen of chemotherapy. After the first rounds proved ineffective, he signed up for a second, this time experimental, round. When people who knew what he was going through asked how he was, he replied, "Apart from dying of cancer, I feel just fine." He was only intermittently in great pain, but chemotherapy can be to cancer what psychoanalysis often is to neurosis: the illness, as Karl Kraus said, for which it purports to be the cure.

Edward must have lost fifty pounds, his eyes stared out of his head, he began to shuffle, he looked particularly fragile from behind. Whereas before the intrusion of cancer, Edward, for the twenty-odd years I knew him, seemed a permanent age sixty, he now looked all of his eighty-four years and more. Among the other penalties exacted by cancer—by the chemotherapy, really—was that he lost his sense of taste. He told me that he would fantasize about dishes, then order them or prepare them himself, only to find most of them tasteless. One day I brought, at his request, a jar of spinach borscht called schav, which he ate with great dollops of sour cream. "I don't know how much longer I'll be alive," he said to me, "but however long it might be, I shall never eat this horrible soup again." Our last meal together, before he took to his bed, was a cold smoked pheasant followed by a special brand of chocolate ice cream, each of us eating the latter out of separate pint-sized containers.

Edward told me that he felt he had, over the years, acquired the character to face death without terror. And so he did, little as he wished to leave life. Except for only occasional lapses into delirium, he kept his lucidity to the end. The extreme weight loss caused the very shape of his face to change. His nose, which was normally fleshy at the end, now came to seem longish and slightly aquiline, which made him look like a very distinguished Roman senator. To me his face always suggested great playfulness, and I have seen him in a state of intellectual passion, after a day of solid work at his desk, when he seemed to me nothing less than radiant. But he never seemed more beautiful than at the end of his life. Until the end, he continued to see students. Old friends, my wife among them, came in a week or so before his death to bid him good-bye. As my wife said, he did all the work: telling her how much her friendship had meant to him, how he would miss her, instructing her not to grieve for him but to remember the lovely times they had had together. I had taken to kissing his forehead when I came into or departed his bedroom. He would lift my hand to his mouth and smile.

Four or so weeks before he died, I told him that he had been a very good friend, the best friend I expected ever to have. He told me that I had been a dear friend to him as well and added the qualification: "even though we rarely spoke together of things of the heart." I tried not to show shock at this, and I have since pondered its meaning. He also once told me that tact and candor were the essential qualities of friendship and that he thought he and I, in our friendship, had them in the right proportion.

We shared a happy intellectual candor, as only two people whose general views are congruent can. From early in our friendship, we told one another the amount of fees we collected for lectures and for magazine pieces or what we paid for this or that article of clothing or meal. I felt there was nothing I could not say to him about other people, we could even analyze the personalities of

persons we both admired, and, such was his tact, I never had to
tell him that anything I said was *entre nous*—he could make those
delicate judgments nicely enough on his own. Our loyalty to each
other was complete. And yet, at the end, Edward felt that "we
rarely spoke of things of the heart." What did he mean?

What he meant, I have come to believe, was that we chose
not to speak to each other, except in the most fleeting way, of our
doubts and disappointments and griefs. We didn't, in part because
neither of us was therapeutic in our impulses—better, we both
felt, to eat than to spill the beans—and in part because we each
lived by a code in which a man does not whine or weep, even on
the shoulder of his dearest friend.

Edward applied his own high standards to himself, and if he
found so many contemporaries wanting, he knew that, as good as
he was, he was not as good as he wanted to be. He left unfinished
vastly ambitious manuscripts; and as excellent as his published
work was, he always felt it could have been better. In his intellectual life, Edward suffered what I used to think of as encyclope-
dism: he wished to get all around every subject he took up. This
could make him sometimes garrulous in conversation and cause
him to bring in manuscripts forty or fifty pages longer than the
possible outer limits of the space available. He was immensely
tolerant of my editing of his manuscripts, which chiefly entailed
radical cutting, and he used to joke about bringing out a book consisting entirely of things that I had cut from his essays. (I gave the
book the working title *From the Abattoir Floor.*) Powerful as so
much of his writing is, and permanent though I believe his contribution to the study of society has been, he would, I do not doubt,
have preferred to have left behind a single masterwork. But, alas,
he didn't. It was not something we talked about.

He hungered, too, for a richer family life than he had. He
loved the *idea* of Christmas, for example, though he didn't do
much about it; and his notions here may have derived as much
from Dickens as from the sad reality of the rather hopeless binge
of gift giving that this holiday has become. By the time I knew
him, Edward had long been divorced, though he had had chief responsibility for raising his only child. In all the time I knew him,
he never told me that he had been married twice, and I only

learned this from an enemy of his who told it to me to spite him. Yet, such are the paradoxes in the human heart that, despite his love of family, Edward may have been one of nature's true bachelors, with his frequent travel to international conferences, his penchant for working at all hours, and his domestic schedule open to invasion by students, visiting scholars, and old friends.

Along with his hunger for family, Edward had a genuine regard for religion. He once described himself to a devout Catholic acquaintance as a "pious agnostic." He just couldn't make the leap into faith. I don't think this was by any means the central drama in his life. Faithfulness to his own exacting standards provided that. But he believed in religion, as he believed in family, because he thought both enhanced society by strengthening its bonds, preserving its traditions, making it deeper and richer. We spoke often of these things, Edward and I, but usually in a detached rather than a personal way.

Any but a fatuous man will be disappointed by his own life—will feel that he could have done more and better than he did. The truer test is whether a man has disappointed others. An entry from my journal of April 13, 1973, very soon after I first met Edward, reads:

Dinner last evening with Edward Shils. Always a pleasure: very good food, even better talk, and a lovely overall feeling of intellectual glow that lasts for hours afterward. What an impressive figure he is, by turns serious, severe, wildly humorous, marvelously anecdotal, and above all disinterested. While on the one hand he seems unconnable, on the other he can be—and often is—a great appreciator.

When Edward was in Chicago, we spoke over the phone every day, usually for forty minutes or longer. In twenty-two years, we never ran out of things to say. My problem now is that I still have so many things to tell him. I remember wanting to call him to laugh together about the story in the *New York Times* about Tip O'Neill's pals in North Cambridge—Skippy McCaffrey, Pinky Sullivan, and Mickey O'Neil—who met to remember their friend Tip at their favorite bar, a story Edward would have loved. I wanted to call him to tell him the joke I heard about Yeshiva University's rowing team, on which one man rows and the other twelve yell.

For the remainder of my life I shall have stories that I shan't be able to tell to Edward, and this will make them less satisfying.

Edward taught me how best to peel an orange, where to buy olive oil, how to spot intellectual fraudulence, and how to laugh in dark times. Since his death, a word, a phrase, a formulation will occur to me that has his own lovely comic spin on it, and I know that it is Edward speaking through me, as he so often did in life. Edward's life was devoted to the fundamental, the primordial truths we all know and are ever in danger of forgetting. Chief among them is that only a life lived with courage, passion, and honor is worth living. This was, precisely, the life Edward lived, indomitably, right up to the very end.

one

A GALLERY OF ACADEMICS, MAINLY IN CHICAGO

THE UNIVERSITY OF CHICAGO IN THE EARLY 1930s was a wonderful place for a young man without social airs and without social ambitions, poor, rather ignorant, serious, and intellectual, launched on a quest without knowing what he was looking for. It was a great place for me to grope with confidence that I would not go astray.

It was a very different kind of place from what I had imagined a university to be. Even as an undergraduate I had still thought of a university as a place where the professors knew clearly what was right and what was not right. Perhaps that was because I retained from my tenth year the belief that the knowable was finite and that genuine professors had mastered that; perhaps it was because I had formed, from what sources I do not know, the notion that German professors were the true professors, the very idea of professors, and German professors, I thought, were dogmatic and commanding. That was not the way it was in Chicago.

The two best men at Chicago at that time were always tentative and disarming by their tentativeness. They were both men of very clearly formed character. One of them could be querulous and as persistent in a discussion as a bulldog; he was sharp and subtle and had an exceptional acumen in detecting contradictions in others' and in his own positions. While he always complained about the errors of others, he never ceased to confess his own ignorance. He had an exasperated certainty when he referred to what was unlikely to be true, but when it came to the truth of his own assertions he was modest to the point of humility. The other professor who brought me at once into his vast, bewildering intellectual universe was like a bear—built like a bear, hunched over like a bear, putting his nose into everything like a bear, and growling and grunting like a bear. The first was Frank Knight; the second was Robert Park.

When I came to Chicago on September 22, 1932, Park was prowling about in the Orient and Frank Knight was in the depths of a deep depression about the state of and prospects for liberalism. When the 1932 presidential campaign was coming to an end, the Communist Club announced that Frank Knight would lecture under its auspices on "An Ex-Liberal Looks at Communism." I do not know what the officers of the Communist Club could have been thinking of when they asked Knight to speak. Did they think that Knight would announce his conversion to Communism? They might have done so because many intellectuals in the United States were then turning in that direction, prefiguring the policy which the Communist party would follow in the second part of the decade—that the party should attach to its retinue as many intellectuals as possible, whatever their views, as long as they would be willing to be associated, however loosely, with the Communist party and as long as they would attack the existing regimes of the Western countries. The head of the Communist Club was a square-faced, bespectacled student of divinity. His was no great brain. He seemed to be an earnest, ignorant, and simple fellow with a tone of righteousness; he was a forerunner of many a defecting clergyman in the decades to come.

The meeting was to be held at 8:00 P.M. in the large lecture room in the Social Science Research Building. As was characteristic of rooms in that building in the evening, it was stiflingly hot, the lights were dim, and the radiators clanked in a fitful and lugubrious way for most of the evening. Frank Knight, whom I had never seen before, came in timorously yet defiantly—I later saw this combination of qualities quite often. He was wearing a dark woolen shirt, a sombre necktie. He was bald and had a closely clipped, bristling little gray mustache. He wore silver-framed spectacles. His face was pink and round yet with nothing soft about it.

He looked like a very intelligent little rodent, rather adorable to look at but well capable of giving one a nip which would not soon be forgotten.

The room was nearly full when Frank Knight entered. He walked toward the front, sat down in a seat on the aisle, and waited. No one came over to speak to him, or seemed even to take notice of him. The students, most of whom were undoubtedly not Communists or fellow travelers, obviously came with the expectation of hearing something very interesting. I had the impression that they did not recognize Knight. Since I myself was new at the university, I did not know anyone except for one friend who was a great admirer of Knight and who pointed him out to me.

I can no longer recall what Knight said in any detail, but the main point of his lecture was an affirmation of the principles of liberalism—individual freedom, rational choice and action, rational discussion to settle political disagreements, the functioning of the competitive market as the most productive, the freest, and the socially most beneficial mode of organization of economic life. Communism was tyranny; it, like nationalism, appealed to what was basest in the human mind, the mob spirit. Knight said not a word in favor of communism, except that liberalism had proved itself untenable because human beings were incapable of rational thought, even about their own advantage; they did not wish to act on their own responsibility. They wanted leaders who would comfort them with illusions and who would make unrealizable promises to them. They wanted to subordinate themselves; they wanted the security of being part of a mob and of sharing in the mob spirit.

Knight said there had been a time when it looked as if mankind, having advanced toward freeing itself from tradition, superstition, and despotism, had turned toward the ideal of a free society. It had become clear, however, that mankind did not wish to live in freedom and according to the light of reason. He spoke with sombre regret about the failure of education, including higher education, to overcome the human desire for self-deception and its readiness to turn its problems over to demagogic leaders for solutions. That was why communism—in which he seemed to include fascism—appeared to be on the verge of triumph in the world. He spoke about this with genuine grief and painful bitterness, although there were many sardonic remarks and sober bits of rural wisdom at which some students laughed. He blamed no individuals. He thought that the human race was just not up to living in a free society. He criticized liberalism because it had not understood the limited powers of human beings and it had also not seen the potentialities for deterioration in its own ideals—the fact that competition was not between equals and that it contained the danger of monopoly, or that discussion tends to deteriorate into argument and propaganda in which the objective is victory rather than truth.

But it was not so much what Frank Knight said that impressed me or even the oddity of this profound and honest man speaking under the auspices of a band of novices naive in intellectual dishonesty and chicanery. There was much in it which I could not fathom, since his kind of clear-minded liberalism, so trenchantly asserted, was new to me. What impressed me was a man so honest that he could reason himself into paralyzing uncertainties, an idealist so lofty in his aspirations that anything that fell short of them was oppressive disappointment. Yet all the while he was humble about his own ignorance, deep in his understanding of human imperfections.

Frank Knight did not mention sociology in that lecture. When I began to attend his courses the next year, he never mentioned sociology or sociologists, except for Max Weber. Although he had not himself studied very much sociology—he was by training an economist—Frank Knight offered a great deal to a sociologist. He had reflected profoundly about the market and he was aware that the behavior of human beings was not exhaustively described when one had described the market. He saw, too, that the operation of the market depended on certain conditions, such as the family, which were not part of it, and that it produced consequences which were inimical to its further working as a competitive market. He was also a stringent critic of behaviorism (which then as now had fanatical proponents), of ethical positivism, of scientism (which he called "scienticism") long before Friedrich Hayek and Karl Popper were pointing out its deficiencies.

I was entranced by Knight. His grim humor was an additional

merit but the main thing was his curiosity, his freedom from cant, and his refusal to accept mealymouthed intellectual compromises and reluctances. He was terribly difficult to come to grips with in an argument; arguing with him was like wrestling with an intellectual porcupine.

Frank Knight was a ruminator, a mutterer, a brooder. He was obsessed by a vision of society but his mind ranged over an immense field. He was an individualist who saw the limits of individualism, a rationalist who saw the limitations of rationality and its meager prospect of universal adoption. He was preoccupied by religion, although he was not a believer. He was a writer of extraordinary clarity on particular points; he had a lucid and mordant wit. A genuine liberal—not at all a collectivistic liberal—he used nevertheless to say that "one cannot twist the tails of the sacred cows of society," by which he meant that humanity will resist the invasion of reason and scientific knowledge into those domains that it thinks are sacred. He read omnivorously, and captiously annotated everything he read—underscoring, refuting, and lining the margins of the pages with exclamation points and question marks.

Frank Knight said many things which at the time I could not understand. Yet even some of what I could not understand I was certain contained much which ought to be understood and which I might be able to understand later. This in fact has turned out to be the case. For example, one Sunday he was at lunch with us in a flat which I then shared with two older graduate students. There arose some question about the correction of one or another defect in American society. In the unthinking idiom of the day—which I employed unthinkingly—I said that it was necessary to fight to bring about the desired change. I did not mean violent fighting; in fact I did not mean anything except persistence, but I had not really thought hard about what I did mean. Knight, in his cranky, whining way, expostulated: "But that is just what is wrong; it can't be done by fighting!" I can't even now convey the implications of this statement as I received it, but it moved my mind a little further toward the idea of the moral consensus around which Robert Park, too, had been circling.

I attended most of Frank Knight's lecture courses and seminars for a number of years. Much of what he said escaped me, either because I did not have a good enough understanding of economic theory or because he spoke of it with such oblique subtlety and so inaudibly that I could not always follow him. But now and then I caught sight of the paradoxes of existence which were always in the forefront of his mind. He was not an easy man to be with. There was certainly no small talk between us; he was about a quarter of a century older than I was at a time when such a discrepancy still made a difference. In any case, we never talked about private matters; our conversations proceeded by my timorously asking him his opinion about some ill-formulated problem or by his speaking about what preoccupied him, which were almost always the same things: the obduracy of human beings to reason as manifested in the persistence of Christianity, or of the tariff, or, later, of Marxism; the terrible difficulty of applying reason because of the uncertainty of the passage from abstract principles to more particular propositions; the vexingly inevitable ambiguity in the application of rules; the absence of any better alternative to the judgment of a wise and experienced person, and the rational inadequacy of this position.

This is no fair account of the strenuous and impassioned exertion of the mind which I witnessed in Frank Knight, and of his inability or unwillingness to reconcile himself to the imperfections of the human race, which he saw with such unhappy clarity. Not long before his death a young colleague met him on the street and asked him what he was writing. He replied that he had stopped writing, and when asked how he spent his time, he replied, "Meditating on the follies of the human race." He never lost his rationalistic impatience with those follies.

Frank Knight was brought up by God-fearing parents who were adherents of an intellectually narrow sect—the Plymouth Brethren. On one side of his character Knight was a thoroughgoing antinomian who no longer expected the coming of the Millennium. His antinomianism went further than that of the Plymouth Brethren because he was very anti-Christian and hostile to all religion, which, like Clarence Darrow and other freethinkers of the older generation, he regarded as the epitome of superstition. Yet he studied Scripture, read theological books constantly, and two theologians at the University of Chicago were among his closest friends. In his old age—he died well into his eighties—I once inquired about his health and he told me that he was very tired and slept very poorly. When I gave him some of my home remedies for falling asleep, he said, "No, it's not that I can't fall asleep. It's just that I wake up in the middle of the night and think about religion. It's that damned religion. I just can't get it out of my mind."

Knight was an economic theorist who in his time was one of the great figures of his subject. His doctoral dissertation became a classic. Many of his papers on interest and capital were studied by economists everywhere and greatly appreciated as among the important writings on these subjects in the history of the discipline. He complained bitterly against the failure of institutional economists to understand economic theory, but he was also preoccupied with the limited intellectual and ethical jurisdiction of economic theory. This was one of the reasons for his interest in Max Weber.

Knight was surely one of the first persons in the English-speaking world to be attracted to Weber's efforts to supplement economic theory with sociology. He translated Weber's *Wirtschaftsgeschichte* when Weber was only slightly known in the English-speaking world for his famous essay on the Protestant ethic and the origins of capitalism. He knew German well—his thesis for the degree of master of arts at the University of Tennessee in 1912 was on Gerhart Hauptmann. In about 1935 or 1936 he announced a seminar on Max Weber. The members at first were Milton Friedman, George Stigler, Allen Wallis, Herbert Goldhamer, Michael Sapir (the son of Edward Sapir, one of the best linguists and cultural anthropologists of the time), and I. I think that most of the others, except for Herbert Goldhamer and me, attended irregularly or ceased coming after a while. The procedure was a line-by-line reading of the first three chapters of Weber's *Wirtschaft und Gesellschaft,* with comments by Knight and a few hesitant observations by me. I myself studied the text every day; I was overpowered when the perspectives opened up by Weber's concepts brought together things which hitherto had never seemed to me to have any affinity with each other. I could not assimilate it all or bring it into a satisfying order. But reading Max Weber was literally breath-

taking. Sometimes, in the midst of reading him, I had to stand
up and walk around for a minute or two until my exhilaration
died down.

I also began to go to John Nef's lectures on the economic
history of England. Nef lectured mainly from the proofs of his fine
book on the coal industry in Great Britain, and I was dazzled by
his learning, his general literary and artistic culture, and the order-
liness of his lectures. He offered more material than I could absorb. It appeared to me to be the kind of thing which sociology
ought to be: the study of the interconnections and the inner work-
ings of institutions. I also attended, for some reason I cannot recall, the lectures of Harry Millis on labor organizations, labor legislation, and the like. Not knowing what sociology was supposed
to be, at least as understood by sociologists, I thought it should
be about whole societies—as in Werner Sombart's *Der moderne
Kapitalismus* and Mikhail Rostovtzeff's *Social and Economic History of the Roman Empire,* both of which I assumed to fall within
the province of sociology. I went to a course with Ernest Burgess
in a long, dark gothic room in the east tower of Harper Library.
Ernest Burgess was a gentle little man, with a soft, shy smile. He
spoke in a whisper. The course was centered on the Park and Burgess text, *Introduction to the Science of Sociology,* which I had
heard referred to as "the green bible." It was a huge book consisting of long passages by all sorts of writers from many countries. Each chapter was preceded by an introduction and at the end
there were topics for further inquiry and a long bibliography
which testified to the extraordinary range of Park's reading. Burgess went through it chapter by chapter, expounding it in a way
which showed that his heart was elsewhere.

On one occasion, I spoke up in class and mentioned Emile
Durkheim, whose writings were still fresh in my mind after my
short but exhaustive study of his books and articles several years
before. I do not know what the point was. I suppose that I was
simply showing off, since Durkheim had never held my sociological affections. But that interpellation made me a marked man
among the students. Imagine a student who could read French and
who did so even though he did not have to! After that class, one
of its members, a stocky, broad-shouldered man about thirty-five

or forty years old, with an aquiline nose and shining black hair, came up to me, remarked on my mention of Durkheim, and asked if we could walk home together. I was flattered by his attention; he was obviously a European and I had never spoken with an educated European before, although I had revered them from across the ocean. He told me that he was Dr. Josef Davidsohn, and when he gave me his card—until then I thought that only businessmen had cards—I saw that he was *Privatdozent* in sociology at the University of Copenhagen. I felt close to Copenhagen, having studied Georg Brandes's writings and with whose *Recollections of My Childhood and Youth* and essays on Kierkegaard, Drachmann, and other gloomy Danes I was intimate. Davidsohn was also a gloomy Dane, very grave and courteous. I guess that he was homesick for a bit of Europe and the closest thing to Europe the poor man could have was a young man who knew Durkheim's writings (at this time the only work of Durkheim's in English was *The Elementary Forms of Religious Life*). When he went back to Denmark at the end of the year, he gave me as fond a farewell as only a timid man in far from congenial company could give to a person with whom he had no affinity other than a shared knowledge of Durkheim. From Copenhagen he sent me a copy of his *Habilitationsschrift*, on Durkheim, and there our contact ceased. Nearly thirty years later, Fröde Jakobson, who had been the commanding general of the Danish Home Army during the Nazi occupation, told me, in response to my inquiry, that Davidsohn and his wife, both of whom were his friends, had committed suicide one night while the Home Army was attempting to smuggle them out of the country into Sweden.

I had become acquainted with Louis Wirth on my first day in Chicago. I had read Wirth's *The Ghetto* while I was an undergraduate and liked it; I had also looked over his annotated bibliography in *The City*, a book of essays on urban sociology which had been assembled by Park and Burgess with important contributions by both of them. Wirth's bibliography was intoxicating. It mentioned so many interesting works about every aspect of urban life throughout the world and, having come to Chicago from a year of enthusiastic weltschmerz in New York, I was fascinated by it and by all the great cities of the world. Park and Simmel, two sociologists, grasped exactly what riveted the imagination of youth about cities.

Wirth was a small man, plump without being fat. He had rounded cheeks, a chin and a nose like small cones; his brow and the top of his head also formed a cone. He had a sweet smile and an extraordinarily mellifluous voice. He told me that he had recently returned from Germany—as far as I was concerned, no experience could have been more desirable. The Nazis were not yet in power and I occasionally allowed myself the luxury of a daydream of studying in Germany. It was ridiculous. I had no money and in the Depression no prospect of having any. I had come to Chicago with the generous backing of an enthusiastic friend, himself nearly impecunious, and was soon supporting myself as a social worker in the Black Belt, working for the Cook County Bureau of Public Welfare.

Meeting Wirth was, for me, to be in contact with Germany. To be in contact with German universities was to be in contact with the great tradition of learning. Not that I felt elevated by anything that Wirth said. He told me that in Frankfurt he had visited Karl Mannheim, who was very interested in American sociology. Wirth asked me if I knew about Mannheim, whose articles I had seen in the *Archiv für Sozialwissenschaft.* Of course, I knew about him, but I had to answer that I had not read anything by him; I said that I intended to do so. I told Wirth that I had thought of submitting a monograph in the competition on the sociology of knowledge conducted by the Viennese Sociological Society but had dropped the idea. This was true, but I did not tell him that I had been spending my time studying Sorel with the intention of writing a book on him. (The only result of this was the introduction to a reprinting of Hulme's translation of the *Réflexions sur la violence* which I published nearly two decades later.) The interview with Wirth ended pleasantly. It was the first time that I had ever had a conversation about an intellectual subject with a professor. At the University of Pennsylvania, professors—at least those that I studied under as an undergraduate—did not speak to students outside of class and the students did not expect them to do so. This was not the way it was at Chicago.

I did not see Louis Wirth again until January 1933 when I

began to attend his course—at 8:00 A.M. three mornings a week—on the history of sociology, or the history of German sociology, I forget which. The course was one of the oddest I ever attended. The texts for the class were the three little green-bound volumes of Franz Oppenheimer's and Gottfried Salomon's *Soziologische Lesestücke*. Wirth would come into a room in the Social Science Research Building which had a large oval table, and make a few desultory comments; then on most days he would begin to read excerpts from one of the little volumes—in German. Sometimes he would read a whole page, sometimes more. He did this throughout the hour. There must have been some days when he spoke on his own for most of the hour, but I do not recall any of them. He sometimes made rather good comments, linking the passage read with the work of some other sociologist. I think I was probably the only member of the class who read German fairly well, and I also had the advantage of having the text in front of me while it was being read. Yet the students adored Wirth and not least for his reading to them in German, even though they could not understand what he was reading. They thought him a true scholar. In fact, he often said some clever things and I learned something about *Volksgeist* from the course.

In about June 1933, at a public meeting of social workers at the Goodman Theater, Louis Wirth asked me if I wished to be his research assistant. He said he had received some money for a study of "the methodological presuppositions of German sociology." Being a social worker, I occasionally went to meetings at Hull House and elsewhere, where the inadequate public provision for the unemployed was discussed. Louis Wirth himself had been a family caseworker for the Jewish Charities of Chicago before he went to teach sociology at Tulane, and he took an intense interest in social problems; his wife was a leading social worker. It was inspiring to be asked to accept such an honor. Although the acceptance of the appointment would require a reduction of my monthly income from $125.00 to $86.11, I had no hesitation. I was crossing the barrier between the outside and the inside. I have for most of my life had a sensitive imagination for that barrier—the invisible line separating periphery and center—and I thought that I was now in the process of passing over the line. I did not think that it was any merit of mine which had brought it about, and I had no idea of what the research could consist of. It was unprecedented to be pitched onto the peak of the sociological Parnassus. *Voraussetzungen*—presuppositions—was a very high-toned word among those of my undergraduate friends who knew a few words of German. (Theodore Mommsen was the first to speak of *voraussetzungslose Wissenschaft* at the beginning of the century.) It was the very center of intellectual activity to be aware of one's "presuppositions." Here I was about to enter this vital domain of my heart's desire.

It did not work out very well. Louis Wirth was very kind, but he could never tell me what I should do. I read countless books and essays and formed an intimacy with German social science which remains with me—not to any great intellectual benefit, except insofar as it made me intimate with a great period of modern intellectual history. Even now when I speak or correspond with a young German scholar working on some aspect of German academic history, I am sometimes asked whether I lived in Germany at that time—the period before the First World War!

Several things of importance happened in my early years at the University of Chicago. The first was that I began to study Max Weber's *Wirtschaft und Gesellschaft* in dead earnest, as well as his political and, of course, his methodological writings. His writings on religion came a little later. The other was that I attended the last course given by Robert Park in Rosenwald Hall, which was entitled "Collective Behavior." I remember Park growling as he paced up and back across the front of the room. He always looked into the distance when he spoke; he spoke slowly as if he were reading out his thoughts from a distant script which he could not easily decipher. Sometimes he spoke as if from the midst of the things he was talking about. He did not lecture to us; we were just present while he pondered aloud on what he had seen or was seeing while he spoke. Yet this course must have been partly a seminar, because I delivered a paper there on the socialist and communist movements—the course gave much attention to social movements since these were of major interest to Park. The presentation was a success and Park singled me out for special attention. That is the way he was. If a student's subject interested him, he did not limit his interest to the classroom.

Park spoke from time to time of consensus, of social unity such as exists in a mob with a common mood, or *Stimmung*. He thought that the mob or crowd, released from the control of institutions, manifested certain features of "emotional unity" which were fundamental in the life of society under more ordinary circumstances. In his idea of moral order, inchoately expounded by him and inchoately apprehended by me, he went more deeply into the fundamental substratum of the bonds which form individuals into societies than any other sociologist of his time or since.

Park combined this brooding reflectiveness about the basis of society with a passionate sensitivity to the humble facts of ordinary life. He loved to walk the streets to watch ordinary human beings, to strike up conversations with them, to ask them questions, and to ponder on their lives. When a student did a dissertation under him, he lived in that student's subject, imposed himself on the student, went to the district where the student was doing his fieldwork, adding his own observation to the student's. He cross-examined his students and thought aloud with them about the things he and they had observed. If a graduate student worked on an interesting subject—usually a subject suggested by him— he interested himself unrestrainedly in the student's work. That is how it happened that important studies were published from the dissertations which he supervised by authors who never afterward wrote anything of any interest whatsoever. He had no reservations about telling a student, "I am interested in you." He once said that to me.

If students faltered, Park kept after them with kindness and sometimes with brutality. One graduate student in the department, a Negro, had formerly been a policeman in a large city of the Northwest; he had aroused the interest of one of Park's former students, who was then teaching at a university in that area and who sent this man to work under Park for an advanced degree. He was a thick-chested, large man, of the shape which used to be characteristic of American policemen; he was also a jovial person, quite clever, and Park wanted to make something of him. Park farmed him out to another professor who was writing a book on

Negro politicians, and the former policeman did much of the fieldwork but he was not always a faithful worker; there were periods when he was indolent, too convivial, or pursued women. One day Park took him to task for his neglect of his duties and his waste of his talents. He launched into the student—then a man of about thirty-five. He started with reprimands, then began to shout at him, and finally the man burst into tears. There the interview ended and the crushed object of Park's censure went back to his room, much the worse for the encounter. About an hour later, Park appeared at the man's door, to cheer him up and to apologize for having spoken to him so roughly. He explained himself by saying that the student would benefit by the chiding he had received. "Conflict brings out what's in a man" was his final consolation to the sorry fellow.

Park was not a lucid expositor of his own ideas; he proceeded by giving hints about glimpses, but his growling ruminations about what he glimpsed were so vivid and so emphatic, so many-sided, that I understood things from him which he never said. After the class he would walk home, about three-quarters of a mile from the university. I often accompanied him and he thought aloud all the way. Having been in the Orient for much of the previous year, he would tell me about what he had seen there and what it signified. Rickshaw pullers, small merchants, priests and temple custodians, gamblers—everybody and everything interested him. He also wandered about the streets of Chicago in districts through which he had tramped in the past, observing and reflecting unceasingly. He spoke to me with horror of what he had just seen on the West Side. In what was then the idiom of American sociology, he spoke to me with horrified astonishment of some of the younger inhabitants of one of those areas: "They have no norms; they have no norms at all." He did not intend to be prophetic but he was. I said very little in response to the interesting things he told me.

Although retired after this last course, Park continued to come to the department of sociology on most days, and I saw a lot of him because he came frequently into Louis Wirth's room while we were revising my translation of Karl Mannheim's *Ideologie und Utopie,* which Wirth had asked me to do. (This had become a substitute for the "methodological presuppositions . . ." which soon ran into the ground because neither Wirth nor I knew what we were looking for.) Park would come into Wirth's room several times each day when he was at the university, usually very excited about some new aspect of an old idea which had occurred to him while reading or writing. He continued to read the most miscellaneous books which seemed to bear on his interest in the unity of the crowd, the normative element in human action, the composition of conformity, the incessant disruptions of order in every sphere of social life. He never sat down, but paced back and forth in the small room, in a lumbering ursine movement, gesticulating with both hands outstretched in front of his chest, moving up and down. I cannot recall the things he said, but I received from those frequent interruptions a sense of Park's unquenchable wonderment and curiosity. I also came to understand why Park's writings are so incoherent. Wherever an idea came to him in the course of writing it, he transferred it to conversation, talking until he used up his stimulation. He would then go back to his manuscripts and would begin again where the conversation had left off. I am not certain of this, but after seeing him in action so often in this way and reading his penetrating but discontinuous essays, this explanation seems plausible to me.

In about 1935 or 1936, Park went to live at Fisk University, where his beloved pupil Charles Johnson was professor and later president. He had a special interest in black men and women and had lived in Tuskegee for some time as Booker T. Washington's associate, writing much of Washington's famous autobiography, *Up from Slavery*. I did not see him again except very briefly. He died in 1944 while I was away from Chicago but he left a most formative impression on my way of looking at society and societies.

One day in the summer of 1936 Louis Wirth came down into the room in the Social Science Building which Herbert Goldhamer and I shared. He was accompanied by Talcott Parsons. The first thing that struck me about Parsons was the look of refinement on his face, which was not common among sociologists. He looked well-bred, and gave the impression of pacific concentration of mind. Most sociologists looked very ill-assorted. They were no longer clergymen; they were not businessmen; they were gawky, awkward country boys, however old they were. Parsons looked a little like a genteel easterner, although, like many sociologists, he too came from the Middle West, having been born in Ohio.

Talcott Parsons was very conscious of his mission to bring intellectual order into sociology, but he was neither priggish nor arrogant. By 1936 he was well on the road to the completion of the first stage of his journey and he knew that he had traveled a great distance. In the summer term of 1937 he came to teach at Chicago, and the huge typescript of his *The Structure of Social Action* accompanied him. It was already complete; he lectured with parts of the typescript in front of him but he did not look at it. He spoke very slowly in a low, dry monotone, as from a vision. He spoke with some pride and with confident modesty of his intellectual accomplishment in demonstrating, with great meticulousness and rigor, the structure of traditions behind Durkheim, Weber, Pareto, and Alfred Marshall. He also spoke with pride of his observations of the relations between physicians and patients. The association with the highest stratum of the New England medical profession at the Massachusetts General Hospital, which he had studied so closely, had entered into his self-confidence.

Until *The Structure of Social Action* was completed, Talcott Parsons knew exactly where he was going. When it was over he did not stop, but his direction became less clear. This was the time when he wrote his best things on relatively particular subjects— on social stratification, on kinship and family, on age in the United States, and on the rise of totalitarian nationalist movements. These were excellent essays and sociological in the best sense, but the extent to which they were guided by, or subsumed under, explicit and abstract theoretical ideas was rather slight.

A few years later, Parsons's paper on social stratification brought us a little closer together. He had sent the paper to the *American Journal of Sociology* with a view to publication. Ernest Burgess, who was then the editor, asked me to read it for the *Journal*. I did so, writing about twenty foolscap pages of sharply critical comments and suggestions for revision in content, style, and organization. It was toward the end of the 1930s, and I was myself very much engaged in the study of social stratification and had a few not wholly commonplace ideas on the subject which I put into suggestions for Parsons's revision. Not long afterward we were together traveling on a train from Detroit to Chicago after a meeting. Talcott Parsons and I went to the dining car for a cup of coffee. He thanked me as warmly as it was in his very restrained nature to do for my comments on and proposed revisions of his paper, and he said that he had accepted them all. He did not mention the subject of the paper and I did not at first know what he was referring to. Then, as he continued, I recalled his paper on social stratification and my comments, and I was a little anxious because I recalled that some of them were rather censorious, even harsh. I therefore pretended that I was being mistakenly thanked for someone else's labors. He was not to be dissuaded by my dissimulation, however, and told me that Ernest Burgess had sent him my criticisms and suggestions and that he had recognized my handwriting and the yellow foolscap legal paper on which he knew that I always wrote. I tell this long-winded story to underscore the point that Talcott Parsons was one of the humblest and least vain of men of genuine intellectual accomplishments.

Talcott Parsons was a saint of sociology; his life was consecrated to it. He had a vision of social action which he sought ceaselessly to differentiate and to unify. He was a good man in all his relationships, but sociology was the center of his concern. Not an insight here and a cleared area there but a unified understanding of society was the ambition which dominated him. During the time when we collaborated on *Toward a General Theory of Action,* we often worked until midnight discussing and drafting, discussing and redrafting; then often as early as seven o'clock in the morning of the next day, he would be on the telephone with me, raising a question about what we had done the preceding day, suggesting a new formulation, a new distinction, or a new connection which we had failed to make. He sought to find systemic patterns and the interconnectedness of all things in society, and yet he never lost any of the modesty which I noticed in him on the first day we met. When toward the last years of his life all sorts of miscreants took to abusing him for being a reactionary, a "servant of the interests," he never once complained. He was saddened but never embittered. He never slackened in his devotion to his calling. Max Weber would have appreciated him as a *Berufsmensch* who did not lose his depth of vision.

No account of the intellectual atmosphere in which I lived in Chicago in the 1930s would be complete without a few words about Harold Lasswell, who has recently died. By the time I first came to Chicago, he was already fairly high in the firmament of the social sciences—at least in Chicago. He had written a brilliant doctoral dissertation on *Propaganda Technique in the World War* and he had also published, in 1930, *Psychopathology and Politics,* which he wrote when he was about twenty-seven. I had read it when I was an undergraduate. At that time, I was not interested in psychoanalysis, but any author who knew about Robert Michels, Max Weber, Mosei Ostrogorsky, as Lasswell did, was obviously a man for me. At the University of Chicago, I came into contact with him only after some delay. I knew a number of his students and I was put off by them. They spoke in extremely obscure, very portentous language of things which I thought I knew much better than they did. None of them read German and French as well as I did—if they read them at all—and they therefore knew the work of the authors they spoke about only through having heard about them from Lasswell.

When I first heard Lasswell lecture in one of the public lecture series of the division of the social sciences I was put off by his deliberate pose of omniscience, conveyed with an amusingly diabolical archness. Yet I could not deny that not only did he seem to think that he was the real thing but that in fact he was the real thing. As far as I was concerned, he too was a man of the great world. Europe and the Soviet Union were objects of easy reference to him. He had gone to Europe in the first half of the 1920s and he took special pleasure in not being a Middle Western yokel. Before his students, he referred to European politicians as if he knew them personally without at the same time saying anything specific about any meeting with them which could be confirmed or denied.

In fact, Lasswell came from a pious and respectable family in southern Illinois. His father was a clergyman, his mother a schoolteacher. Both parents lived with him in a small philistine house near the university. None of us was ever allowed to visit him there and once, when we returned from a long night in an Italian restaurant on Taylor Street, he would not permit the cabman to pull up in front of the house; he insisted on stopping about thirty yards away. Religion never entered his thoughts except as an object of psychoanalytic interpretation. I was at first surprised, and then not surprised, to learn after his death that in later years he became convinced of the reality of occult phenomena. He read in all fields of social science and history and affected intimacy with all; but he was, in fact, intimate with quite a number of them. He was in the great tradition of those thinkers who looked forward to the time when social science would guide society to a hitherto unattained state of social and psychological well-being. He did not allow himself to give any appearance of moral concern, and it is very likely that at this time his moral sensibility was extremely faint. He liked to appear as a cold-blooded social-scientific surgeon, delighting in designing social arrangements for the attainment of indeterminate ends.

Although he was only in his early thirties when I first met him, Harold Lasswell's closely cut and somewhat bristling hair was a mixture of gray and black. His black eyebrows, always raised when he spoke, his smile of pursed lips, his sharply pointed nose, thick at the middle and narrow and sharp at the end, and his grin—as if he were in conspiracy with his audience in an immense unspoken "leg-pull"—all gave him a devilish tone. He was kind and even affectionate, although shyness hidden by a cascade of words and his hints of being on the inside of all sorts of things gave a different impression.

Lasswell had a genuine reverence for Robert Park. Park was a man who knew the world as a journalist in Detroit, as a student at Michigan, Berlin, Heidelberg, and Strassburg, as an assistant of William James at Harvard, as a wanderer and seeker who had no pretenses and whose earnestness forbade any pretenses. Park was always open to whatever was "interesting"—one of his most frequently used adjectives. It was evidence of Lasswell's genuine intellectual discrimination that he took to Park in a way that he took to none of his elders—and for the right reasons. He also admired Frank Knight very much but he kept his distance from him. Knight abominated scientism; he was contemptuous of the pretensions of social scientists to be scientists, and he was very capable in acrimonious disputation. Lasswell, with all his effort to appear imperturbable and beyond any ordinary sensibility or hurt, was, I think, reluctant to be put into a position in which he would have to face Knight's often extremely offensive complaints about the intellectual ineptitude of his interlocutors.

I find it hard to estimate the significance which Harold Lasswell had for me. I doubt whether I acquired any fundamental insight from him, such as I acquired from Robert Park and Frank Knight. Lasswell's view of society, as I encountered it in the 1930s, was much under the influence of Pareto married to Freud. For him, politics was a struggle for power and what could be acquired through the use of power. Nothing was stable; elites were in continuous circulation. Lasswell's view was the Hobbesian view tempered by the psychoanalytic theory of identification which brought individuals otherwise isolated from each other into groups, which then pitted their collective strength against each other by whatever means they had available and which they thought they could apply successfully. All beliefs were ideologies. The psychoanalytic theory was put into the service of the theory of *homo homini lupus.* Lasswell's was a unique amalgam which was made before the popularization of Freud and Marx. The individual authors who went into Lasswell's synthesis were all known to me and I liked neither the intellectual result nor the moral overtones of the synthesis. But I learned something from it nonetheless. I was certainly made more aware of the possibilities of psychoanalytic interpretations, and it was in the atmosphere which he created that I was led to study this theory sympathetically and hence to take from it what little I still retain in my thoughts.

Like Park and unlike Knight in his economic writings and Parsons in all his writings, Lasswell was not gifted with the capacity of continuous, logically coherent exposition. His extraordinary fluency was not in character with the brokenness of his written exposition. Lasswell's two main books, *World Politics and Personal Insecurity* and *Politics: Who Gets What, When and How,* both published in the middle of the 1930s, were not well-rounded expositions of his outlook on society. In fact, he never succeeded in writing such a book. Nevertheless, for me these two books were extraordinarily beneficial. The very fact that the books were unsystematic—unlike his later book on power and society and the numerous works which he published after he became professor at the Law School of Yale University—permitted him a freedom of imagination and insight which greater ratiocinative inclinations and powers would have inhibited.

Like Knight and Park, Lasswell was a great teacher. Unfortunately his pedagogical fruitfulness ended early. He left the University of Chicago in 1938 after Robert Hutchins refused to approve of his promotion to a full professorship. For about six years he had a marginal existence on the edge of federal government agencies and he saw some hard times; the strength of his facade helped to keep his interior structure from crumbling. Fortunately for him, he came into contact with Professor Myres MacDougall, a distinguished international lawyer at Yale. He spent the rest of his career at Yale, producing many books but adding little to wisdom or knowledge. The Yale law students were interested in the traditional Yale training as the precondition for large incomes gained through work on behalf of business. Lasswell attracted relatively few of them; his students and collaborators became mainly foreign students who were not of a high quality, and the stimulation which he had gained at Chicago from his clever, hardworking students who really believed in his Paretian-Freudian synthesis was no longer there.

Of course, no one knows what would have happened to him had he stayed at Chicago, but I regret bitterly that he did not, for his sake and for mine. Lasswell and I were at first very wary of each other. Later on—after 1936—I became relatively well-acquainted and friendly with him. Bit by bit I came to like him until, after several decades, I came to feel a real affection for him. But from 1935 onward, we began to deal with each other as two sovereign powers—he a larger state, I a smaller one, even though he was already a prolific author and an associate professor and I a poorly paid assistant who had published little more than nothing. After the Second World War, I came to feel very warmly toward him, with an affection based on recollections of a treasured experience shared many years before. Unfortunately, by this time he was confirmed in a schematic, utopian belief in the feasibility of social engineering. I thought that if he had remained in Chicago, I could have helped him to avoid that fate.

I said at the beginning of these pages that the University of Chicago was, when I came there, in the beginning of the fourth decade of this century, a wonderful place for an intellectually serious young person. Some say that it still is. Perhaps that is not for me to say, since I am now older than were any of the persons I have discussed when I was in close contact with them before the Second World War. The traditions of seriousness about important things and of the freedom to study them according to one's best lights have persisted. The soil from which the traditions embodied in Knight, Park, and Lasswell grew has become somewhat more stony in recent years as the social sciences have become more professional, more rigorous, more specialized, more preoccupied with contemporary questions, and more dependent on the interests and whims of the federal government and the large philanthropic foundations. Despite these constraints, those two traditions on which I was nurtured in Chicago are still there, still alive, and still flourishing. I owe a great deal to them.

two

RAYMOND ARON

RAYMOND ARON HAD MANY GREAT VIRTUES as an intellectual and citizen. Among these numerous virtues were a penetrating, pervasive intelligence operating over a very wide range, an exceptional speed in focusing his mind on fundamentals in the midst of a chaos of particular facts, an immense stock of knowledge in philosophy, history, economics, sociology, and politics, a vast capacity for unceasing and strenuous work, a quiet and tenacious courage, and sobriety and lucidity of outlook and style. All of these were in the service of a steady matter-of-fact patriotism and a firm and discriminating devotion to the ideals of the Enlightenment. Yet what made him unique among the intellectuals of his time was his practice as a scholar, observer, and analyst, year in, year out, day in, day out, of what Max Weber called the ethics of responsibility—*Verantwortungsethik*—in contrast with the ethics of conscience—*Gesinnungsethik*. The ethics of responsibility requires the unflinching effort to discover the truth and the readiness to accept disagreeable truths; it requires the courage to act in the light of knowledge, and to be aware at the same time of the inadequacy of that knowledge, while bearing in mind the limited range of possibilities of action and the costs as well as benefits of any action. It presupposes freedom of action within these limits. The primacy of the obligation of intellectual, ethical, and political responsibility that lay upon politicians and citizens, teachers and students, literary men and philosophers was the dominant note in Raymond Aron's active career as a university teacher, scholar, and publicist—a career that ran for more than half a century.

Raymond Aron's inquiry began in his dissertation, *Introduction à la philosophie de l'histoire,* which was a study of the possibility and the limits of knowledge of history and society as these were treated by four German authors of the late nineteenth and early twentieth centuries; it was also a study of the historical consciousness and of the place of historical—and sociological—knowledge in action. It was a work of clarification regarding the powers of the mind to apprehend the reality of human actions and institutions in the past and in the present.

The central theme of Raymond Aron's dissertation—the conditions and limits of valid knowledge of history and society—remained with him throughout his unusually variegated career. It was joined with an active practical concern for the dignity of his country and the well-being of his fellow countrymen, which was not merely a contemplative interest. That interest was inseparably intertwined with the knowledge of the inevitable imperfection of knowledge itself and the ineluctability of choice and decision. It began to take form in the 1930s after he returned from several years in Cologne and Berlin. That combination was brought more sharply to the forefront of his consciousness in 1932, when he first began to give form to his political views in writing. He had been given an audience by an under secretary of the Ministry of Foreign Affairs at the Quai d'Orsay. He had expounded his strongly held views about National Socialist Germany and French foreign policy and especially about the danger of war if Hitler came to power. The under secretary replied, "The Minister of Foreign Affairs is a very exceptional person and he enjoys much authority. The moment is propitious for any initiative. But what would you, who have spoken to me so well about Germany and the dangers which are looming, do if you were in his place?"

That question never left Raymond Aron's mind. That question was always present in his analysis of contemporary politics in France and in the world. Decisions must be made and the actions that they require are always taken under the constraints of limiting conditions and of limited resources and with very imper-

fect knowledge; decisions, moreover, must be made with an awareness of risks and costs—but they must be made. Such decisions
require courage in politicians, and they require courage in those
who analyze the actions of politicians and who attempt to understand the world as an intelligent politician would see it. Raymond
Aron very early came to know the sterile vanity of moral denunciations and lofty proclamations, of demands for perfection and of
the assessment of existing situations according to the standard of
an unrealizable perfection.

Although he was a socialist (in fact, he was a member of the
Section française de l'International ouvrière, the French socialist
party) while he was a student at the École normale supérieure,
and although throughout his life he retained the humanitarian,
secular, democratic, and progressive views of social-democracy,
Raymond Aron also saw from the beginning that the government
of the Popular Front of the middle 1930s was pursuing unattain-
able ends by ineffective and self-defeating means. He retained his
sympathy and admiration for Léon Blum and for the kind of socialism Blum represented, and he preserved his intellectual interest in Marxism until the end of life; but he became, in fact, the
most persistent, the most severe, and the most learned critic of
Marxism and of the socialist—or more precisely Communist—
order of society of the present century. It was not prejudice that
led Raymond Aron to perform this task. He accepted the task because of his respect for truth, his devotion to freedom and to the
kind of society that sustains freedom and well-being, and his rec-
ognition that the world is a hard place, where ideals can be ap-
proached but can never be fully realized.

In an important sense, Aron was a man of his time but not
a product of the opinions that prevailed in the intellectual circles
of his time. He was an anguished witness to the weakness—decadence, he called it later—of French society in the 1930s and of its
humiliation under conditions of defeat and occupation in
the Second World War. When he returned to France in 1944, the
agenda for the rest of his public life was made firm. It included the
rehabilitation of French society, the effectiveness of its political
conduct, the renewal of its self-respect, the protection of its unity
in a regime of liberal democracy that makes provision for free dis-

agreement, its integration into the wider civilization of humane and progressive liberal democracies, and the protection of that civilization from the encroachment of totalitarianism and the destructiveness of war. These were his daily preoccupations from 1947 to 1977 as publicist in *Figaro*, as well as in many other journals, and in *l'Express* from 1977 until his death. They were also his preoccupations in the academic career that he resumed in 1955, when he became professor of sociology at the Sorbonne, and later, when he became a director of studies at the École pratique des hautes études in 1960, and when he was professor of the sociology of European civilization at the Collège de France from 1969 until his retirement in 1978.

Raymond Aron did not direct his mind to the ultimate problems of human existence—he was too much an heir of the Enlightenment to think about transcendental realities; he directed it to the problems of his time, and he did so from a stable point of view. This point of view was defined by the prizing of reason and liberty and of the institutions, the society, and the civilization in which reason and liberty could be practiced and maintained and in which human beings could lead a decent life and have some influence on their fate.

II

At the time of his death on October 17, 1983, Raymond Aron was the most prominent and the most esteemed writer in the world on modern society and contemporary international politics. He was accepted as a towering figure in intellectual circles in France, Great Britain, Germany, and the United States, in Italy, Israel, and Latin America—indeed, wherever reason, learning, and moral responsibility are respected. He was never confined to the academic world by his professional obligations, which he observed with animated devotion and with a genuine concern for the university as an intellectual institution. He was known and deeply appreciated far beyond the boundaries of academic sociology. He had, in fact, become a celebrity known by the broad public that knew of Arnold Toynbee, Albert Schweitzer, and Teilhard de Chardin. He was the author of forty books, most of which were translated into English and many of which were translated into other languages both in Europe and in Japan. For a third of a century he regularly wrote many hundreds of articles on the current political and economic problems of France, as well as of the whole world. He was an honorary graduate of Oxford, Cambridge, Jerusalem, Chicago, Columbia, and other universities. Honorific lectureships, above all the Gifford lectureship, and honorific prizes—the Goethe Prize, the Erasmus Prize, the Tocqueville Prize, the Ordre pour le Mérite and countless others—were conferred on him. He was a member of the Académie des sciences morales et politiques and a foreign member of the British Academy, the American Philosophical Society, the American Academy of Arts and Sciences, and numerous other honorific learned bodies.

I think that no academic of this century—certainly no academic social scientist, with the possible exception of John Maynard Keynes—was so widely known and appreciated as Raymond Aron. In France, above all, leading politicians read his articles and sometimes invited him to discuss their problems and their policies. When he came to the United States he was sought out by the highest officials in the fields of foreign policy and national security. He was listened to attentively by the political elites of France, and by Robert McNamara, Henry Kissinger, and many others in the United States.

With all his eminence, with all the attention he received in high political circles, he was nonetheless isolated in the French intellectual world. Of his close friends at the École normale, one, Paul Nizan, became a Communist, two others, Jean-Paul Sartre and Maurice Merleau-Ponty, became arrant, if singular, fellow travelers of the Communist party and powerful and popular proponents of the Soviet Union. Le Monde, when it was not hostile, kept him at a distance. It was common, when a fellow-traveling, highbrow leftism ruled the roost in the French intellectual barnyard, to speak of Raymond Aron as a "reactionary." In the 1950s, I heard a refined young Trotskyite call him a "fascist." This same young man, when he became older and more sensible, became a devoted "Aronian." It was hinted, because Aron was critical of the

Soviet Union, that he was an American agent. His entry into the Sorbonne was not an easy one. Some professors did not want him because he was, so they said, a journalist; others did not want him because he was critical of Marxism and the Soviet Union.

His life was not an easy one. It was sustained by the warmth of his domestic circle and a small number of affectionate friends, some of his own generation, like André Malraux and Manès Sperber, others of a younger generation, like Jean-Claude Casanova, François Bourricaud, and the group that gathered around him first at *Contrepoint* and then at *Commentaire*. It was only in the last ten years of his life that French intellectual opinion about him became more positive; there had always been a certain fearful awe before his intellectual power and his vast, easily summoned knowledge. The new attitude was more respectful, more admiring, even reverent. It was certainly not respect for age—he never gave the impression of being an old man—which caused this change. It was a genuine appreciation of the power of his mind and character.

Raymond Aron himself attributed the change in French opinion—not about himself but about Marxism—to the obvious gap between Marxist promises and the squalid record of the Soviet Union. He attributed the change in French opinion to the undermining of Marxist beliefs following Khrushchev's speech of February 24–25, 1956, and the shock of Solzhenitsyn's *Gulag Archipelago*. Aron himself never drew any conclusions about his own rise in standing before French opinion from his observations of the changes in the standing of Marxism. Some of the change in attitude toward him should undoubtedly be attributed to these two large causes. In my view, however, the change in the French intellectuals' attitude toward Aron was simply that, even in an intellectual stratum as frivolous and as irrational as it has been in France for some decades, a vein of seriousness and rationality is inexpungible. That seriousness could not resist the evidence of three decades of rigorous reasoning and dispassionate mastery of facts, fairness to opponents in argument, and, above all, integrity and liberality. Raymond Aron finally gained a more just assessment from French intellectuals because even they could not long deny the force of his imposing virtues or the claims of their own long-repressed, better selves.

III

Raymond Aron's life, like all lives and especially those in the twentieth century, was much affected by accidents and by events over which he had no control. After the superlative achievement at the École normale supérieure, where he stood out among the most brilliant young men of his generation, including Sartre, Merleau-Ponty, Lagache, and Nizan, and taking first place in the *agrégation* of that year, he went to Germany. He took advantage of the opportunity to go there in a junior post at the University of Cologne because he was uncertain about what to do with the rest of his life. In Germany, he interested himself in the philosophy of history, discovered Max Weber, perfected his fluency in German, and witnessed the descent of the Weimar Republic and the rise of National Socialism. After a stay of about three years, he returned to France and taught at a lycée as a replacement for his classmate and friend, Sartre. For several years he accepted miscellaneous academic employments, and in 1939 he was appointed to a professorship at Toulouse. He could not take up this appointment, however, because he was called to military service. After the disintegration of the French army, he managed to make his way to London. Shortly after his arrival, General de Gaulle, under the influence of André Labarthe, decided that an intellectual review to uphold the idea of France in cultural matters should be published in England. Aron, who had meanwhile rejoined the French forces, became the review's political commentator, each month writing an article and a survey of the internal situation in France; he was also in effect the managing editor until his return to France in 1944.

There he became a publicist, at first with *Combat* and then with *Figaro.* He was pressed to join the staff of *Le Monde,* but he chose *Figaro* because, being a morning paper, its schedule of work would allow him to concentrate on his scholarly studies in the mornings and to give the later part of each day to journalism. During much of this time he also lectured at the École nationale d'administration and the Institut d'études politiques. When he returned to the university, he continued his career as a publicist with undiminished activity.

It was a unique career. There were academics who had been journalists—Franklin Giddings at Columbia and L. T. Hobhouse at the London School of Economics, among the sociologists of the two generations before Aron, had been editorial writers—and there were academics who became journalists. There were many academics who wrote frequently in newspapers: Harold Laski and Denis Brogan and Arthur Schlesinger, Jr., in English-speaking countries, Alfred Grosser and Maurice Duverger in France. Max Weber was an illustrious predecessor in this kind of occasional journalism by scholars. There has, in fact, been no shortage of these academic occasional journalists. This crossing of the boundaries between journalism and the university has indeed become a commonplace phenomenon, and television has further blurred the boundary between journalism and university teaching in history and the social sciences. In the case of Raymond Aron, the remarkable thing is not that he did both but that he did both so extraordinarily well.

This combination of two different kinds of activities and the unremittingly high level at which both activities were carried on undoubtedly contributed to his fame. The fact that he was known to be a productive and scrupulous academic philosopher and sociologist must have formed around his publicistic writings the aura that is even now seen as encircling a great savant. Whatever the dominant leftist literati in France said about him throughout the 1950s and 1960s and well into the 1970s, he was always regarded with great respect in the main academic circles of the United States, Great Britain, and Germany. His sociological achievements were justly known; the deference accorded to him was heightened by awareness of his subtle and realistic analysis of the affairs of the great world.

IV

Raymond Aron's combination of academic and publicistic careers was unique. He was a university teacher from the time of his resettlement in Paris after the Second World War until his retirement at the age of seventy-two from the Collège de France. Even before that he was an academic, in charge of a research center—the Centre de la documentation sociale—at the École normale supérieure from 1934 to 1939, when he entered the French army. It was indeed only during the war that he was not active in academic life.

He began his publicistic activities very hesitantly in the 1930s; they began in earnest when he became editor de facto of *La France libre.* Thereafter they went on steadily until his death, being interrupted only by his illness in 1977.

Aron himself felt a tension between these two careers; he sometimes thought that he had not done the right thing in becoming a publicist. He yearned to devote himself exclusively to his academic work. He would have liked to produce more books like the two that he wrote in the 1930s on the epistemology of historical knowledge and the two major works on war and peace that he wrote in the last two decades of his life. That was what he would have preferred. But for nearly four decades he regularly and frequently wrote short articles on topics of the political arena, domestic and international. He also wrote numerous long sociological and philosophical essays, and he published many books, some of which were formed from his already-published longer essays. None of these books is simply a gathering of unconnected papers within a single binding. Each is unified by a common theme, and all are integrated by the "signature" that is always present in whatever an important artist or writer does.

In his later years, Aron felt occasional regret about his failure to write those longer, deeper, more scholarly works that could not be written because of that obligation to comment regularly on public questions which he had imposed upon himself. Yet such was the force of his intellectual personality that there was, in fact, no separation of these two different occupations. The same fundamental values, the same way of thinking, the same preoccupations were present in all he wrote.

Something should also be said about the wide diversity of Raymond Aron's intellectual interests. In his journalistic work, he wrote with the detail of an expert and the penetration of a sage about the economic problems and internal political affairs of the United States, Great Britain, the Federal Republic of Germany, Italy, the Soviet Union, Israel, Japan, Communist China, and India. He wrote with equal mastery of detail and wide perspective about the international economic and military order. He discussed military strategy and military weapons. His writings commanded the careful attention of specialized scholars and persons in responsible positions in many countries, yet they could be instructively understood by the intelligent layman. As an academic, he wrote with unquestionable scholarly authority on the main German thinkers in historical and sociological theory, on the structures of modern societies, on military strategy and international relations, on Thucydides, Montesquieu, and Machiavelli, on Marxism in its variant forms, on intellectuals, on economic and social development, and on current economic policies. The list of topics he wrote on could be much extended. He did not experience any tension in keeping in balance this exceptionally broad range of subjects, each of which has its own large body of literature. There were good reasons why he felt no strain in mastering so many different fields of intellectual interest.

Yet he did experience a tension about the duality of his professional life. My own view is that he had, despite his own feelings about it, no grounds for a sense of strain in contemplating his dual career. There was a genuine unity that embraced all his activities; it was imposed by the unity of outlook that pervaded all his very diverse intellectual interests. That same unity of outlook made his dual professional career into a complex but single intellectual activity.

There were other heterogeneities in Aron's existence about which he at times felt a strain. One of these was his consciousness of being Jewish while at the same time being a Frenchman. This was not at all salient in his mind until his first sight of National Socialism in the last years of the Weimar Republic. Although he was a non-practicing, non-believing Jew, he was conscious of being of Jewish origin, but he did not regard that in itself as setting him apart from other Frenchmen. Nevertheless, in the 1930s he was inhibited from trying to tell Frenchmen the truth about Hitler because he was apprehensive lest, because he was a Jew, his objectivity would be questioned. So it continued until President de Gaulle in 1967 made his disparaging statement about the Jews. This evoked in Aron's mind the anti-Semitism of Drumont and of Vichy France, and he wrote a powerful denunciation of de Gaulle's statement. But by this time he had ceased to fear that his objectivity or good faith could be placed in question.

There was another heterogeneity in Raymond Aron's intellectual constitution about which he had no reservations or doubts whatsoever. The inner heterogeneity of being French, European, and "transatlantic" was one that he accepted entirely without self-consciousness. He was a Frenchman and a French patriot to the depth of his spirit. He was attached to France as a whole and positively; he was not one of those spurious patriots who espouses his own country only as a reflex of rancor against other countries. He was also a citizen of Europe—not in the narrow sense of being in favor of the Common Market, but in the way in which it was once said of Georg Brandes that he was a "good European." Aron was practically as at home in Great Britain and in Germany as he was in France. He was as at home in the United States as he was in Germany and Great Britain. He was more than a "good European"; he was a citizen of Western civilization.

He had never been in Great Britain until 1940, when he came there from Bordeaux to rejoin the French army, scattered elements of which had reassembled in England after they escaped from Dunkirk. He scarcely knew English when he arrived, but in a fairly short time he became very fluent in the language. He did not live in the confinement of exile; he soon became well known to leading British academic figures. The tradition of sympathy with British institutions that ran from Voltaire and Montesquieu through Tocqueville and Halévy became part of Aron's second nature. After the war he came frequently to England in various capacities to deliver lectures and to receive honorary degrees. Thereafter Britain joined Germany as part of his wider spiritual homeland.

Aron's relationship with the United States began later. I think he came there for the first time to participate in the summer school that Henry Kissinger conducted at Harvard. From the latter 1950s, he was frequently in the United States and was very much at ease there. He understood American politics in the same quick and sympathetically realistic way that he grasped all situations.

No other intellectual of the present century has had the familiarity and sympathy with the major Western countries that Raymond Aron had. Denis Brogan knew France and the United States, and Isaiah Berlin acquired a very acute knowledge of America in the war years. But neither of them knew Germany as deeply as Aron did, and neither of them took the welfare of these foreign countries into their care in the way in which Aron did. They were part of his larger family—they were not kinsmen who intermittently entered into his consciousness, they were steadily there. They were a third circle—beyond his own immediate family and his intimate friends, and France—a circle of wide radius, the perimeter of which was always close to the center of his own existence.

The fact is that, despite the multifariousness of his activities, the diverse objects of his intellectual exertions, the duality of his professional careers, and the plurality of his attachments, there was a fundamental harmony in Raymond Aron's life and in his outlook. Without that harmony, he probably would not have been able to sustain himself so fruitfully in the face of his own sense of the tragic character of human history, his isolation from the long-dominant circles of French intellectuals, the attacks made against him by those intellectuals, and the obstacles placed in his way by the academics among them.

V

Raymond Aron, once he found himself in Germany, had wanted to be a scholar, a philosophic contemplator of the world as it really is, with his contemplative powers strengthened by his knowledge of modern sociology and economics. First the war intervened. Then, after the war, his attachment to and solicitude for France impelled him to attempt to contribute in his own intellectual way to the rehabilitation of French society by the clarifying guidance of public opinion and the constructive criticism of politicians and of governmental actions. Nevertheless, during his first decade as a journalist, he did succeed in writing several books that were not collections of articles but were in fact elegantly constructed, eloquently argued books: one on the wars of the nineteenth and twentieth centuries, another on nuclear warfare, and another— the most famous and perhaps the most enduring—*L'Opium des intellectuels,* on the alienation of intellectuals from their own society and their negativistic self-indulgence in the politics of perfection.

All this was not enough for him. He wished to be a professor, to teach intelligent young men and women, and to write books of depth of analysis and scholarly thoroughness. When, finally, in 1955 he was elected to a professorship of sociology at the Sorbonne against some resistance, he entered a period of even greater productivity. He published a major book on the great figures of sociological thought from Montesquieu to Max Weber, which is now one of the most authoritative works on the subject, and three small books on modern liberal-democratic and totalitarian societies. These four books were based on lectures delivered to his students, and they are evidence of his sense of pedagogical responsibility as well as of the power of his thought. He also published at this time a work that has since become a classic on peace and war among states. During this decade and a half of extraordinary intellectual exertion, he also continued his publicistic activity in *Figaro* at the same high level and with unchanged frequency, ceasing only because of changes in the ownership and control of that newspaper. Three of his most impressive achievements as a publicist occurred in this period. These were his writings on the necessity of French decolonization of Algeria, on President de Gaulle's disparagement of Israel and the Jews, and on the "student revolution."

Aron was not, however, satisfied with these accomplishments, and he resigned from *Figaro* in order to concentrate on his scholarly works. In 1970, he was elected to the Collège de France, a distinction that had not been accorded to even the renowned Durkheim. During his tenure there he wrote his great book on Clausewitz and military strategy that showed what the learned world had lost, through the publicistic diversion of his enormous energy and his powerful mind, to the hurly-burly of politics.

In 1977, after the vexatious experience of his last months at *Figaro,* he suffered a stroke that deprived him of the power of speech and, indeed, threatened his life. He recovered completely all of his powers of speech and mind, resumed his journalistic activity in *l'Express* and *Commentaire,* and continued to write with his habitual clarity and fluency. His *Memoires*, which appeared in the last year of his life, is in itself a monumental account of the substance of sixty years of European and American intellectual life. It is also a vivid, often touching portrait of a very exceptional moral and intellectual personality.

Toward the end of his life, Raymond Aron permitted to be published a series of interviews, fragments of which were broadcast on French television. Two young persons, both of leftist political convictions, undertook to cross-examine him. They had studied his writings, of which they disapproved, and they were determined to put him in the dock. The result, *Le Spectateur engagé*, is a fascinating, quietly dramatic unfolding of the history of Raymond Aron's intellectual and political development and a fresh revelation of his constancy of demeanor and conviction. It is also a portrait of a noble moral personality, modest and self-questioning, of a delicate courtesy, of frankness and courage. It is such a testimonial to Raymond Aron's transparent and unshakable honesty, his patent determination to know and tell the truth, and above all his willingness to discuss—not just to expound—his convictions that, by the end of the interviews, the two young leftists who had come to demonstrate his faults, became his friends and admirers.

VI

Raymond Aron's accuser-interrogators repeatedly intimated in these interviews on television, as their elders have said before, that Raymond Aron had no heart, that he was without compassion, that he was a conservative without any feeling of sympathy for the poor in France and elsewhere in the world. His response to their charges and all his writings on modern societies showed just the opposite.

Indeed, one reason why he was such an outstanding observer of French life was that he had an embracing consciousness of his fellow countrymen. Without that fellow feeling he could never have understood his fellow countrymen, including those with whom he disagreed, such as the conservatives and the socialists before the war, the Vichyites, and, to some extent, the Gaullists during the war, and the Communist leftist intellectuals after the war.

Raymond Aron in his lifetime was accused by his detractors, who became fewer and fewer as the years went on, of being indifferent to the unhappiness of human beings. Nothing could have been further from the truth. He had, on the contrary, a remarkable tenderness and refinement of sentiment; it was expressed with such dignity and courtesy that persons who were not in his most intimate circle of friends might mistake it for an utter absence of sentiment, as no more than a polished instance of the *politesse française* that has now become so rare. Others, who knew him only from his writings and who had become used to the emotionally effusive rhetoric of those who think that passionate sentiment is all, and who think that a good purpose is served by wearing their bleeding hearts on their sleeves, also thought that Raymond Aron was a detached observer of an icy coldness. They were wrong. They mistook a dispassionate consideration of the merits and defects of alternative possibilities of action as moral indifference.

Raymond Aron never engaged in moralistic denunciations of those with whom he disagreed. He wrote against their arguments, not against them personally. He distinguished between persons and arguments. He did not discuss the motives of his adversaries; he examined their arguments. He was never abusive even when he was abused; he wrote polemics, but they were factual and logical, and he never insulted his adversaries as they insulted him. The same courtesy that was characteristic of his conduct in dealing with whomever he met was present in his dealings with those with whom he contended in writing. There was a tone of deeply felt sentiment in his voice, but what that voice said was invariably about intellectually stated arguments, his own and those of others. He was profound and affectionate in his personal attachments, and he remained faithful to the friends of his youth even when, as in the case of Sartre, the friend made himself into an abusive adversary.

It has always been a charge of the romantics against the Enlightenment that its cold rationality had driven enchantment out of the world. Raymond Aron was a direct continuator of the Enlightenment. He believed in and practiced the exercise of reason and the realistic assessment of possible courses of action in public life.

The virtues that he praised were impossible to realize in societies in which rulers thought that they had the ultimate and correct answer to every problem and would not permit the free exercise of reason and the free pursuit of truth that might lead to conclusions differing from their own. He also prized the freedom of the individual to pursue, within the limits of his resources and his obligations to others, ends that he thought right. That is why he espoused the cause of a pluralistic society, of competitive political parties, free elections, representative institutions, and a free press. That is why he opposed those who regarded the Soviet Union or some variant of it as the ideal. That is also the reason why he opposed the expansion of the Soviet system to other societies.

Although he regarded the free exercise of reason, the free pursuit of truth, and the freedom of action of individuals and groups as among the chief criteria by which the merit of a society should be assessed, he was acutely aware of the imperfection of even the best societies—and Western liberal-democratic societies, not least. He had no confidence in claims of perfection. No society, he thought, could be perfect, and every society was justly subject to criticism. He did not exempt Western liberal-democratic societies from these strictures. He was well aware of their imperfections with respect to equality and justice, but he thought that their merits and demerits must be realistically assessed in the light of plausible alternatives.

He was not a rationalist. He was conscious of the possibility of error in reasoning; he was, above all, conscious of the insufficiency of knowledge of the present and of the unforeseeability of the future. Theories or doctrines that claimed certainty were intellectually and temperamentally repugnant to him. That is why Marxism-Leninism and their variants, which confidently claimed to foresee the future as the culmination of an inevitable historical process, were even more unacceptable. He was a man of reason and truth who understood the frailty of reason and the obstacles to gaining knowledge of reality. Doctrines that asserted "the meaning of history" and expounded the correct way to realize that meaning were inimical, he was convinced, to the free exercise of reason and to the free pursuit of truth as well as to responsible and realistic action.

Utopias did not attract him because he thought that their proponents avoided, for the sake of an ultimate and unrealizable condition of perfection, a seriously taken responsibility in judgment and action. He himself eschewed the unqualified censure of politicians from the standpoint of an ideal that he regarded as unrealizable. He emphasized constantly the constraints of political action and decisions. He was always simultaneously critical and constructive. He knew that no politician or government could act without constraints; in every situation there were, according to his view, a small number and a narrow range of alternatives, and every one of these carried with it costs that should be borne in mind in the making of decisions. A government or any politician in office had to consider the state of opinion, the attitudes of rivals and adversaries, and the strength of the support that could be mustered for the realization of a decision. The limited power of politicians and governments, arising from ignorance—from inevitable ignorance, not avoidable ignorance—the impossibility of foreseeing the future, and the limits imposed on its powers by the limits of the support it enjoyed from its supporters and allies and the resistance of its adversaries, whether they were domestic or foreign, confirmed Raymond Aron in his conviction that no government, and least of all a government in a liberal-democratic society, could act in a way that would satisfy intellectual opponents whose criticisms postulated the realizability of a vaguely conceived but nonetheless absolute and ultimate ideal.

These are among the reasons why he so patiently and painstakingly remonstrated with the intellectuals of the Left. It was not that he was unsympathetic with humanitarian ideals—quite the opposite—nor that he was unsympathetic with the more recent demand for "human rights." It was not at all that he ignored the misery of human beings or that he viewed with indifference their death from starvation and disease or their extermination by the brutality of war. On the contrary, justice in distribution of rewards and opportunities was in fact for him a vital criterion in the assessment of the goodness of a society.

In one sense Raymond Aron was the heir of the best elements in the outlook of the Third Republic. He retained a deep sympathy for those who came to the support of Captain Dreyfus and who continued that tradition. He retained, in a somber, less optimistic way, their appreciation of progress—progress in the sense of the increasing material well-being of humanity—their belief in the rightness and goodness of freedom, their conviction that reason and knowledge are proper guides of choice and action, and their French patriotism. Of course Raymond Aron was more aware of the seamy side of the technological progress that was necessary to the material well-being of mankind; he was far more aware of the limits of knowledge. He was even a "man of the Left" in his humanitarianism and in his hatred of war. But he had no confidence that the "international working class" could be counted upon to prevent wars, and he had no confidence at all that public ownership of the instruments of production would improve the lot of men and increase their freedom. He had studied the writings of Marx and Engels too closely to believe that they were valid. He knew too much economics, he knew too much history, and he had studied international politics and military strategy and technology too closely to continue to accept the traditional doctrines of international and French socialism and communism. And of course he was never in the slightest degree a man of the Left as that term came to be understood after the formation of the Communist International. He was never blind to the mendacity and deceitfulness of the Communist party, and he was too intelligent not to see through the manipulation of the gullibility of the fellow travelers.

Nevertheless, although it was the Left that reviled him and sent him to Coventry, he had a soft place in his heart for it. It was his strong intelligence, his acute scholarship, and his moral courage that caused him to reject its false beliefs and its lighthearted self-deceptions.

VII

It is very difficult for me to take a just and final leave of a man whom I knew for over forty years, with whom I agreed on nearly everything he wrote and said, whom I admired greatly, whom, especially in later years, I saw infrequently, towards whom I was drawn by warm affection, and from whom I was nonetheless remote. I had so many common intellectual interests with him. I shared intellectual traditions that were very important to both of us in our separate ways. It has therefore not been easy to attain the detachment necessary to do justice to such a complex and many-sided character, to such a richly learned and such a polymorphous and yet utterly straightforward intelligence.

I first encountered Raymond Aron in his little book, *La Sociologie allemande contemporaine*, which was published by Alcan in 1936. As soon as I learned of its existence, I ordered it from G. E. Stechert, who at that time was the major importer of European books into the United States. I myself was spending a lot of my time on the writers with whom Aron wrote, and my judgments had been much the same as those he arrived at. The prominence he gave to Max Weber, at a time when very few sociologists knew how important Weber's work was, caused me to feel a kinship with him over the four thousand miles that separated us. The book was very much a *Jugendschrift*. Yet even at that early date, I could sense the courage that was one of his major characteristics over the remainder of his life. There was almost no interest in German sociology in France in the middle of the 1930s and no more knowledge; among the German sociologists whom Aron came across in Germany in the early part of that decade, Weber had nothing like the prominence he now possesses. It needed courage for a young man, in his first book, to fly in the face of his elders by praising so fully, in France, an almost unknown German writer and by praising, in Germany, a dead writer whom living Germans did not want to appreciate.

I met Aron for the first time in the early months in 1943. We were introduced to each other in front of the offices of *La France libre*, which were in a fine residential building in Queensbury Place. I had come there with a Polish friend, Eugene

Friedwald—a "petroleum journalist" who wrote on economic subjects for *La France libre*. Friedwald, or perhaps Karl Mannheim, must have told him about me; he appeared to know that I had studied Max Weber's writings carefully and had translated some of them. He knew that I had translated Mannheim's *Ideologie und Utopie*. He made a brief reference to our common admiration for Max Weber. He seemed pleased by my passing reference to the chapter on Weber in his little book. Then he went off with Mme Moura Budberg, the fabulous, then still beautiful friend of Maxim Gorky, H. G. Wells, and Bruce Lockhart, who performed some sort of administrative function at *La France libre*. I went off with Friedwald. Our meeting was very brief, but I still retain my original impression of his quick, yet sad and gentle, smile, the fraternal benevolence of his brief conversation.

After his return to France in the late summer of 1944, I did not see him again until the spring of 1947. Thereafter I saw him frequently in Paris throughout the remainder of the 1940s and until 1967, when there was a temporary suspension. He never varied from his, at least for me, somewhat shy friendliness and his humor, which was never injurious. There was a melancholy sonorousness in his voice. He never slipped into "personalities." He never flaunted his connections with prominent politicians. If he knew secrets, he never disclosed or hinted at them. He did not tell me things "in confidence." He avoided giving any impression of being on the "inside." Just as in his writings, in his conversation he drew on information that was openly available to anyone who went to the trouble to obtain it. The only time I ever heard him refer with pride to any of his writings was just after he had completed *Paix et guerre entre les nations*; his reference was not to its content, of which he could very well have been proud, but rather to the fact that he had written that very thick book, based on much study, in what was for me an astonishingly short time. He never referred to the honors that had been conferred on him or made other acknowledgments of his achievements.

Although during much of the period when I was much in his company he was treated by most French intellectuals almost as a leper was treated in antiquity, I cannot recall his ever voicing a grievance against his detractors. I remember a lunch in the late autumn of 1951 in a *cabinet particulier* at Lapérouse. Present were Georges Davy, a dreary Durkheimian professor of sociology at the Sorbonne and dean of the faculté des lettres; Georges Fried-mann, a very decent, once-Communist professor of sociology at the Conservatoire des arts et métiers; Aron; another person, whom I do not recall clearly; and myself. At the time, the "Gilson affair" was much talked about in the press and in conversation. Etienne Gilson earlier in the year had been visiting Notre Dame University. Gilson, who was a great authority on medieval philoso-phy, was much preoccupied with politics and was a vehement "neutralist." He had been writing for several years in a furious style against American foreign policy and most recently against the North Atlantic Treaty. Early in 1951 there appeared in *Figaro litteraire* an "open letter" addressed to Gilson by Waldemar Gu-rian, then professor of politics at Notre Dame, in which Gurian said that Gilson had declared that Aron was a "paid American agent." Gurian admitted that he himself had not heard Gilson say this but had it only at second hand. I knew Gurian well and he came often to see me in Chicago; on one of his visits he told me of the incident and he assured me of the reliability of the person who had reported Gilson's remark to him. This was well before the "open letter" was published in France. The discussion about Gilson's charge reverberated in France for a long time after the appearance of the "open letter," and it emerged in the course of our lunch. Aron uttered no recriminations against Gilson, al-though he did not deny that Gilson might have made the charge; nor did Aron attempt to refute the charge that was obviously base-less. I recall above all that Aron insisted that Gurian should not have written as he did on the basis of secondhand evidence and that he wished to dissociate himself from Gurian's accusation, re-gardless of whether it was true or untrue. He was pained by the introduction of personal considerations into a political discussion. Although his own honor had been impugned, he would not accept a vindication by improper means.

I have, of course, not read all of Raymond Aron's hundreds and hundreds of articles in *Figaro* or even the smaller number in *l'Express*. I have, however, read a very large number over the years, and I have also read most of his writings published in book form.

What impressed me most, along with their sense of responsibility, their transparent cogency, their complete sobriety of judgment, and their amazing informedness, was the avoidance of any display of his "personality" and the absence of any claim to authority other than the authority of facts and rational arguments.

His reticence about himself was equaled by his consideration for others. His patience with Sartre, along with his generosity toward him, despite Sartre's brutal denunciations of him, is only one instance of his freedom from rancor. He always tried to speak of others in an understanding way. I once asked his opinion of Bertrand de Jouvenel's conduct in the first year or two of the German occupation. Jouvenel had been accused of being a *collaborateur* and in 1941 had written a problematic book that accepted the unification of Europe under German hegemony. Aron answered in something like the following words: "The defeat of the French army and the subjugation of France by Germany had deeply shaken and disordered the spirits of those who had to live under it. It was easy for me because I had to leave France being a Jew and so I could maintain my intellectual equilibrium. But for those who remained behind, the situation was very much harder. Furthermore, well before the Germans were driven out of France, Jouvenel had made amends by serving the *résistance*." His appearance in court on Jouvenel's behalf in a legal action instituted by Jouvenel against an author who had accused him of having been a Fascist in the 1930s was another instance of his determination to be never less than truthful or just. (Aron died almost immediately on leaving the courtroom.)

I could go on and on in trying to be just to this extraordinary man, this model of civility, of selfless sobriety, and of deep and learned reflection. What stands out in my mind, in addition to his great qualities as a scholar and as a philosophical observer of human societies, was his indomitability. He was indomitable in the face of personal misfortunes, public obloquy, and the severe trials of the society and the civilizations that he sought to serve and strengthen. One of the greatest sons of the Enlightenment, he believed that reason could not be extinguished from the human mind and that his appeals to the reason of others would not be in vain.

Many years ago, Raymond Aron, Professor Arvid Brodersen, and I were standing on a street corner in Paris after lunch, continuing our conversation about the affairs of the human race. In response to a remark of my own, he said laughingly, "*C'est un pessimiste jovial.*" I now return the compliment but without doing anything like full justice to the richness of his mind and character, by saying, "*C'était un optimiste triste.*" With that I take my unhappy leave of Raymond Aron.

three

NIRAD C. CHAUDHURI

THE AUTOBIOGRAPHY OF AN UNKNOWN INDIAN ("an autobiography of a kind of life—not of a man") brought us to the point where Mr. Chaudhuri failed in his examination for the degree of Master of Arts at the University of Calcutta, refused to sit for it a second time, and therewith concluded that he must renounce his ambition to become a scholar, a historian on a grand scale, and a college or university teacher. This was in 1921. Thereafter followed more than fifteen years of intermittent despondency, penury, and contumely; during about seven of these years, Mr. Chaudhuri was unemployed and almost utterly destitute, depending on relatives for support offered disapprovingly. He was sensitive to the contempt in which others held him when he was in a weak position and to their envy when he was in a better position. From the middle of the 1930s, his critical attitudes towards Indian nationalist politics and his denunciation of Nazis, Communists, and Fascists, as well as his support for Churchill's demand that Great Britain increase its military strength, exacerbated the animosity directed against him. His large knowledge and his insistence on high intellectual standards were resented, as was his occasional display of a sartorial dandyism. About thirty years after his first reversal of fortune, on the foundation of *The Autobiography*, which was published in 1951, he acquired a small reputation in England and America; in India, on the same foundation, he became the object of even more raucous hatred and more vehement contempt.

Despite the appreciative and denunciatory attention which Mr. Chaudhuri received after 1951, his life did not change significantly. His reputation has grown, but it has remained small and to some extent unduly preoccupied with the unconventionality of his views and with what is thought to be his deliberate provocativeness. The slow, hard grind did not cease; his life was still very difficult. Now, in his ninety-first year, with the publication of *Thy Hand, Great Anarch!* (published this autumn by Addison-Wesley)—the seventh of the series of books which began with *The Autobiography*—it can no longer be denied, even by his late detractors, that he is a stylist of the first order, a scholar of great intelligence, learning, and subtlety and a courageous, wise, and honest man.

The first thing to be said about Mr. Chaudhuri is that he is indomitable. He cannot be imposed upon by man and he does not break under the vicissitudes of fate. He has always followed the intellectual path which has been an interior necessity for him. When he left the University of Calcutta in 1921, after his failure in the examination, he was humiliated as well as prospectless. The only prospect before him was the mortifying one of an "unemployed university graduate"—a condition very common and much feared in Calcutta—but he was not diverted from his intellectual interests; they remained practically undiminished and undiverted. When, through the intercession of a relative, he did find employment in the military accounts department of the government of India, his demonstrated capacity to perform the successfully assigned tasks, the high prestige of "government service," the relative sufficiency of his salary, and the absence of any alternative appointment could not prevent him from resigning after five years because he regarded the work not only as boring but also as alien to the vocation which had become clearer to him in the course of daily tedium. Then followed a period of several years of unemployment, no less distressing and very much longer than the first period of humiliation between the failure at the university and the appointment at the military accounts department. Still

his intellectual propensities never relaxed; he continued unceasingly to read widely and intensively. He was determined on a career of authorship; he still wanted to write a great historical work.

Mr. Chaudhuri's first published work in English was an essay
on a Bengali poet of the eighteenth century; the next, also in English, was a reflection on the inevitability of the Westernization
of Indian culture and the insubstantiality of the "Hindu revival."
His first ambition in the 1920s was to be a literary critic of the
type of Sainte-Beuve, or at least one like Jules Lemaître or Anatole
France. In the midst of the worst years of his self-exile in the de-
sert of Calcutta, he was a co-editor of a lively Bengali literary magazine *Sanibarer Chithi,* founded and conducted by a small circle
of close friends with the intention of deflating the pretensions of
a circle of self-proclaimed innovators in contemporary Bengali literature. This brought him very little if any income, but it was an
intermittent relief from the griefs of an embarrassing dependence
and sheer impecuniousness, made worse by surges of uncontrollable bibliophilia breaking out in extravagant purchases of French
and English books beyond his capacity to pay for them. The period
of unemployment which ran from 1926 to 1928 was succeeded by
about five years of service under Ramananda Chatterjee, a great
Indian journalist, who employed Mr. Chaudhuri as an assistant
editor of two influential journals, one in English, *The Modern Review,* the other in Bengali, *Prabasi.* He resigned from this post in
1932 in order to take up an editorial post which promised to be a
more remunerative one; that promise soon faded away. From 1933
to 1937 he was again without regular employment, pot-boiling
with very meager returns and receiving a very small amount of
financial assistance from his brother. He suffered much at this
time. He was already married and he was often literally penniless.
Mr. Chaudhuri has had a wonderfully devoted, uncomplaining,
and intelligent wife. She has sustained him by her quiet devotion
and levelheaded judgment about his abilities and about all other
matters as well.

It was only in 1937, after more than a decade during which
Mr. Chaudhuri was in steady employment for only about half of
the time, that he became, first, literary assistant to Dr. Satya
Churn Law, a man of great wealth and prominence in Calcutta

who was also a distinguished ornithologist and, then, secretary-cum-amanuensis to Sarat Chandra Bose, an eminent lawyer in Calcutta and a leading politician in Bengal. For about five years he combined his work for S. C. Law and Sarat Chandra Bose with work as analyst in Bengali on international politics for the Calcutta station of All-India Radio. His financial situation became better than it had ever been before. In 1942 he was invited to serve, in Delhi, as military analyst in English on the overseas service of All-India Radio. In 1952 he retired at the statutorily required age of fifty-five without even the derisory pension of an Indian civil servant of the middle rank. He would once more have been in very narrow financial straits had not the French ambassador to India, Count Stanislas Ostrorog, appreciating his knowledge of French literature and his skill as a writer, offered him a small income for writing the news bulletin which the French embassy in Delhi produced for circulation in India. He did this until 1966. The income from the French embassy, together with income from his writings, maintained him at a very modest standard.

After a late beginning, Mr. Chaudhuri finally succeeded in becoming an independent author. *The Autobiography* and *Passage to England* were published and well received in England; less so in India, although his success in England made some of the denunciations less vociferous. Other books followed in fairly steady and rapid succession: *The Continent of Circe, Scholar Extraordinary: Friedrich Max-Mueller, Hinduism,* and *Clive of India.* Now, Mr. Chaudhuri at the peak of his powers—and ninety years of age at the date of publication—has produced the long-delayed, long-awaited second volume of his autobiography *Thy Hand, Great Anarch!: India 1921–1952*—a book fascinating as it is long. There is no parallel to this achievement in old age.

In a sense, all of Mr. Chaudhuri's life has been a preparation for this book. The alertness of his observations, and the imaginativeness of his insight, the accumulation of his knowledge from reading and experience, the detachment of his large perspective, and the gravity and penetration of his reflection and judgment—none of these could have been achieved very much earlier in his life. Fortunately, his memory is as good as his curiosity, and his observational and receptive powers such that his narration of events of fifty years ago, like the descriptions of East Bengal in *The Autobiography,* retains the freshness of accounts of things recently seen or experienced.

Mr. Chaudhuri's life has been lived in only a few places. He has not traveled much except through his mind, but through that kind of travel he has embraced the whole world. Until his first trip to Europe in 1955, Mr. Chaudhuri had lived all his life in Kishorganj, Calcutta, and Delhi, except for trips to his ancestral and maternal villages and for visits to such places as Benares and Puri.

Mr. Chaudhuri is a puritan. A Victorian sense of privacy precludes the conventional sort of autobiographical self-revelation which "lets it all hang out." I must emphasize that although Nirad Chaudhuri led a hidden life, the world was not hidden from him. He watched it all the time. He lived to understand the world. His private life was respected, but it was made to fit into the relationship which he wanted to establish to the world: to observe it, to know it, to render judgment on it, and to avoid its corrupting temptations. Mr. Chaudhuri has dispelled the buzzing, booming confusion of the world and has never hesitated to formulate his own opinions on what he has seen. Except for a small number of friends, he has lived aloof from the world; he has not sought out the mighty and great and he has above all never sought their attention. Thus, much of the autobiography is an account of the observations which he made about Indian society as he lived in it in the happiness of childhood and the vicissitudes of keeping intellectually alive and true in adulthood.

The world has never ceased to be interesting to Mr. Chaudhuri. He is still alert to it, even in his very advanced years. He is still at heart a Brahmo liberal of the Victorian age, although he has disavowed the doctrinal beliefs of the Brahmos, and has elaborated his own views of faith, of man's life in the cosmos, and of the responsibility of individuals. He remains a liberal, and it is from that standpoint that he assesses the world as it is now. There are touches of old-fashionedness in Mr. Chaudhuri's idiom, especially in his liking for metaphors about the animal kingdom seen from an evolutionary standpoint, but he has never failed to see each event afresh.

Mr. Chaudhuri was never distracted from his concentration

on his intellectual vocation, because he was able to render unto Caesar what was Caesar's—but not more—and to render unto the spirit what was the spirit's. He was able to keep misery and boredom from seeping into the sphere of what he regarded as his vocation. His vocation, which he discovered and decided early on, was to understand the world, to appreciate the great and beautiful things in it, and to write into clear and concise English exactly what he saw with his own eyes and with his mind's eye and what he thought and appreciated—and, in so doing, to live a life in accordance with his inner necessities. This does not mean that there were no periods when he was not almost paralyzingly enfeebled by lack of self-confidence and ill health. Yet he never stayed that way long.

He never allowed himself to be deaf to the voice of his vocation. Once he gave up his academic ambition, the idea of being a writer, not just a writer who earns a living from writing but a writer who lives up to the standard which he has discerned in the greatest writers, dominated his life. Still, until he was in his early fifties, he had little to show for his extraordinary knowledge of history and literature. He had persisted in his long-held desire to produce a work of historical scholarship, but it made no progress. He would not seek anything below the highest standard, and he felt it was too difficult to undertake tasks which might end by falling short of that standard. In his fiftieth year he began to write his autobiography. Writing the first chapter on his boyhood in East Bengal brought his powers into full play; he finished it in 1949 and it was published in 1951. He had crossed the barrier. It marked his entry into a new phase of life. Now, after many periods when the idea seemed unrealizable, and when he would not settle for less, he has come through in triumph.

II

Mr. Chaudhuri in his *Autobiography* wrote, "I have only to look into myself and contemplate my life to discover India; my intellect has indeed at last emancipated itself from my country but taking stock of all the rest, I can say without the least suggestion of arrogance: *l'Inde, c'est moi."* Mr. Chaudhuri's Indian critics angrily repudiate this assertion in all its various forms.

About four years after its publication, while I was working in Calcutta, I attempted to turn the conversation with my host, whom I was interviewing, to *The Autobiography.* He stamped out of the room in a sputtering fury. The next day he apologized to me for his rude conduct the previous day, explaining that "it is impossible for us to talk about Nirad Babu. He has said so much to wound us." "Anti-Indian" was the main theme of the denunciations of Mr. Chaudhuri in India after the publication of *The Autobiography.* There was great resentment about his criticism of the present state of affairs in India. It was not rendered more acceptable by Mr. Chaudhuri's willingness and even pleasure in letting the chips fall where they may. Mr. Chaudhuri never uses invective, but he never hesitates to say things which many Indians think are directed against them. And they are not entirely wrong; Mr. Chaudhuri has taken no pains to avoid provoking these rancorous responses. The clarity of his style makes it easier for Indians to take umbrage at what he writes about them. The criticism has become less bitter in recent years; there is now more willingness among Indians to acknowledge his gifts as a writer, but the belief that he is hostile to India persists, as does resentment against him. It is alleviated to some extent by a smiling derogation of his admiration for England, as no more than an eccentricity, which implies that he does not have to be considered seriously as an intellectual personality.

Yet the belief that he is anti-Indian is not true. It is true only in the sense that there are certainly features of Indian society of which he disapproves very severely. He dislikes Indian politicians for their corruption and mixture of infidelity and sycophancy where personal advantage is in sight and for their readiness to fall into factional disputes. He thinks that Indians generally are deficient in their capacity for politics. He dislikes Indian officials, whom he regards as subservient and willing to serve any powerful authority as long as it rewards them with money, status, and power. Unlike many Indian and foreign observers, he is no admirer of the Indian members of the Indian Civil Service, who continued to serve the government of India after independence. He thinks that they were time-servers concerned only with their own well-being. He adds to this the further observation that Indians were always willing to aid foreign rulers in the subjection of other Indians. He disapproves of the widespread admiration and greed of Indians for money; he dislikes the superficiality and vulgarity of the modes of thought and conduct which contemporary Westernized Indians have taken from Western culture; he deplores their preoccupation with status, their supineness in the presence of superordinate authorities, and their harshness and lack of sympathy with those who are subordinate to them. There is no moral conviction in their Westernization: "Behind it lies hidden a dangerous void of faith, ideas, courage and . . . energy."

He thinks Indians are xenophobic. Indians were xenophobic even before the establishment of Moghul rule and their xenophobia became more intense under British rule. It simmered through much of the nineteenth century, when it was held in check by the assimilation into Indian thought of Western liberal and humanitarian ideas. Then, with Gandhi's first "non-cooperation" campaign, it came to the forefront of Indian life. Thereafter it moved cyclically, rising and subsiding and rising; it rose to a crescendo in the murderous outbursts at the time of the partition of British India into India and Pakistan.

Mr. Chaudhuri regards contemporary India as torpid. The defects of India are, he thinks, not of recent birth. At one time he thought that India of the nineteenth century was the heir of ancient Indian civilization, but in looking into the sources in preparation for the scholarly history of Indian civilization, which he once intended to write, he concluded that there had been a "complete break between ancient Hindu culture and our life and culture . . . in the eighteenth century." He now thinks that India is incapable of a vital civilization of its own unless it is subjected to foreign influence. Without the Aryan, Muslim, and Western influence, India would not have ever developed a significant civilization.

He is convinced that Indian spirituality does not exist. It is a figment of the Western imagination. He thinks that there is no creative power left in India. The Hindus are "a combination of putrified flesh and fossil bones." The industrial working class in the big cities of India "do not form a stable or coherent social class, but constitute an amorphously piled up and featureless detritus of the stratified human rocks of rural India." He is "thankful that the vast majority of the common people of India remain in their villages." The survival of the Hindus "is due to the fact that nine-tenths of Indian society consists of an inert element which is impervious to the active malignancy of the one-tenth." Indian society is a degenerate society; that is why it has been subjugated by foreigners. He himself, when he was younger, believed, as many Indian nationalists did, that the degeneracy of the Indian society was the result of subjugation by foreigners. Now he thinks that the degeneracy of the Indian character was the cause of the subjugation by foreign rulers, rather than the other way around. As early as 1936, he "wholly rejected the idea of a transfer of power to Indian hands by Britain as a possible solution of the Indian problem. On the contrary, I thought that power in Indian hands would be a calamity for the Indian people."

This all adds up to a very severe condemnation of Indian society. Yet, according to Mr. Chaudhuri, it has not always been that way. Indian life in the nineteenth century was for a time aroused from its torpor. Under the influence of Western ideas, brought into India by the consolidation of British dominion over India, Indian thought became animated. Both conservatives and liberals benefited from this first contact with Western knowledge, beliefs, and ideals; they thought that the "entire fabric of Indian society" had to be rebuilt. Earnest movements for the improvement of Indian society were set in motion. These movements for reform aimed to transform Indian society. The reformers sought to bring about the cessation of widow-burning, the right of remarriage for widows, the improvement of the status of untouchables, education—especially education for girls and young women—the promotion of science and technology and the diffusion of scientific and technological knowledge, the introduction of literary genres previously not used in India, and not least the improvement of the intellectual substance of Hindu religious belief and the eradication of superstition. The pursuit of those objectives and the public discussion of them gave an elevation to Indian life, especially in the great urban centers of Calcutta, Madras, and Bombay, which lasted well into the first quarter of the twentieth century.

For Mr. Chaudhuri, Bengal was the heart of modern India. It was there that a new impulse came into Indian life. That Indian culture, enlivened and deepened by Western ideas, was the light of India. That light has been extinguished, and Bengal, which was the leader in this movement, has now "passed out of Indian history." But it had not been that way in the Bengal in which Mr. Chaudhuri was and still is rooted. Men of that age "had a positive love for the concrete features of India or Indian civilization, e.g., landscape, literature, art, or music, which was always present in pre-Gandhian nationalism." The older generation of Bengali liberals had "a well developed political sense and awareness of official and political duties." He never met any of the members of this older generation of Anglicized Bengalis. "Even so," he writes, "I miss them."

Politically, Bengal was eclipsed by Gandhian politics, but the end came when Bengalis gave their unqualified support to Subhas Chandra Bose. The new type of Indian nationalism, which replaced the liberal nationalism and the conservative nationalism, both of which had flourished in Bengal under the fructifying influence of British and other European ideals, was intellectually retrograde. The new "Indian national movement was carried on in a growing cultural void." The promising movement for the reform of Indian society was forced into obscurity and then extinguished by the upsurge of Gandhian nationalism which emerged after Gandhi's return from South Africa.

Mr. Chaudhuri was at first swept into an enthusiastic devotion to the new type of nationalism; he was also suspicious of it. When, as early as November 17, 1921, there was a huge and violent manifestation in Calcutta to protest the arrival of the Prince of Wales in India, he saw the British soldiers, "alien soldiers, belonging to the army of our foreign rulers," as "the sole defenders of civilization." Nevertheless, he remained devoted into the early 1930s to the new nationalist movement. He had begun, however, to understand it better. He concluded that the new type of Indian nationalism had no positive content; it was driven by a "negative obsession." It was only after 1932 that he understood more clearly what had repelled him about the movement.

His historical studies gave him a long perspective on public life in India and much to think about; this and his own observations of contemporaneous events in India caused his own attachment to the nationalist movement to become more and more disabused. He had a "profound distrust of undisciplined mass movements." He despised the explosive folly of crowds; he was always distrustful of those who arouse crowds and who seek their approbation as well as by those who join them. The Indian masses, in his view, have two sides to their character: one is simple morality and piety, the other is violent action and hatred. Gandhi, he believes, appealed to the latter side. It was Mr. Chaudhuri's understanding of this bifurcation of the Indian peasant and the urban lower class of India that led him to develop a very interesting general proposition about the ebb and flow of Indian nationalist politics as a recurrent but unenduring surge of hatred in cycles of ten years. He himself did not see this until the subsidence of the "non-cooperation movement" of the early 1930s. His definitive detachment from that movement can be dated from that time.

Looking back over the Indian nationalist movement, he has little admiration for the contribution made by Gandhi to Indian public life. Gandhi, Mr. Chaudhuri thinks, was resolved "to abandon all civilized life and to revert to a primitive existence." He has concluded that Gandhi "had not the slightest understanding of the higher features of Hindu culture and its complexities." He thinks, moreover, that Gandhi's ideas have been without any influence in contemporary India. The movement created and led by Gandhi for three decades rested on a basic xenophobic irrationality which is endemic in India; it was propelled largely by an intensely emotional hatred of the British and British rule in India. It destroyed the promising Indian liberal reform movement and the conservative reform movement, both of which were intent on improving the social and moral life in India.

Mr. Chaudhuri became much more critical of Indian politics and politicians and Indians by the end of the 1930s. He disapproved of both Gandhi and Subhas Chandra Bose, the radical Congress politician who ended up as a would-be military ally of the

Nazi-Fascist coalition. Whether this precipitation of his critical attitude was affected by the fact that he was standing almost alone at this time among Indian intellectuals—in Bengal as elsewhere in India—in his condemnation of nazism, fascism, and communism, and his concern about the dangers which they presented to European civilization, it is difficult to say. He was deeply repulsed by the acclamation of Hitler and Mussolini by educated and middle-class Indians and by the admiration for Soviet communism among the intellectuals, even by those who were not Communists. Mr. Chaudhuri fervently desired the British and the French to resist Hitler—he was very familiar with the military and political situation of Europe and was probably able to follow it with greater comprehension than anyone else in India—and he was practically alone in this desire. The danger to European civilization alarmed Mr. Chaudhuri, while the hatred of his fellow-countrymen towards British rule in India blinded them to the likelihood of war. In any case, they welcomed the difficulties and distractions which were besetting the British.

The genuineness of Mr. Chaudhuri's attachment to India may be seen first of all in his distress over the partition of India. It is not only that he regrets the frightful murders of the time of partition—he tells a little of this in *Thy Hand, Great Anarch!* There he draws extensively on his two articles in the journal *Now* which are the best ever written on the dreadful events. What he regrets above all is the breaking up of the country. It may, of course, be true that he is especially sensitive to it because of the final partition of Bengal and the separation of East Bengal from India. If, as his critics aver, Mr. Chaudhuri hates India, why would he suffer from the separation from it of a part of Bengal in which he has not lived for about seventy years? It is, however, not only the separation of East Bengal from India; it is the detachment of so much of Northern India from what was British India as a whole that causes him pain. Mr. Chaudhuri was an Indian patriot from the beginning, and he has always remained one. He had a sense of being an Indian more than of being a Hindu, although the Hindu idiom recurs persistently in his discourse and he understands it with the intimacy of one who has grown up and lived in its midst. He is "socially at home only" among Indians. He refers on numerous occasions to his love of India. He acknowledges that Hindu monism, "which proclaims the individual soul and the universal soul to be one," is "the starting point of my faith. . . ." In his final elaboration of his faith, he writes, "I have had the advantage of being born a Hindu and of being brought up in the Hindu ethic."

The fact is that Mr. Chaudhuri, although he has written a great deal about politics, does not believe that politics is the be-all and end-all of human existence. He is above all not a believer in democratic politics. This goes very much against the Indian intellectual grain since Gandhi, and most of all since independence. This is another of the sources of animosity of many Indians against Mr. Chaudhuri.

Anyone who has read Mr. Chaudhuri's description of the town of Kishorganj and the countryside of East Bengal, his accounts of his family and neighbors there, his observations on Benares and Puri, his descriptions of street scenes of Calcutta and of the houses he lived in there—which he says oppressed him—his portrayals of his calm, silent, solicitous and thoughtful father, of Mohit Majumdar, of Sarat Chandra Bose, of Bhibuti Banerji, and of Ramananda and Ashoke Chatterjee, or his discussions of Bengali literature will agree that such things could not be written by one who lacked fellow feeling for his countrymen. Mr. Chaudhuri's description of the three great rivers of Bengal—although far briefer than Mark Twain's portrait of the Mississippi—could not have been written by anyone who did not love the country in which he lived. Only a person profoundly attached to what is essential in India could have written with such concreteness and penetration about India and about the two foreigners who had so much to do with the formation, political and intellectual, of modern India—namely, Robert Clive and Friedrich Max-Mueller.

III

Simply to have criticized India would have been sufficient to arch the backs of Indian intellectuals. But Mr. Chaudhuri has not left it at that; he has been practically alone among Indians who have dared to express publicly their favorable views of Great Britain and the British Empire. This has deepened the animosity of many

Indian intellectuals against him. This has, however, not deterred him. It has, rather, fortified his contemptuous attitude towards those Indians who are self-blinded by their nationalistic prejudices while, at the same time, vaunting their Western mode of life. All this was accentuated during the war, when British bravery deprived the detractors of Britain of "the pleasure of gloating over British cowardice." Mr. Chaudhuri writes, "I felt even more proud when the British people went on fighting alone, in this, too, depriving my countrymen of their second expectation of joy."

Mr. Chaudhuri's relations with England are no less complicated than are his relations with India. In both cases, deep attachments stand alongside unsparing criticism. From fairly early in his life, Mr. Chaudhuri took root in an England which he never saw until 1955 and in which he finally settled in 1970. Naturally, he has not become a native Englishman any more than he could cease to be a native Indian. There is little about him which could enable him to pass as a contemporary Englishman. But then no Englishman who was born around the beginning of the present century could be a perfectly up-to-date, contemporary Englishman.

Mr. Chaudhuri is essentially a late Victorian Englishman who assimilated as much of the intellectual culture which England had inherited down to the 1920s as any native-born Englishman. Although he was a small boy at the end of the Victorian age, the English culture which he acquired during the reigns of Edward VII and George V was the Victorian variant of that culture, richly filled with all that had gone before intellectually while being distinctly Victorian in its moral and political outlook. Mr. Chaudhuri's participation in the English intellectual tradition has been acquired mainly from books, but that is also true of the native-born Englishmen who possess that kind of culture. There is no other way in which it can be acquired.

Mr. Chaudhuri has made his career as a writer in the English language. The mastery of a language brings its master into the nationality which uses that language. It was not Mr. Chaudhuri's first intention to become a writer in English. He first wished to write in Bengali and "never thought of trying our hand at English for anything but livelihood." He goes on to say that "why from this early conviction my thoughts finally turned to English has its own history." Mr. Chaudhuri does not go into details about that history, but it is worth speculating about it because an answer would illuminate the singularity of Mr. Chaudhuri's relations with India and Great Britain.

There might be many plausible reasons for Mr. Chaudhuri's having chosen English as his medium of intellectual expression. For one thing, Mr. Chaudhuri began to write about public matters and ceased to write about literature. The national language of literary creation is almost always the language of the author's original nationality; there are, of course, exceptions, such as Conrad, and, at a lower level, Nabokov and Koestler, Apollinaire and Julien Green. But for writing about public or political matters, a foreign language is often used effectively. This was certainly true in India up to independence. English was the closest thing to a national language in India, and it was therefore an appropriate medium for reaching readers all over India about matters of public concern. It also offered the possibility of reaching an audience far beyond the boundaries of India, and therewith offered also the possibility of a larger income from writing. He might through English also reach an audience which would not spurn him for his political views, as Indian audiences were already doing in the 1930s and 1940s.

Mr. Chaudhuri was raised in a Bengali-speaking household, more rather than less observant of the Hindu piety and observance which had entered into the tradition of the Brahmo-Samaj. His father was a sensible man, a solicitor, not highly educated, a good father to his family, careful about the education of his offspring, attentive to their well-being; he was neither an Anglophobe nor an Anglophile. Mr. Chaudhuri's family was, mutatis mutandis, a Victorian family, and the great achievements of English literature were esteemed in his home. In his childhood, Mr. Chaudhuri learned the plays of Shakespeare and some of the other chief works of English literature. His first love was English literature, and he became intimately familiar with English history. Later, as a result of his reading of English literature and history, he came to admire such British moral values as rectitude, bravery, straightforwardness, and public-spiritedness. In the First World War, he was, in his sentiments, a strong supporter of the British.

Although Mr. Chaudhuri's intellect ranged very widely over

world history and English and French literature, he met very few Englishmen and probably even fewer Continental Europeans. He had no contacts with Englishmen until he went to Calcutta to study in about 1917. A kindly Anglican priest, Father Prior at the Oxford University Mission, took an interest in him. In 1931, he was lent a gramophone and recorded European music by Christopher Ackroyd, an Englishman who taught in a college in Calcutta. In the military accounts department where he was a clerk, his remoter superiors were Englishmen but he had no close contact with them. There were undoubtedly others, though they were surely not very numerous. It was not part of the normal course of life in India for Indians to meet Englishmen. His self-respect forbade his seeking out the company of Englishmen. Despite his limited contacts with Europeans in Calcutta, Mr. Chaudhuri acquired a very rich English and Continental culture. (His accounts of his purchases of books—English and French—in many fields of litera ture, art, and scholarship endear him to me. He and I were purchasing simultaneously, in Calcutta and Philadelphia, the same deluxe edition of the collected works of Anatole France.)

Mr. Chaudhuri's intellectual life is much in debt to Calcutta—and not just for its centrality in Bengali culture. A modestly cosmopolitan, somewhat Francophile culture existed in Calcutta. Mr. Chaudhuri drew from it all that it could provide. There were good bookshops which offered large numbers of books published in England; there was at one time even a shop specializing in French books. Mr. Chaudhuri was an avid, perhaps spendthrift, purchaser of European books on many diverse subjects. Then there was the Imperial Library, of which Mr. Chaudhuri made rewarding use. Calcutta was full of zealous readers of Bengali and European literature. There were some highly cultivated Bengalis of sophisticated literary tastes who knew a lot about European literature and thought. Some of these were intimates of Mr. Chaudhuri. The Indian intellectuals whom Mr. Chaudhuri mentions in *Thy Hand, Great Anarch!*, his friends and associates who in the depths of his misfortunes, sustained him by their personal loyalty, seriousness, and liveliness, were all Bengalis who wrote in Bengali and who loved the Bengal and its literature, which he, too, loved. None, however, had his openness to the world outside Bengal or could equal him in his familiarity with European culture. In fact, not many Europeans can equal him today in his knowledge of the classics of European literature, history, and philosophy.

British rule made available to Indians through Bengali literature and the teaching of English literature, in Mr. Chaudhuri's words, an image of "British character with its courage, honesty, stamina, capacity for work, as well as gentlemanliness." It did this by directing Indian attention to those qualities as they existed in England and as they were represented in English literary and historical works. The knowledge and appreciation of British virtues which he got from his reading of British history, of English literature, and by inference from some of the things which the British did in India, made British rule in India worthwhile to him.

The greatest Indians of the nineteenth century—those whose ideas and ideals were expelled from Indian nationalism "by the negative rancour of the Gandhian brand of nationalism"—appreciated the benefits of the British connection. Mr. Chaudhuri writes: "No Indian with any education and some regard for historical truth, ever denied that, with all its shortcomings, British rule had, in the balance, promoted both the welfare and the happiness of the Indian people. The general assumption then was that an Indian regime succeeding the British would also promote these as assiduously. I however began to doubt this from the Thirties onwards, and therefore I became more of an imperialist than a nationalist." He concludes that the British Empire "had a meaning for civilized human life as its disappearance is showing all over Asia and Africa today." For India, too, it was beneficial. "British rule in India ... I regarded as the best political regime that had ever been seen in India."

Yet, as Mr. Chaudhuri does not gainsay, it was far from a wholly pleasing scene. Mr. Chaudhuri had little immediate experience of the maltreatment of Indians by Englishmen in India. But the haughtiness, rudeness, contempt, condescension, and sometimes physical manhandling of Indians by Englishmen is very prominent in his mind. He thinks that by and large Englishmen in India behaved very poorly. They were obsessed by fear that the Indians would get out of hand. They feared a violent uprising against British rule. They over-reacted to Indian terrorism, which they could have dealt with quite easily and without excessive force; in fact, they did so quite handily, thanks in part to the ineptitude of the Indian terrorists. He still has not forgotten the rudeness of the resident Britons—especially the British businessmen and journalists who despised and feared Indians and who never had a good word to say to or for them. He disliked especially their apprehensive condescension towards Indians.

Mr. Chaudhuri says, against the British detractors who insisted Indians learned Shakespeare and the rest, in order to gain a "better" marriage, etc., that, in fact, Indians loved Shakespeare's writing in a genuinely appreciative and disinterested way. (He is certainly right in this.) He repudiates the contempt of the British for the educated Indian's appreciation of English and European culture. "When after reading Bergson or Croce, Mr. Hardy or Mr. Wells, with a sense of kinship, an Indian comes across some instance of ignorant superciliousness in a European . . . his primary enjoyment of a European writer becomes to him a cankering reminiscence of his humiliation." Although he forgives much, he does not forgive that.

This British misconduct, based on unrealistic fear and racial prejudice, did harm to both the Indians and the British ascendancy in India. Indian xenophobia was exacerbated by such degradation. "British officials . . . did more to discredit British rule in India than any nationalist could," Mr. Chaudhuri writes.

Nevertheless, in the beginning of the twentieth century, educated Indians, although humiliated by political subjection, still recognized that "apart from peace and protection from blatant oppression, which it had brought, it had also emancipated their minds, so that they could turn to social and religious reform and cultural creation." Mr. Chaudhuri believed and still believes that Great Britain brought to India an outlook which made for a tremendous improvement in Indian society. It improved Indian intellectual and spiritual life. In the words of the famous dedication of *The Autobiography of an Unknown Indian*, "To the memory of the British Empire in India which conferred subjecthood on us but withheld citizenship; to which every one of us threw out the challenge: *'Civis Britannicus sum'* because all that was good and living in us was made, shaped, and quickened by the same British rule."

It was this challenge which led to the greatest advance made by India because it resulted in the creation of a modern Indian life which espoused the ideals of personal uprightness, of a dignified sense of Indian nationality, of an appreciation of scientific knowledge and rationality, and of an ordered public life in which individual freedom was combined with a sense of responsibility for the common good.

Mr. Chaudhuri's repudiation of the poor conduct of Englishmen in India towards Indians "never made any difference to my historical judgment on British rule." He was long of the opinion that the finest phase of Indian history was the Indian liberalism which resulted from the assimilation and adaptation of British and Continental ideas; his regret about the present Westernization of India rests on his conviction that the particular Western ideas and practices which Indians have in fact adopted are departures from those which had elevated Indian life in the one period when India seemed to have taken a turn towards a better future.

Although for much of his life Mr. Chaudhuri wished India to be ruled, sooner or later, by Indians, he had not expected that to happen very soon; on the whole he did not bridle at the thought that the British would continue to rule India for an indefinitely long time. He probably held this attitude while he was a supporter of the Gandhian politics in the 1920s and early 1930s.

At the same time, he also began, as he matured in insight and judgment, to see that the British were losing their imperial sense and the will to continue to rule India. Mr. Chaudhuri does not think that the British had to grant independence to India if they had been minded to continue to rule it. He said once to Count Ostrorog, "If the British had the guts to spend only one thousand cartridges in 1947, they would have kept their empire for two hundred years more." He suggests that if they had been "ready to spend one hundred cartridges in 1946–47, they might have prevented "the slaughter of hundreds of thousands of Indians by Indians themselves."

In the end, Mr. Chaudhuri's pride and confidence in Great Britain have been disappointed. "At the end of the war, I felt that the heroism, intellectual competence and scientific inventiveness which was being displayed by the British during the war would be extended when peace came to the creation of a better world. . . . But my confidence in the British people and my hopes for a greater future for them was shaken in less than three months after the end of the war with Germany." The victory of the Labour Party in the election of 1945 marked the turning point. It made clear what had been happening below the surface of events. He was confirmed in this by the British withdrawal from India. He had already seen signs of this in the 1930s.

Present-day British society pleases him about as little as does contemporary Indian public life. The British people have lost their greatness. He writes: "Journalists, broadcasters, TV producers, and writers or intellectuals generally . . . are all clever and their mission is to ridicule all British greatness and virtues with ribald jests. . . . They are as rabid as the maddest leftist dog." And: "It is set against all forms of British greatness and [is] working in favour of British decline."

Mr. Chaudhuri has concluded that Great Britain is in a state of decadence and he foresees no reversal of the trend. The decadence consists in the refusal to acknowledge great achievements of great individuals. Disrespect for great achievements is a result, in his view, of the lack of courage to attempt them.

IV

Mrs. Chaudhuri had wanted her husband to go to England and to settle there ever since India became a sovereign state. She thought that he could practice the profession of authorship much more satisfactorily there because he would be nearer to his publishers and to his appreciative readers, and because in India "my abilities were neither recognized nor rewarded by those who employed me." He did not follow her advice because his three sons were still of school age and he was not willing to leave them and Mrs. Chaudhuri in India—as Mrs. Chaudhuri proposed—while he went to England. Furthermore, he still had before him five years of service on All-India Radio until he reached the statutory age of retirement at fifty-five. More than two decades later, Mr. Chaudhuri did act on Mrs. Chaudhuri's advice. By 1970, his sons were grown up; one of them was living in England.

I recall that sometime in the early 1960s, Mr. Chaudhuri told me, in the course of a conversation, that he looked forward to taking up residence in England, but I did not pursue the matter. The question remains as to why he has done so. It is, of course, unusual for a person approaching the middle of his eighth decade to transplant himself from his native country, but then Mr. Chaudhuri has never been a usual sort of person who is daunted by the possibility of doing something that is unusual. Had he done only what is usual over the course of his long life, he would not have become Nirad Chaudhuri.

England was as much the source of Mr. Chaudhuri's intellectual life as India, and it was a better place for his serious studies. He now lives in a village near Oxford, where he has access to a great library and to excellent bookshops. England offers advantages which India cannot offer. He does not feel himself to be an object of hostile opinion, he is near his publishers, and he also has opportunities in England to write in papers and journals of the sort which are not available to him in India.

Perhaps more important, England is not a foreign country to Mr. Chaudhuri. His deep knowledge of English literature and his familiarity with British history are far greater than that of most Englishmen. True, present-day England appears to him to be decadent. He is no admirer of "swinging London" or the "permissive society." He dislikes the slovenliness of contemporary English speech. He is saddened by British decline from its earlier greatness. Yet contemporary England is not the only England. The greatness of England in literature and architecture remains. The past is as real to Mr. Chaudhuri as the present. He does not draw from the daily newspapers or from television the spiritual sustenance which keeps his spirit fresh.

He has not renounced India. The best of the liberal India in which he came to manhood still lives in him. He has brought it with him in his vivid, discriminating, and capacious memory. Mr. Chaudhuri lives in a much larger world than do practically all of his contemporaries, and he lives in a much larger epoch. He lives, as he put it in the first volume of his autobiography, in "the fall of ancient Athens and in the breakdown of the empires of the Mauryas, the Guptas, and the Moguls, of the disintegration of the

Egyptian empire, the passing away of the Babylonian empires, the unfulfilled promise of the Alexandrian empire and the decline and fall of Rome." He is at home everywhere, yet he also thinks of himself as living in exile.

V

How did Nirad Chaudhuri, small and frail and having to surmount so many obstacles physical, linguistic, national, financial, and professional, achieve as much as he has, and how did he come to be so at home in the great world?

To begin with, it called for enormous self-confidence, which he gained only as the years passed. He never renounced his vocation. Although he had always felt himself superior to most of his contemporaries, he could not for many years overcome the inhibitions about putting his thoughts into a major book. He did not think himself fit to meet those tasks which he regarded as worthy of being undertaken. He lacked, as he says, a "prompting passion." He attributes this in part to his lack of physical strength, in part to a weakness in willpower. (I accept the former explanation but the latter only with qualifications.) He said that he needed an external instigation such as Mohit Lal Majumdar, his old teacher of English at school, had provided for him when he was a very young man and when he was a member of a circle which published *Sani-barer Chithi*. After that, Mr. Chaudhuri seems to have gone on without the stimulus of a circle of like-minded intellectuals. He had some friends in Calcutta, but by the later 1930s his position was already so singular that there were no fellow travelers who could accompany him on his intellectual journey.

The Gandhian movement was another such instigation. Its stimulus—sometimes a negative stimulus—gave him an object to which he was at first attached and from which he detached himself by an intellectual effort to examine his own mind and to bring to the fore insights which his first enthusiasm had hidden from himself. Fortunately for him, he was driven by cognitive passion. Even though he still lacked the "prompting passion" to write, his curiosity to know and understand never flagged. During the worst times in his periods of unemployment, he continued to read and

observe. Mr. Chaudhuri's English and French culture was acquired
by an impetus working on him from within. It was his curiosity
about the world and his pleasure in beautiful works of literature,
art, and music and in scholarly works of history and philosophy
that drove him forward. There was no one else like him in India
to arouse his imagination and to embody before him a standard,
compelling emulation.

Indian society and its relations with Western ideas and practices provided the objects for his curiosity, observation, and reflection. He gained little stimulus from any intellectual community from whose members he could learn and by whom he could
be stimulated. Mr. Chaudhuri's intimacy with English and of Continental culture and his original views about India were very much
products of his own force of intellectual character and of the survival within himself of the traditions left by the surviving fragments of the Bengali opening to the West in the nineteenth century. These qualities still did not make him into an author of the
books which he had always wanted to be.

When he finally came, at roughly the age of fifty, to write his
first book, it was about India and the West, framed in his autobiography; the second volume, the great work which just has been
given to us, is of a similar pattern. Mr. Chaudhuri has shown that
he can write with great penetration about subjects other than himself or about those which are not immediately connected with his
own path of life; it has however been about India and his relations
to it that his great books have been written. His *The Indian Intellectual* and his several volumes of essays are about the India of his
own times. *The Continent of Circe* and *Hinduism* and the books
about Robert Clive and Friedrich Max-Mueller are also about India, albeit in a way different from the books which deal with the
interaction between India and the West which Mr. Chaudhuri has
experienced and observed at first hand.

Remote from Mr. Chaudhuri in time, the two subjects of his
biographies represented in their lives certain fundamental aspects
of Indian life and culture and their relations with the West with
which Mr. Chaudhuri has always been preoccupied. *Clive of India*
is about the life of an Englishman who, by his courage and
strength of character, achieved more than anyone else to set the

pattern of the British Empire in India; *Scholar Extraordinary*, his book about Max-Mueller, is about the life of an Anglo-German scholar who, impelled by his sense of vocation, brought India and Europe closer together by helping to disclose India to the West and by helping to restore to modern India knowledge of its own intellectual traditions. *The Continent of Circe* is about Mr. Chaudhuri's contemporary India, as observed immediately and by reading, but it reached far into the past of India and into the physical properties of its territory to explain certain important features of contemporary Indian life. *Hinduism* is about the most fundamental beliefs of Indian society in the midst of which Mr. Chaudhuri lived as a boy and which has never been out of his field of vision, even though, as he informs us in the second volume of his autobiography, he "lost faith in the gods and tenets of Hinduism by the time I was eighteen."

Mr. Chaudhuri's being an Indian and a Bengali, and a European and an Englishman, all at the same time, is unique. He is perhaps the only one of his kind and there is no established name for the likes of him. Perhaps the old designation of "citizen of the world" is the only one available. There have been "good Europeans" in the past, persons who were entirely at ease in several European societies, who knew their languages, their literatures, their arts, and their institutions. Georg Brandes comes to mind, so do Ernst Robert Curtius, Karl Vossler, Count Harry Kessler, and, most recently, Arnaldo Momigliano. Being a "good European," however, although it demanded exceptional qualities, was an easier kind of thing than what Nirad Chaudhuri has accomplished, for there was already a common culture and a long history of the free movement of intellectuals from one European society to another, all within the setting of a common European civilization.

Mr. Chaudhuri is the real thing. His didactic manner and his obvious and justified pride in his mastery of the substance of several civilizations sometimes conceals their unique and genuine fusion. He himself is aware of what he has accomplished. In writing about persons like Max-Mueller, in whom he might be said to see his own prefiguration, Mr. Chaudhuri noted, "It is wrong to say that they become mentally, socially and culturally *deraciné*. . . . They can develop a very high capacity to assimilate themselves into any environment and move naturally in it. This is true cosmopolitanism which, in spite of its diverse elements, is a stable, though compound, product. . . . Such a life is no more ill-organized than a symphony but it is not easily put together."

More specifically about himself, Mr. Chaudhuri wrote that his experiences during the Second World War made him "a fuller *homo sapiens* than I was before, although all my life, I have tried to remain one. In making me that, it has not taken away from me any particularity I may have had. I remain a Bengali, an Indian, an Englishman, while being a citizen of the world. I have not had to give up anything in order to become cosmopolitan. My cosmopolitanism is deeply rooted in all the particular soils—material or mental—in which I have grown."

Nevertheless, Mr. Chaudhuri is well aware of the strains of this attainment. He knows that his detachment has had heavy costs. His transcendence of parochialism, his rejection of that feature of primordial attachment "which makes every human community to look on all others as 'They,' and therefore as enemies," has damaged his own standing in India where he is accused of having renounced his loyalty to India. "The only loyalty which I admitted I owed to my people was that I should warn them about the danger that faced them at the risk of being unpopular. This duty I have performed all my life, and therefore, I have now to live in exile."

More painful for an outside observer to contemplate than Mr. Chaudhuri's exile is his conviction that Europe is decadent and Great Britain not least. All his life he opposed those anti-European, anti-British Indian nationalists who proclaimed "the failure and bankruptcy of European civilization." Now that he has thrown in his lot with Europe and Great Britain, it has turned to ashes in his mouth. Mr. Chaudhuri might be right about the decadence of Europe and Western civilization—there is certainly some evidence that he is right—or he might be wrong. Right or wrong, it does not lighten the tragedy of the man who, while remaining an Indian, assimilated so much of the best of European civilization and whose reputation in India has been badly besmirched by his devotion to the West, and who, towards the end of his life, has come to think what he does about Western civilization. This tragedy does not, however, diminish the grandeur of his own achievement.

Decadence for Mr. Chaudhuri is cravenness, lack of individual and collective self-respect, lack of dignity, a deficient sense of honor, no appreciation of national greatness. An individual or a collectivity with courage, the willingness to exercise power and to take the responsibilities incumbent on its exercise is not corrupt. He adapts Acton's maxim into "loss of power corrupts, and loss of absolute power corrupts absolutely" to describe or account for British decadence. It was in the unwillingness to live up to the responsibilities imposed by national greatness that the decadence of Great Britain can be best seen. It is the lack of self-respect in the powerful that Mr. Chaudhuri despises. He is no unqualified condemner of empires; he admires the builders and rulers of empires and great generals. Churchill he admires above all political figures of the twentieth century for his courage and his sense of historical greatness. It is not power as such that Mr. Chaudhuri admires. He admires the virtues which are often necessary for the acquisition and exercise of power. He esteems the courage which leads to great achievements and the pride in such achievements— individual and collective, intellectual, political, and military. Mr. Chaudhuri sees the decadence of Great Britain in the present state of British manners and speech; the frivolity of public amusements, the triviality of interests and indecorous conduct are part of this decadence. He quite correctly sees them as of a piece with the renunciation of power and of the aspiration to greatness.

The tragedy of arrival at such a condition is real for a man who staked his public reputation on the assertion of the belief that there were qualities of greatness in the British people.

VI

Mr. Chaudhuri's achievements are not those he sought at first. Would it have been better had he been able to follow the path which he originally laid out for himself? Was it really such a misfortune for him to have failed the examination for the degree of Master of Arts at the University of Calcutta, to have resolved that he would not attempt the examination a second time, and then to abandon his halfhearted efforts to try again some years later—although that second try was what his father wished and what he himself decided to do and then decided not to do?

It is nonetheless interesting to speculate on what might have happened had he been as successful in the first or second examination for the Master of Arts degree as he had been in his examination for the baccalaureate. Let us suppose that he would have been successful in gaining an appointment to the University of Calcutta or to a leading college in Calcutta—at best, at the Presidency College or at one of the superior missionary colleges, at worst at one of the many others, missionary or private, then not so numerous as they later became, and on probably a higher standard then than they observed during the years of the great expansion of higher education just after India became independent. Mr. Chaudhuri probably would have been a very successful teacher of the most intelligent students, gaining their devotion by his great learning and his own devotion to the life of the mind. He would probably have attracted a small number of faithful, intelligent, and hardworking disciples. Other students probably would not have liked him so much because he did not teach primarily with an eye to the preparation for the examination.

The relations with his colleagues would have been strained by the superiority of his knowledge and his contentious disclosure of their mistakes. He probably would have drawn to himself much animosity from his colleagues, because he would not have hidden the light of his learning under a bushel. Indian academics are even more given to intrigue and cabal than their European and American colleagues. His liberal nationalism and his critical attitude towards Gandhism, socialism and communism, fascism and nazism would have stirred the resentment of his colleagues against him. He would also have by this time been thrust into the position of a reactionary by the Marxists who were more numerous among intellectuals in Calcutta.

Would he have become the great scholar which he had wanted to be, a scholar who held before himself the ideal embodied in the achievements of Adolf von Harnack, Eduard Meyer, Theodor Mommsen, Charles Seignobos, Albert Sorel, Ernest Lavisse, and other great scholars of that order? The probability is not high that he would have done so. Indian colleges and universities have never been congenial places for research, outside of Indological studies. Mr. Chaudhuri's views on India, as they developed in the direction which was necessary for him, given his values, his own research, and his fearlessness, would have closed the ranks of the European and Indian Indologists against him.

To do research on European or ancient classical civilization would have been extremely difficult, even if his teaching burden did not take up all of his time and energy; he could not afford the time or the money to travel to Europe to work there in archives and libraries, so that his scholarly productions would have had to be based on published sources and on those available in the Imperial Library and in the library of the University of Calcutta; hence he would not have met the standards of scholars in Western countries. (There was also a reluctance of the latter in those years before the independence of India to take any Indian scholar, especially if he did not write on Indian subjects, at all seriously.) He would have been further handicapped by his disregard for departmental and disciplinary boundaries.

The Europeans, who would not have deigned to notice him because he was Indian, would have found additional reason to keep their backs turned on him because he knew so much beyond their conventional academic jurisdictions. British scholars in those days were always ready to disdain the work of scholars who liked to "generalize" or who had "theories" or "ideas." An Indian with a penchant for doing so would have been even more handicapped—nothing could be less welcome to British scholars of those days than trenchantly stated works of erudition produced by a Bengali babu. The outcome would have been an unceasing series of frustrations compensated only by the regularity of employment at a small salary and limited by compulsory retirement at the age of fifty-five.

At the very time that he would have retired from an academic career, Mr. Chaudhuri's life in fact took a new turn. He wrote *The Autobiography of an Unknown Indian* in what would have been the last years of his academic career. It is very doubtful whether he would ever have written that book had he become a college or university teacher. As it turned out, *The Autobiography* gained for Mr. Chaudhuri a small number of admirers abroad, mainly in the world of letters and not much in universities. That book is beginning, very justly, to take its rightful position as a classic of autobiography. *Thy Hand, Great Anarch!* is certain to do so. Hence, looking back over Mr. Chaudhuri's painful failure of nearly seventy years ago, those of us who did not suffer it have very good reason to be grateful, or at least not to be especially regretful, for that failure.

About the careers of Sidney Hook and Raymond Aron—two men very different in their external features, in their societies, in their mode of life, and in their intellectual achievements from Mr. Chaudhuri's—I have recently asked whether they would have "done better" (whatever that means) to have followed more strictly academic careers than they did, and to have written more academic, philosophical, and sociological treatises, rather than given so much of their time to publicistic activities and to polemics about immediately contemporaneous events. In both cases, I asked the question about persons who had, in fact, distinguished academic careers and who had indeed raised this very question in their autobiographies. In the case of Mr. Chaudhuri, I ask not whether a shift of balance in a more academic direction would have been better but whether an academic career at all would have been a better alternative for him.

Mr. Chaudhuri's erudition was never poured into molds that corresponded to his ambition. It turns out that the greatest achievement of Mr. Chaudhuri's nearly eight decades of intensive study and precise observation is the record of the first five and a half of these decades. This is a great achievement because it is a record, clear and honest, of the activities of an intelligence of very great eminence, of a personality of clear and admirable lineaments in a situation of world-historical significance. Mr. Chaudhuri's autobiography is a work which gives pleasure by opening to us the village life of the East Bengal of his childhood, the Calcutta of his maturity, and the Delhi of the years of the Second World War and the first half decade of India as a sovereign state. Nevertheless, replete though *The Autobiography of an Unknown Indian* and *Thy Hand, Great Anarch!* are with learning, they are not academic works.

Mr. Chaudhuri never entered upon an academic career, and he therefore did not face the dilemma which Professors Hook and Aron faced. Yet, retrospectively, the three situations are the same, and about all three of them I render the same judgment. In each case, the best alternative was taken; in each case, the result was better than it would have been had the other path been followed.

A person of strong character has certain necessities of rationality and morality. It is not a matter of blind uncontrollable passion, of pigheaded obstinacy, sheer contrariness in the presence of temptation. The task which any person of strong intellectual character undertakes is the task defined for him by his intellectual and moral convictions, within the framework of the intellectual and social traditions in which he has been placed and in which he deliberately places himself.

There is an unswerving entelechy in Mr. Chaudhuri which never changes its direction. It was impeded and it could never find the form he had hoped in his youth to give it—namely, to write a supremely erudite work. In its course, that entelechy led him to acquire, and thanks to his power of memory to accumulate, a prodigious erudition. The person who has such an entelechy in him does what he has to do. Not everything that has to be done can be done. But for a person of strong character, what he is triumphs in the end.

The most frequent fatality of all intellectual activities in our contemporary societies is the gratifying ease of reiterating what is currently fashionable. Falling in with fashion is very easy—all the clichés of thought are readily available—and to do so, with a few spuriously idiosyncratic wrinkles, is also advantageous to one's acceptance and hence to one's career. To run with the intellectual mob is a common pitfall into which many intellectuals fall and in which they remain. They are acclaimed and rewarded for this with real money and spurious honors. This did not happen to persons like Sidney Hook and Raymond Aron, and it has not happened to Nirad Chaudhuri. Whatever they do, what is essential to their vocation gets done. They discover their beliefs by hard and studious intellectual exertion, they refine them by reasoning on experience, and they adhere to them.

Their beliefs are not the momentary products of enthusiasm—Raymond Aron, Sidney Hook, and Nirad Chaudhuri have, all three of them, washed enthusiasm out of themselves by reflection on experience and events. Dry and rueful judgment on the fallacies of enthusiasm is a salient feature of all three men. (Mr. Chaudhuri expresses this in his frequent invocation of the sagacious formulations of the *moralistes* of the seventeenth and eighteenth centuries.) They tell about the world as it is disclosed to them by the exercise of their intellectual powers. Whatever careers men like Mr. Chaudhuri follow, their minds shine forth. If they follow careers, as university teachers or as publicists or as free-lance writers, they always speak the truth as they see it, and, being what they are, the truths they speak are true about serious matters.

Thus, in the end, it probably has not made a great difference whether Mr. Chaudhuri became the great erudite whom, when he was young, he had hoped to become or whether he has become the author of two great autobiographical works. Whatever he would have done would have borne the stamp of his deep intelligence, his unceasing intellectual curiosity, his independence of spirit, and his unimpeachable moral integrity. *The Autobiography of an Unknown Indian* and *Thy Hand, Great Anarch!* give unquestionable evidence of these qualities.

And in arriving at this destination, after detours and delays and long periods of obloquy and insult, Mr. Chaudhuri has also been able to look back without embitterment and with a certain pride in the moral achievement of survival. Having become a citizen of the world, Mr. Chaudhuri is in the painful situation of seeing the world into which he has grown as being far poorer than he had hoped it would be. For a human being of poorer substance, it might have been an embittering experience, but that has not happened to Mr. Chaudhuri.

— *four* —

SIDNEY HOOK

I

John Dewey's philosophy has its limitations, but it was a great good fortune for Sidney Hook when he discovered it. It might have been designed for him. In him it found its best embodiment: its level-headedness, its rationality, its openness to new experience and readiness to consider every argument and any alternative in the light of experience and reason. In Sidney Hook's hands, it is emphatic in argument but never dogmatic in beliefs. John Dewey's philosophy is a generous one. It never excludes its opponents as irredeemable. It excludes no one—neither individuals nor strata—from the range of its sympathies.

Despite the facts that Sidney Hook has lived most of his life in New York and that intellectuals living in New York have made up most of his friends, interlocutors, and opponents, he has a genuine sense of affinity for his fellowman and for American society—unlike many of his fellow intellectuals in New York who unceasingly bore in their consciousness the burden of being Americans in a society in which they did not feel at home. Neither Paris, nor London, nor Moscow, nor Berlin has ever been the center of the world for him. One gets the impression that Sidney Hook never yearned to live in another century or in another society. He has never thought that it would be better to be a Frenchman or an Englishman or a German or a Russian. He knows that there is much in American society that needs improvement, but he does not think that the improvement requires a fundamental, disjunctive transformation.

Sidney Hook does not have the rhetoric or the voice of piety, but he knows very well what it is. When he speaks of his teacher Morris Cohen's attitude, he expresses it in the words of Santayana: "Piety was 'reverence for the sources of one's being.'" He then goes on to present Cohen's view of those who "went beyond rational criticism and reform and denounced America—either from the standpoint of an impossibly perfectionist ideal or, more often, as defenders of the foreign policy of the Soviet Union—[who] appeared to him to be violating the adage not to spit in the waters from which one has drunk." Hook seems to allow Cohen to represent his own views when he says that Cohen's "sympathy, as well as his understanding of the American heritage, became stronger with each passing year."

Sidney Hook is a quiet patriot. He takes for granted being American; he is careful to distinguish patriotism and love of country from chauvinism, jingoism, and nationalism. He has received and affirmed the traditions of the equality of opportunity, of the rule of law, and of individual freedom, pondered them, affirmed them, and taken them as the highest of goods in his outlook on the world. He accepts traditions; he emphasizes that his radicalism has been a traditional American radicalism. Although, in principle, Sidney Hook has regarded philosophy as a solvent of tradition, and has said less about philosophy as a means of discovering and improving traditions and finding out what is sound and fruitful in them, his attachment to America is not just to the America of the present or to an America of the future. It is also to a conception of America that includes its past.

Unlike so many of the American intellectuals with whom he has been associated—in the *Partisan Review*, for example— Sidney Hook has never railed against bourgeois society. He has never hated bourgeois society. Although his philosophy says little for tradition, he accepts and espouses many of the traditions of the society and the civilization in which he grew up. Even when he was a brash adolescent in high school, and a less brash but nevertheless radical undergraduate, sympathetic toward communism, he never gave any impression of hating Western society, and least of all American society. Sidney Hook always felt at home in America; he never yearned for "abroad," though he has experienced a more cosmopolitan culture than many of his lofty xenophilic contemporaries. Sidney Hook never pretended to be a superior European intellectual. He greatly admired Dostoyevski, but he did not turn him into a prophet of the end of bourgeois civilization. Sidney Hook is no prophet of the end of bourgeois civilization; he has never written melodramatic, bloodcurdling diagnoses and prognostications. He does not have any of the airs of an intellectual who sneezes in New York when it rains in Paris or London.

II

Sidney Hook has entitled his autobiography *Out of Step.* "Out of step" with whom? An outstanding person is always "out of step" in some respects. If he were entirely "in step," he would be no different from anyone else and hence, by definition, not outstanding. So with whom was he "out of step"? He was out of step with American academics in that he was probably the first American university teacher to study thoroughly the writings of Marx, Engels, and Lenin, and he was the first American university teacher to publish a scholarly book on the subject. (Vladimir G. Simkhovitch was an economic historian at Columbia who had studied Marx and Engels but never in the systematic and comprehensive way that Sidney Hook had done; E. R. A. Seligman was also moderately familiar with the writings of Marx and Engels when he wrote *The Economic Interpretation of History.* There was a doctoral dissertation by Morton Bober at Harvard in the 1920s on *Karl Marx' Interpretation of History.* It is interesting to note that three of these four early authors of books on Marx were connected with Columbia University.)

Sidney Hook was out of step with other proponents of Marx of his own generation inasmuch as his interpretation diverged from the then-dominant scientistic interpretations of the ideas of Marx.

Although he was not entirely unsympathetic with communist ideals or with the Soviet Union or with the Communist party of the United States in the late 1920s and early 1930s, he was never a member of that Party or a wholehearted supporter of the Party; nor was he ever unqualified in his admiration for the Soviet Union, even in the time of his greatest admiration for it. These things happened before the stampede of the fellow travelers; and when that began, Sidney Hook was among the small number who attempted to discourage the stampede. If the metaphor of a marching stride is appropriate in speaking of a stampede, Sidney Hook was also "out of step" with the stampeding intellectuals of the 1930s. He continued to be "out of step" with the "secret battalion" of the fellow travelers and their now-dispersed but still-influential successors who are more insistent that the United States disarm than that the Soviet Union should do so. He is certainly "out of step" with the "anti-anti-communists."

There are, however, things in life and society that are far more important than the beliefs of Karl Marx or the Communist party of the United States or even the Soviet Union and its fellow travelers in the liberal-democratic societies. After all, these things are all of negative value, and the last of them is of very negative value, so that being "out of step" with them is being "in step" with something of much more positive value. Sidney Hook was never out of step in those things that are really important: the maintenance of civil society, the well-being of his own country, academic institutions, and, above all else, the cultivation of truth as the object of intellectual activity and for truthfulness in conduct. Sidney Hook was never "out of step" with the central values of liberal-democratic society.

III

The New York—more precisely the Brooklyn—in which Sidney Hook was a schoolboy, the Manhattan of his college days at City College and his days as a graduate student at Columbia, was never a city for clergymen's daughters. It was a rough city, although more orderly than it is now, a city of hard work, respectable poverty, ambition, and hope. Sidney Hook came from a poor Jewish family that encouraged him to study. He was a bookish boy and youth, bored by his teachers and mischievously mocking their ignorance. His early life was an enclosed life from within which the larger life of the city was looked upon with respect and even awe. The Jewish boys and girls with whom he became friendly were readers, eager to know about the wide world of which they had no experience. They began as outsiders looking in. The world on which they looked was an austere one that had little interest in them. Their teachers were dry, inflexible, rigidly mechanical in their teaching; they must have been put off by their unrefined, uncouth, eager pupils, and they kept them at a distance. Sidney Hook's teachers were parts of that remote, still Christian firmament which Hook's own generation looked upon from afar, as through the looking glass, with distrustful awe, apprehension, resentment, and respect.

Nothing seems further from the United States of the 1980s than the New York of the 1920s and 1930s. The solid parts of American society were still very stolid. As a whole, much of American society and culture was still puritanical. It still had a center. Large parts of the society on the periphery looked up to that stolid center. At the center, puritanism and patriotism were combined with a rather unimaginative anticipation of a continuing increase in material well-being. There was little doubt about the value of scientific knowledge and its advancement. There was truculent pride in American society and confidence in its moral rightness in the world. It was a time of patriotism, on the one side verging into xenophobia and self-righteous chauvinism, on the other into regrets over a lost paradise and "the search for a usable past." The xenophobia and self-righteous chauvinism were more prominent in the beginning of the period; the regrets about the lost American past became accentuated and, as the period went on, brought out a hatred of the American present. Once the country settled down after the First World War, American society resumed its prior compound of individual diligence and ambitious striving in most of the society, with vigorous entrepreneurial activity, shortsighted self-interest among businessmen and farmers, and a mixture of corrupt conduct, civility, and efforts to be efficient in the political and governmental spheres. High stiff collars, rimless spectacles, and felt hats were the sartorial manifestations of the dominant tone of the times.

In parts of the periphery, and especially in the bohemian circles of New York, puritanism and patriotism were angrily criticized. Radicalism had always been a peripheral phenomenon, which had become much reduced through most of the 1920s. But by the end of that first of the two decades between the wars, a new kind of radicalism came onto the scene. Political radicalism, which had previously been to some extent an affair of a very small section of the educated classes, grew through the 1930s on a scale which American society had not seen before.

In the 1920s, criticism of American society was confined to a small number of publicists who wrote so vaguely that their criticism could scarcely be discerned—among them were Waldo Frank, Lewis Mumford, and Harold Stearns. There was H. L. Mencken, the jocular, good-natured philistine-baiter. There was also a small number of critics in universities—most notably Irving Babbitt and the remnants of the genteel Anglophile academic—whose voice was seldom heard in public. None of them had much of a following. Among literary men and women, the numbers were greater, but few of them were popular except among other like-minded persons.

Further out in the periphery, the Jews of Eastern European origin were beginning to stir out of their orthodoxy, driven and harassed by their monetary worries and desires and their ignorance of the language and the culture of the great world. They were linked to the center by their grateful patriotism and their hampered will to acquire its language and manners; they shared with the center its belief in the rightfulness of ambition and respectability. The first appearances from the cocoon took place in the generation born between 1900 and 1905, whose parents had come to the United States mainly in the decade before the turn of the century. Sidney Hook was such a chrysalis. Ernest Nagel was another. Lionel Trilling still another. They were the best of that generation, and they were also superior to the next generation, which had its path laid down for it. The world was a little easier for that next generation to deal with. The stolid center had weakened in the Depression; puritanism in economic and sexual affairs was showing many of the cracks of fatigue. But more important in the academic world was the pioneering of Sidney Hook and his friends.

IV

Sidney Hook had no teachers who took any personal interest in him until he went up to City College, where he was already determined to study philosophy. How that interest emerged and grew he does not tell us. The boys read lots of books, and they did much to educate each other.

Some of the boys in Sidney Hook's circle had a lively interest in the great world, although they had no contact with it except through newspapers and books. That world was also the world of the First World War, the Russian Revolution, and the violent suppression of radicals—the "Red raids"—of the first years following the war. Radicalism was prominently displayed in the newspapers. That was the social soil from which Sidney Hook's socialism grew.

It would have been difficult for Sidney Hook not to have been a socialist, given the distance that separated him from his teachers and their own drab distrust of him, and his own omnivorous reading, dawning moral sensibility, and his ratiocinative propensity. Sidney Hook in his youth and early manhood was a very special type of radical by virtue of his intellectual scrupulousness and his capacity for rational argument.

He does not say anything in his autobiography about how he first encountered the writings of Marx and Engels. Of course, socialism and communism were before the mind's eye of anyone who read the newspapers in 1918 and 1919, when the Russian Revolution was receiving so much attention and when radicals were being abused in the press and being physically assaulted by ruffians, policemen, and agents of the Department of Justice. It is likely, too, that some of his classmates came from families in which socialism and communism were supported or at least discussed. There were certainly like-minded students in his classes at the City College of New York. Once he discovered Marxism, he moved into it very easily. In any case, by the time Sidney Hook went up to City College he was already a socialist. He received no encouragement from his teachers there to persist in those views.

Sidney Hook was not one of those brilliant pupils who take a double-starred first in classical moderations or moral sciences, nor did he attend a famous public school or lycée. He did, however, have the luck to be an undergraduate at City College of New York, which for poor boys of Eastern European Jewish stock was an amalgam of Christ Church, Oxford, Trinity College, Cambridge, and the École normale supérieure. Many of the teachers there were at best little more than respectable place-holders. Many were philistines of respectability, defensively ill at ease with their insolent, unworldly, intellectually eager and excitable, sharp-witted, and tactless pupils. Of course, there were many who were simply ambitious to get ahead in the struggle for existence, or to go beyond the status of their impoverished parents who were, to a great extent, workers in the garment trades, small shopkeepers, and small businessmen. The undergraduates played a great part in educating one another by challenging themselves intellectually.

There was, however, one teacher who did educate them and left a very powerful imprint on them. This was Morris R. Cohen, an embittered, rasping, disappointed sage, resembling in some respects an unsuccessful small Jewish businessman, who was also a man of universal knowledge and extraordinary intellectual courage. Cohen's universal scope of knowledge, the cutting sharpness of his criticism of everyone's beliefs, his limitless desire to know, and his demanding skepticism put Hook onto a course from which he never turned back. Cohen's skepticism did not dissuade Hook from socialism, but it kept it from ever becoming dogmatic.

From Cohen, Sidney Hook moved on to John Dewey at Columbia. It was obviously a reinforcement of Hook's intellectual curiosity to pass under his new master, so different from his earlier one. Cohen shared with Hook a love of argument in philosophical questions, which, given Cohen's universal curiosity, included anything in which the human mind could be interested. Cohen's limitless eagerness to know fed and educated Hook's own intellectual passion. His aggressive skepticism sharpened Hook's argumentative capacity.

To live in the atmosphere of John Dewey was quite a different thing. Dewey was more generous and more ruminative than Cohen; he took no pleasure in cutting down an intellectual adversary, and with a student like Sidney Hook, he was very encouraging. Like Cohen, Hook learned to disentangle the arguments of his interlocutors; unlike Cohen, he did not attempt to embarrass them while doing so. Cohen was critical to the point of rudeness; Hook with all his combativeness was never rude or discourteous to his opponents. Cohen sometimes argued by sneers; Hook never did. Some of Hook's rhetorical qualities must have come from John Dewey, who never felt any need to support and reinforce his arguments by debaters' tricks that would discomfit his opponents.

It is certain that Hook must have brought into the presence of his two teachers the inclinations that they helped to form. Nevertheless, the two of them helped to form a mind which had its own style and direction but which also bore the marks of both of these remarkable men, so very different from each other in intellectual mood and procedure. From Cohen, Hook gained an additional impetus to his demand for clear definitions; from Dewey, he gained his willingness to consider generously ideas in their incipiency and to help his interlocutor to discover his own beliefs by the questions put before him.

Since Sidney Hook is not constitutionally a captious, fault-finding man, he had greater affinity with Dewey than with Cohen. Cohen was a noble spirit in his love of knowledge and in his courage to find the truth while traversing so many intellectuals' mare's nests, and on rare occasions he seems to have shown a touch of tenderness and affection. Nevertheless, he was a bit of a porcupine; his quills were quickly stiffened. Dewey was very different. In background he was very far removed from Sidney Hook; he was already a very famous man when Sidney Hook became his student, so that the distance between himself and the young high school teacher—as Hook was until his appointment as an instructor at New York University—was very large. This did not prevent him from appreciating Hook's intellectual power and his desire to introduce the philosophical method into discussions of public policy. He also never disapproved of Hook's political activities; he saw that Hook was attempting to bring philosophical discipline into political discussions rather than infusing his politics into his philosophy. Hook did not try to make Dewey into a Marxist; he tried rather, in his *Towards the Understanding of Karl Marx*, to introduce or discover a fundamental Deweyan instrumentalism in the thought of Karl Marx.

V

The academic world as it was during Sidney Hook's youth and his early career as a university teacher was a world apart from journalism and polemical politics. Academics did not expect their subjects to attract popular attention or to be of interest to persons who had never studied them. Although the publicity of academics outside the university was less common than it is now, within the university there was less specialization. An academic was expected to look beyond his own specialization onto his entire discipline. The subdivision of each discipline into a number of specialized branches, each with a very large body of literature and each having little in common with any other, had not yet come to prevail. The literature of each discipline was sufficiently small in amount so that a diligent reader of "the literature" could study the main classics and contemporary writings in his field; such a reader could keep up critically with much of the contemporary body of publications.

Sidney Hook was interested in the traditional problems of philosophy into which he had been well initiated at City College. When Sidney Hook studied philosophy it was a subject only for persons who had undergone a strenuous and demanding intellectual training; it had not yet been transformed into a subject for academic autodidacts and dilettantes. Philosophy in the time in which Sidney Hook studied and first began to teach was a "*strenge Wissenschaft.*" It was not mixed up with political polemics or literary criticism. It was a subject that could be studied without direct reference to contemporary politics.

The ensuing decade saw a marked departure from this broad and earnest academic isolation. Morris Cohen was interested in public affairs, and he wrote for journals other than academic ones, but he regarded philosophy as apart from the marketplace and the political forum. The philosophy of John Dewey to which Sidney Hook became attached was, in principle, one that denied the validity of the boundary between philosophy and practical affairs. In the five and a half decades since Sidney Hook entered on an academic career, universities have ceased to be as self-contained as they had been; politics, especially the kinds of politics that interest intellectuals, have become more florid in universities. Sidney Hook has courageously resisted the politicization of teaching in universities, although he certainly accepted the notion that problems of political decision should be discussed under the discipline imposed by adherence to philosophical methods. The spirit with which Sidney Hook cultivated philosophy was the same as that in which he conducted his practical political affairs; in both, rational argument and due consideration for evidence were given precedence.

Sidney Hook was an ardent debater about philosophical questions, as he was about political questions; his effort to adhere to the rules that still prevailed in debating philosophical questions when debating political questions was a rare virtue. He was "by nature" a philosopher, seeking clarity of conclusions by lucidity, reason, and evidence in procedure. Sidney Hook's intellectual career has been unceasingly characterized by his self-disciplined practice of clarity, his capacity to exclude sentiments in setting forth his arguments. He thinks that temperament must be adapted to the rules of philosophical argument and not philosophical rules adapted to the exigencies of temperament. Not so much by accidental features of his manners and bearing, but by the main contours of his deportment in intellectual and political affairs, does Sidney Hook belong to the world before the deluge.

If one engages in politics, and particularly if one engages in the politics of intellectuals, which are invariably about large problems and which are often streaked with doctrine, one is bound to be polemical. Sidney Hook has, willy-nilly, been engaged in intellectuals' politics for more than a half century. His engagement has sometimes been organizational, but it has nearly always been polemical. He is probably the greatest polemicist of this century.

Sometimes in political disputes, Sidney Hook has become very vehement, but he has never departed from rationality in argument. To maintain that strict discipline of rationality in political contentions of a sort which have traditionally aroused great anger and savage denunciation is a real moral accomplishment. Sidney Hook has been successful in doing this, and it is no minor accomplishment.

VI

Sidney Hook's choice of mentors was an expression of his intellectual character. Morris Cohen, John Dewey, and Bertrand Russell were his three guiding stars. What he learned from them has stayed with him all his life, but he would not have sought them out and he would not have remained faithful to them if he had not seen in them qualities toward which he already had very strong dispositions. I have already referred to the benefits derived from his association with Cohen and Dewey. Russell, who was a famous philosopher from the first decade of the century onward, was a towering figure made even better known by his political and social progressiveness when Hook first studied philosophy. It was not the latter which attracted Hook, and it was certainly not the fact that Russell was a brilliant figure in British upper class and in refined bohemian circles. In Russell, Hook saw a great embodiment of philosophical power. In the course of time, they even became moderately friendly, but what was most important for Hook in his relationship with Russell was the opportunity it afforded him to discuss philosophical problems unrelentingly and unremittingly. "We talked mostly philosophy and some politics and I drew him out on the philosophers of the past whom he had known, questioning him on details of articles he had written. . . . It was intellectually the most exciting year I had ever experienced."

There was never a period in Sidney Hook's life when his philosophical passion was in abeyance. It speaks in the favor of Morris Cohen, John Dewey, and Bertrand Russell that each of these men possessed qualities that corresponded to Hook's own dispositions. In Cohen, these were fundamental piety of being and an awareness of the limits of rational thinking with a refusal to accept any beliefs about the world that could not be brought into accord with experience and reason. In John Dewey, there was a similar view, less dyspeptic and more optimistic but also aware that nothing, and least of all our knowledge, has finality. In Russell, there was the sheer compellingness of thinking, and of thinking about the most fundamental problems of thinking. It was not the substance of Russell's philosophical views that Hook admired; it was rather his intellectual virtue. In Russell, Hook, alien to almost everything else in and about Russell, found a powerful and disinterested philosophical intelligence at work. It was Hook's own enjoyment of philosophizing that found its gratifying counterpart in Russell.

In all of these three philosophers, Sidney Hook saw a devotion to philosophy not as a profession but as the proper exercise of the mind and as a means of finding truth. Despite Marxism and instrumentalism, he writes, "I had a much more traditional view of philosophy as an autonomous discipline concerned with perennial problems whose solution was the goal of philosophical enquiry and knowledge." He was always convinced of the dignity of philosophy as an autonomous activity with its own proper criteria of truth. His espousal of a Deweyan position as a Marxist was a result of this; his acceptance of Marxism was always limited by that conviction. It was this that kept Sidney Hook committed to reason as well as to experience, in contradiction to his Deweyan instrumentalism.

VII

Would Sidney Hook not have done better to have devoted himself to scholarship and philosophical reflection than to the very exhausting marginal political activities in which he participated, such as the formation of the League of Professional Groups, the American Workers' Party, the Committee for Cultural Freedom, the Congress for Cultural Freedom, the Commission of Inquiry into the Moscow Trials, the Committee for the Defense of Leon Trotsky, etc.? Would it not have been better had he been less preoccupied with the ideas of Karl Marx, if he had been less preoccupied with communism and socialism, if he had engaged in fewer polemics against communist theorists of poor quality, if he had not spent the time he did in organizing the League of Professionals for Foster and Ford, etc.? Was it not all a waste of the time and energy of a man of a very rare acuity of mind and a no less rare moral and intellectual integrity? Would it not have been a gain for Sidney Hook's learning and achievements as a philosopher had he refrained from such busy polemical activity and concentrated instead on writing philosophical works? No definitive answer is possible.

But if one asks whether American public life would have been different had Sidney Hook not participated at its margins for so long, to that question one can give an answer. The answer is that it would have been different and worse had Sidney Hook not done what he did.

At one point in his autobiography, Sidney Hook makes the very penetrating observation that, in the course of his lifetime, what had once been peripheral in American intellectual and public life moved toward the center. What was once an aesthetic, revolutionary bohemianism became a widespread mode of thought and life throughout much of American society. There have been many accounts written about this change. Sidney Hook's careful depiction of what he himself saw and heard over the wide field into which this penetration has occurred is more convincing than any industrious archival research could be.

No one has a more precise and fuller stock of knowledge of the activities of communists and fellow travelers in New York in the 1930s and 1940s. The recent efforts to transfigure the communists of that period (on the part, for example, of such writers as Vivian Gornick and Ellen Schrecker) might be more persuasive without the publication of Sidney Hook's vivid accounts about how the communists acted in the League for Peace and Democracy, the League against War and Fascism, the American Committee for Freedom and Democracy, the New York College Teachers' Union, the Committee of 400, and others. Sidney Hook is an unimpugnable witness to how the communists and the fellow travelers conducted themselves over several decades. No painstaking doctoral candidate writing years after the events, without intimate experience and the perspective that direct knowledge of the persons, times, and places offers can ever replace Sidney Hook's keen observations, made in the course of his unceasing engagements and recollected so sharply.

Nevertheless, I keep coming back to the question as to whether Sidney Hook did not misuse his exceptional moral and intellectual qualities by becoming so active in polemics and organizations that have passed away and are now scarcely remembered. After all, it may be said, the communists are now a negligible force. The Communist party in the United States is all but forgotten; the Party is negligible in Great Britain and in Western Germany; it is of small importance in Spain; and it is shrinking in size and influence in France and Italy. Furthermore, so runs the argument, intellectuals no longer care about the Soviet Union; they do not regard it as the hope of mankind, the center of the universe. One part of the argument is correct; the communist parties themselves are weak and no longer a danger to liberal democracies. It is also true that, thanks to Alexander Solzhenitsyn, Raymond Aron, and Sidney Hook and to the unsuppressible information about the Soviet Union, it, too, is no longer cited as being an ideal by which all other societies are to be measured and alongside of which they come off poorly.

Would Sidney Hook not have been better off if he had spent more of his life in a quiet room writing the philosophical essays and treatises that he was capable of writing? But, then, when I recall that it was Sidney Hook's polemics and organizational work that helped to bring to a halt the stampede of deception and self-deception, I am not so ready to regret the way in which he spent his time. Had Sidney Hook not engaged with communists at firsthand, first with tentative sympathy and then with deeper understanding, which grew from those experiences and his observations and studies, he would not have become the instructor of a generation which has at least to some extent turned the tide of communist mean-spiritedness and duplicity.

There is a close resemblance between Sidney Hook and Raymond Aron. Both of them—men of the same high degree of unimpeachable honesty and courage, of similarly great intelligence—had parallel lives in this respect. Aron for about thirty-five years attended steadily to the flow of events in French political and intellectual life, writing steadily and critically about them, and never ceasing from speaking out courageously, however unpopular and however isolated he became. In the end he triumphed. The inane Marxist and Leninist fever of the French intellectuals has been broken and much of the credit—which Aron, with a modesty no less than Hook's, disclaimed—must go to him for this change in intellectual temper. Hook, in an atmosphere no less tempestuous than that in Paris and for a longer period, has kept at the same task. The re-establishment—to the extent that it has been reestablished—of a more traditional, genuinely liberal liberalism in the United States is a considerable achievement, some of the credit of which must go to Sidney Hook. The Stalinist communism against which Hook contended for three decades no longer has many supporters. Many developments contributed to this; Hook's inexhaustible alertness, courage, and his indefatigable rationality in argument were indispensable to this change of direction.

Raymond Aron in the last years of his life seemed to be uncertain whether he had done the right thing in giving so much of his intellectual energy to the analysis of transient phenomena. Sidney Hook must have asked himself a similar question when he intended, on retirement, to write works of technical philosophy, including a comprehensive and systematic analysis of John Dewey's ideas. I have sometimes asked myself about Sidney Hook: Would he not have done better to be a professor at the University of Chicago or at Stanford University or Harvard or anywhere outside the agitated intellectual atmosphere of New York City? Now, on thinking further about it, I conclude that in this respect all has been for the best in this most problematical of all possible worlds. If it were not for the courageous and steadfast action of such men as Aron and Hook in response to passing events which accumulated into a powerful movement, that movement would not have been brought to subsidence.

Furthermore, the movement against which Aron and Hook set themselves has still not been entirely dissipated. The fantasy of the Soviet Union as the ideal society has permeated deeply into the minds of the intellectuals and those who have been instructed or guided by them. The fundamental image of the Soviet Union is deeper than the factual knowledge of its shortcomings. There are still many Western intellectuals to whom the really decisive feature of the ideal society is the absence of "private property in the means of production." It is the fact that the Soviet Union is not a capitalistic society that is important. Freedom, justice, the rule of law, material well-being, civility, democracy—all of these things, as far as some intellectuals are concerned, are less important, some of them much less important, than the abolition of the stratum of private businessmen. The abolition of private property in the means of production is primary. And that is what the Soviet Union has done. That is what redeems it.

There also remains a dislike of democracy among many intellectuals. They have in most cases accommodated themselves to its existence, since it has become part of the tradition of the war against capitalistic society. At heart, however, there are many to whom the idea of the *vox populi, vox dei* is a confirmation of the appropriateness of atheism. That is why they are so ambivalent toward authority; they dislike authority in their own societies, and they adore its concentration in foreign societies which have abolished private industrial and commercial property. For such intellectuals, socialism—or communism—is not a means of realizing greater justice and greater material well-being and greater opportunity for all citizens to enjoy the benefits made possible by a productive economy. It is the concentration of power abroad that they worship.

Sidney Hook is not one of these intellectuals. He has spent the best years of his life not in the enjoyment of the exercise of his philosophical power and in dialogue with others with the same propensity; he has instead tried to enlighten intellectuals, arguing rationally against those intellectuals who were deceived by others who worshiped power in a society which was not their own.

Sidney Hook is a liberal-democrat, a patriot, and a socialist, and he regarded the quest for truth as the highest good. He has set himself to limit the sway of those who dislike democracy, the freedom of the individual, and their own society and who do not care for truth if it does not serve the purposes of an anti-capitalistic tyranny. To preserve liberal democracy and to advance material well-being and the quest for truth, Sidney Hook has never been willing to share the views of the intellectuals who give precedence to the abolition of capitalism and the concentration of power above all else. Such intellectuals remain very numerous. As long as they are numerous enough to be influential, polemical activities like Sidney Hook's remain as necessary as they ever were. They are of enduring value as long as bourgeois liberal democracy is at stake. That is why Sidney Hook's life has been well spent, and that is why his record of his life remains exemplary. May it encourage others to walk in his footsteps.

five

ROBERT MAYNARD HUTCHINS

ROBERT MAYNARD HUTCHINS was the most handsome man I have ever seen, a man of natural elegance in bearing and manners. It is not just that he was tall and graceful in form and movement, extremely well proportioned in his figure, and with fine strong and regular facial features. He had the most illuminated and enchanting smile, both elevated and kindly at the same time. His voice was a dry, clear monotone; it carried a slight overtone of the speaker's distaste or distrust of his audience. His voice did not distract from the matter which his words treated; it was a perfect vehicle for his lucid, almost geometrical thoughts. He always spoke in sentences which were short and perfectly formed; he never rambled and byways did not tempt him from his theme. When he wrote, he did so in the most economical way. When he replied to questions or criticisms, he never fumbled or evaded; he always had a clear and succinct reply.

I first heard of Robert Hutchins when, as an undergraduate at the University of Pennsylvania, I read in the *New York Times* about his collision with the department of philosophy of the University of Chicago. I knew very little about universities at that time, except that they should be selflessly and disinterestedly given over to learning without regard for practical ends or profit. Veblen's *Higher Learning in America* had not startled me when I first read it as a student. It made it appear that trustees and presidents were obstacles to the realization of the idea of the university, not friends of learning. So that when I read of the philosophers' resistance to Hutchins, I thought he must be one more of those presidents who treat their professors as hired hands. Although Veblen's book was supposed to be about the University of Chicago, it did not affect my conviction, formed—first from hearsay and then by reading books by Chicago professors—that the University of Chicago was the American equivalent of the University of Berlin. Hutchins's troubles with the department of philosophy I interpreted as one more instance of those cases I had read about in which the higher powers of the university torment the lower powers—trustees tormenting presidents and presidents joining with the trustees in tormenting the teaching staff. Despite Veblen I exempted the University of Chicago which I thought to be exceptional in its professors, but I did not exempt its president whom I thought, ignorantly, to be just another university president.

I was wrong about Robert Hutchins. He, too, turned out to be exceptional. In one important respect, however, in his desire to guide his university according to his own lights, he resembled the great generation of university presidents of the end of the century, among them William Rainey Harper, Daniel Coit Gilman, Charles Eliot, and G. Stanley Hall. Nonetheless, he was—like the university which he tried to reshape—very different from all others in his class. The tragedy began when Hutchins's one major legacy from the presidents with whom he otherwise had so little in common combined with his clear and simple intellectual convictions to enter into frontal collision with a body of professors no less tenacious in their own different idea of a university.

One of my contemporaries had gone to Chicago as a research assistant in econometrics, and when he came back to Philadelphia in the summer of 1932, he was full of wondrous tales about the economists Frank Knight and Jacob Viner; he also dropped a few remarks about the young president having set the university on its ear. Nothing more than that. When I came to Chicago, naturally, I heard much more of him, although I was not close enough to the professors to discern the meaning of the hum which was audible but unintelligible to a newly arrived outsider. I saw him once on the walk behind the Harper Library where he had his office. His face bore the signs of awareness that those who looked upon him must be conscious of his presidency and its powers. He also looked as if he thought that the environment in which he lived was inferior to him and that he should not bend himself to it. This was just a fleeting impression.

A year later, when I was a research assistant at the University of Chicago, I lived in a university building. I became acquainted with graduate students in many different fields, and I began to hear rumors that Hutchins was seeking to impose scholastic philosophy on the University of Chicago, that he wished to suppress the social sciences, that he wished to put down science and reduce scientific study to the study of the classical scientific writings of antiquity and early modern times. It was said that Hutchins wished to replace the study of the modern world by the study of the classics of antiquity and the Middle Ages, that he wished to replace research by ratiocination. It was also said that, in addition to giving the armchair precedence over the laboratory bench or the research seminar, Hutchins, though not himself a Catholic, was also attempting to promote Roman Catholicism.

I also began to have opportunities to witness the dispute at closer range. At that distance, the contentions, as I saw them, seemed rather beside the point. There was no doubt, however, that they were being taken as matters of life and death—at least by some of the disputants. Soon after I became assistant to the late Louis Wirth, then an associate professor of sociology and one of the "coming men" at the University, I was made privy to some of the dire things which Hutchins was said to have in hand for the University. Louis Wirth mentioned to me his frequent meetings with Harry Gideonse, Frank Knight, and others, in which the menace presented by Hutchins's conception of the ideal curriculum and his strictures on American university education were gone over with a fine-tooth comb. I was allowed to read memoranda denouncing Hutchins's educational plans, which, according to his opponents, were centered on the undoing of the intellectual advances of modern times. The speeches of Hutchins were worked over with the care which, in later decades, speeches by Soviet politicians were studied by Kremlinologists.

Such courses of instruction as I attended had absolutely nothing to do with this controversy, which seemed to be fought out in memoranda Louis Wirth had occasionally shown me, in the lectures and articles of Hutchins and Mortimer Adler, and in the juvenile partisanship of the undergraduate newspaper, *The Maroon*—I think at that time it was called *The Daily Maroon*—which, at least for one year in the middle of the 1930s, was edited by a youth named John Barden, a sort of poor man's William F. Buckley, Jr., before his time. It is at least fifty years since I last saw any of the editorials written on behalf of Hutchins and Adler by Barden, but I recall them as being exasperating even to one who was not attracted by the views espoused by Wirth and Gideonse; Gideonse used to annotate Barden's writings, and post them on the bulletin board of the College. Aside from being an inappropriate thing for a grown man to do, it encouraged the delusions of the undergraduate editor about the importance of his activity in the stirring struggle for the triumph of the intellect and the unity of knowledge over anti-intellectual specialization and the fragmentation of knowledge, which was what the debate at the University of Chicago was supposed to be about. It was clear to me that Barden was having the time of his life in insulting one group of his elders in order to please another group of them. At the same time, his professorial adversaries were throwing the fat into the fire and dust into their own eyes by resorting to a similar rhetoric.

What impressed me at that time was the vehemence with which the debate was conducted. In alliance with Hutchins, Mortimer Adler was a person of a strong intelligence inclined toward schematic constructions and of an expository skill as pleasing to the ear as a machine gun. His pronouncements in their way were as vexing as Barden's by their dogmatic aggressiveness and in their reduction of the issues to first principles that were extremely simplified and very far from self-evident. The argument as well as the manner forced the debate onto questions which no reasonable man would discuss. Thus the debate raged furiously about spurious issues. President Hutchins did not engage directly in the public debate, as far as I can recall, except through the lectures which he delivered outside the university. His own contributions on those occasions were extremely lucid; they were also very simplistic and exaggerated in their cool and condescending rhetoric. The intensity of feeling and acrimony of expression of the opponents—Wirth, Gideonse, and Knight on the one side, and Barden and Adler on the other—had nothing in common with the detached serenity of Hutchins's assumption of the patent validity of what he said. Nonetheless, Hutchins himself did not improve matters much.

Hutchins, too, argued by hyperbole, distorted the position he opposed, and was as schematic and as unrealistic as Adler. He always argued like a man reasonably explaining obvious things to the wrongheaded, though entirely without the rabid tone which accompanied Adler's unpleasantly self-confident deductions. Although Hutchins was much criticized, I began to see that those who were wrought up by Hutchins were not wrought up as much by Hutchins as they were by Mortimer Adler and to a smaller extent by Arthur Rubin, whom Adler had brought to the University to serve as a member of a committee on liberal arts created presumably on Hutchins's request by Richard McKeon, then dean of the division of the humanities. Richard McKeon was one of the Hutchins party but he did not arouse so much antagonism. Stringfellow Barr and Scott Buchanan, two other prominent allies of Hutchins, were not mentioned often. It was mainly Mortimer Adler who aroused the animosity of the three-man party of opposition of Gideonse, Knight, and Wirth.

I had of course heard about Adler first when I read of Hutchins's conflict with the department of philosophy. I heard more about him after I came to Chicago. As I recall, I first saw him and heard him when I attended a seminar in the Social Science Research Building in the mid-1930s. That seminar still stands out in my memory as one of the more offensive academic performances I have seen. The subject was obviously an impossible one. That it was pretentious and naive in its very title, "Systematic Social Science," and was very sloppy, too, in spite of its implication of deductive rigor, was not the most reprehensible part. What was much worse was the angry imperiousness of Adler's opening exposition. The domineering tone with which he spoke was very disproportionate to the modesty called for by the meager substance of his argument. He slapped the table repeatedly and resoundingly with his palm to add weight to his declarations. He looked very angry; he seemed to surge with impatience. After not many minutes of Adler's exposition, when it was still far from complete, Wirth began a series of interruptions. Wirth, unlike Adler, had a rather soft and melodious voice which always sounded reasonable and thoughtful even when it said unreasonable things about which he had not thought very much.

As far as I can recall, Adler was speaking with angry self-assurance about a subject of which he understood very little, while Wirth, who knew more than Adler about the literature of the social sciences, was defending these disciplines in terms which had no correspondence with what was contained in that literature. Soon the seminar became very unpleasant. Neither of the antagonists would allow the other to finish a statement; each became angrier but Wirth gained the upper hand by his mellifluous interruptions.

After the seminar finished in smoldering incoherence, Wirth strode from the room like a successful street-corner youth who was proud of having frustrated the renowned bully from a nearby street. Adler gave off clouds of fury as he put his papers into his case. Wirth had certainly not made a case for social science against Adler's claim that social science could be practiced only on the foundation of a syllogistic system constituted by question-begging definitions and problematical derivations pretending to be logical. His statements had no connection with what was being done in the social sciences and what could reasonably be expected of them. He should have known better. Adler presented an argument which was of no intellectual value; he seemed to have no grasp of what any society was like. Neither Wirth nor Adler attempted in this seminar to understand the other's argument. It was a dispute in which the antagonism of each disputant toward the other was more prominent than the effort to criticize or to justify—or to propose a better alternative to—what was being done in the social sciences in the building where the wrangle took place.

Frank Knight was the one participant in these disputes who was intellectually far superior to all the others, but he least of all could resist the temptation to be drawn into any discussion with a remote ecclesiastical or theological penumbra. It was that penumbra which obsessed Adler's detractors; Adler did nothing to dispel it. This was a misfortune for Hutchins in these years at the University of Chicago. He had ideas about the organization of the University which would have given rise to opposition in any case, but the opposition would never have been so obstinate and acrimonious had it not been for that unnecessary theological penumbra that Mortimer Adler's and his own arguments lent it.

Knight was a man of deep intellectual penetration. He had been a very distinguished economist of subtle and acute moral perception; he had widely ranging intellectual interests and a rare skill in getting to fundamentals, but he was also easily aroused to cutting disapproval. He was especially irascible in his response to anything in which he suspected even a trace of ecclesiastical dogmatism. He had come from a family of devoted adherents to a primitive Protestant sect and had become a rationalistic unbeliever—almost in some respects a village atheist. Nevertheless, all his life he had been fascinated by religion. He was irresistibly drawn to theology, but he was no less resistant to any belief. He enjoyed the company of a few professors in the faculty of divinity and had great liking and respect for them. (Once, late in his life, he told me that he had difficulty in sleeping and when I asked why, he said, "It's that religion. I think about it all night. I can't get it off my mind.") The odors of Rome were too much for an unbeliever of Protestant sectarian origins, and he regarded President Hutchins as in some way a remote agent of the Pope.

There was another incident of which I was a spectator. That was a debate between Mortimer Adler and Anton J. Carlson, a professor of physiology. Carlson was a crusty old character, much beloved by his students and colleagues; he had the gait and accent of a Swedish-American carpenter. The debate took place in Mandel Hall, the largest hall in the University, and was conducted before an audience which filled every seat. It was a shabby performance; each participant was obstinately inattentive to what the other said. Adler was quicker, more syllogistic in his rhetoric, and gave a quite false impression of rigor and clarity. He also seemed to be unaware of what scientists do. Carlson was simply astonished that something so self-evident as his beloved science could be challenged by a person who was not a scientist and who understood nothing of it. He was intellectually speechless and, in his own rustic, plebeian way, demagogic. It was a vaudeville show, not an intellectual debate. Yet the audience went for it because it enjoyed a brawl.

Mr. Harry Ashmore, who is an experienced journalist, remarkable for his civil courage in the South during the early stages of the struggle for civil rights, has written a long, thoroughly scholarly biography of Hutchins (*Unreasonable Truths: The Life of Robert Maynard Hutchins,* Little, Brown and Company). He has meticulously described the conflicts of which Hutchins was the center at the University of Chicago. Since Mr. Ashmore was closely associated with Hutchins at the Fund for the Republic, the *Encyclopaedia Britannica,* and the Center for the Study of Democratic Institutions in the last decades of Hutchins's life, his history of Hutchins's activities at the University of Chicago is less rich than is his account of the second phase of Hutchins's career. But even about the University of Chicago, Ashmore tells much that is worth knowing. His account of the dispute about the "four-year college" is the best there is. It seems to me to show that Hutchins's program had nothing to do with theology or Adlerian rhetoric.

The story of Hutchins and the College of the University of Chicago begins at Columbia University. In 1917, Professor John Erskine devised a course of study of classics of Western thought and literature for officer-candidates of the United States Army, being trained at Plattsburg, New York. It was introduced as a course in Columbia College in 1921. Erskine and Mark Van Doren were largely responsible for conducting this course. Mortimer Adler was brought into it well after it had become a going concern. When Adler went to Yale in 1927 to see Hutchins, at Hutchins's invitation, to discuss the possible contribution of psychological research to the study of law, the classics of Western civilization had long been established in the general honors program for undergraduates at Columbia College. Between his visit to Hutchins in 1927 and his arrival in Chicago in 1930, Adler underwent something of a conversion from his belief in empirical social science, including experimental social psychology, to metaphysical philosophy. After Hutchins became president of the University of Chicago, he and Adler conducted a class in "the great books" for a small number of undergraduates.

I occasionally met students who had attended this course. They were ecstatic about it. I once attended a class to see what it was like and was sorry to see as harsh a piece of academic browbeating of a student as I have ever witnessed, carried out by Mortimer Adler. Table slapping was as much a part of the technique of interpretation of texts as it had been part of the techniques of exposition of "systematic social science." Hutchins, in contrast with Adler, was indulgent, even affectionate toward the students; he tried to reformulate their stumbling words so that they could discover what they dimly intended, and he did it with a remote but real kindliness. Adler's and Hutchins's procedures, different as they were from each other, made a remarkably effective combination. Those students who survived Adler's harsh schoolmasterly style looked back upon the "great books courses" as a glorious moment in the history of their education.

I do not have the impression that Hutchins had given any serious thought to undergraduate education when he was a professor and then dean at the Yale Law School. His own undergraduate years at Oberlin before his military service and at Yale after it, apparently did not stir him intellectually; nor did he revolt against it. He thought well of his years at Oberlin. He seems to have thought poorly of the undergraduate curriculum and culture at Yale in the 1920s, with its football games, parties, and fraternities and the elective system which was a miscellany of specialized, unconnected courses taught by teachers who abhorred going beyond the boundaries of their special fields. But Hutchins probably did not give any thought to how it could be improved. When he went to Chicago in 1929 to be president at the age of thirty, he probably did not have any definite ideas about undergraduate education. Nevertheless, the reconstruction of undergraduate education became his chief interest once he became president.

The rearrangement of undergraduate education at Chicago had been in hand since the accession of Charles Burton to the presidency of the University in 1923. The idea of survey courses had already been broached. The College Curriculum Committee came into existence early in the second year of Hutchins's presidency, the same year in which he began to teach "the great books" course with Adler.

The survey courses, the "four-year college," and "the great books" course were not identical, but, to the blurred vision of outsiders and to the partisans in the unpleasant wrangles at the University of Chicago, they became somehow amalgamated with one another. Adler, Roman Catholicism, and scholastic philosophy had even less to do with them, but all were thrown into a single pot by Hutchins's opponents, and by some of his partisans.

Much of Hutchins's fame was formed about the survey courses, and much of his affection as well as his hopes went to the College, in which the survey courses were the main thing. There were other features of the College to which Hutchins attached importance, such as the admission of students after the completion of two years of secondary school and the awarding of the bachelor's degree after the completion of what in the older style would be called the sophomore year. Much attention was given to these latter innovations; they were trivial. Their failure was of no consequence that I could see, and their temporary success caused much resentment among Hutchins's antagonists within the University. There was also much passion put into the discussions of the problem about whether all the survey courses should be required and whether a limited range of elections from among them and from other more specialized one-quarter courses should be allowed. As I remember, the question was argued primarily with regard to extreme alternatives.

Hutchins believed that the College should be a completely self-governing body within the University, with its own staff, its own criteria of appointment and promotion, and without regard for the requirements of the specialized departments which made up the four divisions of the University: the divisions of the humanities, the social sciences, the biological sciences, and the physical sciences. Hutchins succeeded in establishing such an arrangement sometime during the war. I think it was a mistake, and it generated much resentment, which flowed into the already overflowing stream of acrimony in which Hutchins was inundated by the polemics of his protégés and partisans and of his equally irrational antagonists. Participation in the disputes was widespread.

As I recall, a sizable fraction of the opponents of Hutchins's proposals were against them because they saw the cloven hoof of Adler getting inside the door. The College was caught in the exchange of fire between two forces remote from each other: those who wished to reorganize learning to place philosophy, as Mortimer Adler understood it, at the center and those in the divisions who were defending their positions even though they were not endangered by the proposed reforms. As a matter of fact, the work of the divisions which covered the third and fourth undergraduate years and all the graduate work went on as it had before. Neither Hutchins nor Adler had any plans for the divisions and, except for a few appointments which turned out to have both positive and negative effects, Hutchins left them to themselves. Under the arching shells and the din, the teaching of survey or comprehensive courses in the College made its way.

Until I began to teach in the College in 1938, I did not know anything about the College survey courses except those in the social sciences. There was certainly no trace of the alleged "medievalizing" or "romanizing" influence which their enemies attributed to Hutchins, Adler, and the rest in the social sciences survey courses—at least as long as Gideonse and Wirth dominated them. I do not think that they contained any assigned book written before the middle of the eighteenth century; and for the most part, the required readings were relatively contemporary. I did not think the social science surveys, as they existed when I first became familiar with them, were on a very high intellectual level, although many very intelligent students—among them Paul Samuelson—have looked back upon them with a profound sense of indebtedness. When, at the end of the decade, I began to have some influence, I revamped "the second-year survey" from beginning to end. The writings of Locke, Milton, and Hobbes were introduced and so were those of Max Weber, Frank Knight, Georg Simmel, A. V. Dicey, John Dickinson, Charles McIlwain, and R. H. Tawney. Again, there was no sign of any "romanizing"—that is, Catholicizing—influence, which Hutchins's antagonists claimed to be his intention. I do not know what he thought about it, but I never had any intimation of his displeasure at what I had done.

The fact that Hutchins wished me to stay at the University of Chicago when I was appointed to the University of London just after the Second World War, and then again urged me to return to Chicago at the end of the 1940s was clear evidence that he did not demand conformity with his own views. He was clearly impressed by a demanding intellectual standard, by the requirement that the students study important books, and that the teachers take the books and the students very seriously. The fact was that Hutchins had no hand in the construction of the survey courses and he did not attempt to take one.

I looked through the syllabuses of the survey courses in the humanities; there was much of Greek literature and philosophy but practically nothing medieval. So much for the outsider's view of the University of Chicago being a place where "Jewish professors teach Roman Catholicism to Protestant students!" So much, too, for the prejudices of Hutchins's opponents within the University itself!

The general drift of Hutchins's attitude toward the College was to encourage teachers who wished their students to read the best literature in their fields and the classical texts rather than secondary works. It encouraged those teachers who wished to work over a broad range and who did not, at least for the time being, wish to teach and do research on very specialized subjects. Hutchins's policy did not say anything about how the texts should be interpreted, although some of his more zealous followers did. The result in general was an atmosphere of extraordinary exhilaration among students and teachers in the undergraduate courses of the first two years of the University. Plato and Aristotle were obviously much better authors to read than Ernest Barker and George Sabine about Plato and Aristotle; it was better to read Locke and Hobbes than some secondary source. The students responded to this mode of teaching, if not with wise understanding, then with the enthusiasm which comes from the sense of doing something of intrinsic importance. It aroused great interest among them and caused them to extend their mental powers.

The impression remains in my mind that part of the high

enthusiasm and the strong convictions of the teachers and the students of the College of the 1930s of the importance of what they were engaged in came from Hutchins's presence and patronage. His public statements repeatedly referred to the College as a vital undertaking. The members of the College staff and the student body were the beneficiaries. Of course, intelligent and intellectually responsive students, well-educated and eager teachers, and very good syllabuses would have aroused enthusiasm and given intense pleasure even under the patronage and presence of a less impressive president. But the auspices of such a famous and scintillating general only added to the pride and delight of the soldiers who served under him.

Apart from the first years of the undergraduate course of studies, the real university was not directly discussed by either side of the great debate at the University of Chicago. The real university was the University of Chicago which had become famous in the first four decades of its existence as the university where Michelson, Millikan, Loeb, Sapir, Bloomfield, Buck, Freund, Breasted, Nitze, Keniston, Craigie, Manley, Rickert, Sherburn, Archer Taylor, Park, Thomas, Knight, Viner, Douglas, Bliss, and the Wright Brothers (Sewall and Quincy) worked. Before the great debate began early in the 1930s, the University of Chicago was a university dead in earnest about learning and discovery. It was the leading graduate school in the country in a very large number of fields. Aside from the regrouping of the departments into four major divisions, Hutchins did not speak about major modifications in the dominant part of the University—the graduate student body outnumbered the undergraduates by two- to three-fold. Research and teaching went on unaffected by President Hutchins's reforming ideas or by Mortimer Adler's flirtations with Thomism.

In the social sciences, the two scholars who were most sympathetic with Hutchins were Robert Redfield, the anthropologist, and John Nef, the economic historian. Both were distinguished scholars, but neither gained in his scholarly work from the Hutchins program for the reconstruction of academic life. John Nef was indeed much affected by Hutchins's ideas at the beginning of the 1940s and, as a result, his outstanding run of scholarly publications was gradually supplanted by social philosophy; his achievements in social philosophy were far from the excellence of his achievements as an economic historian, which showed considerable originality and a remarkable breadth of culture. Although Robert Redfield was an admirer and friend of Hutchins, his anthropological work was influenced far more by his father-in-law, Robert Park, the great sociologist. Hutchins's ideas about the kind of scholarship which should be furthered were encouraging to those with broad interests.

Until the appointment of Leo Strauss—late in Hutchins's administration—there were no other social scientists who were in one way or another close to Hutchins's position. Strauss was all for "great books" in political philosophy, and he was also devoted to St. John's College in Annapolis, where Adler's and Hutchins's more restricted program for undergraduate education was in force. But he had his own ideas about the interpretation of texts. The Committee on Social Thought, which was in the division of the social sciences, had a number of members who admired Hutchins and who thought that he was on the right side in the battle against specialization and the methods of empirical science. The Committee generally was also close to the Hutchins position in the stress which it laid on the intensive study of works of major importance. But the very freedom which Hutchins provided for it meant that it did not run strictly along the lines which seemed to be indicated by his programmatic statements. It certainly had nothing to do with Adler's schemes, which were much more differentiated and specific than Hutchins's own rather general appreciation of the study of fundamental intellectual works. It should also be said that the Committee on Social Thought would never have existed without Hutchins. It was a child of his pessimism about reforming the University of Chicago in the pattern which he adapted with Adler's guidance and of his occasional and despairing toying with the idea of going off and starting something completely new.

The division of the social sciences bore a few negative marks of Hutchins's influence. The department of political science in particular was affected by him. Harold Gosnell and Harold Lasswell, both pioneers in their subjects, could not gain promotion to professorships in the University and they departed. Anthropology and economics went on in their own way, both on a very high standard, but this was because the members of those departments cared about them; I think Hutchins never intruded into their affairs.

Hutchins took no interest in sociology which was at the height of its fame when he came to the University, though he undoubtedly did not like it. He was contemptuous of statistical research in which the department of sociology was strong and in which he had begun to be interested when he was at Yale. He surely did not like Louis Wirth, since Wirth had made himself into one of the most acerbic of the critics of the new regime, as he understood it. The standing of the department of sociology at Chicago certainly did decline during Hutchins's administration, but I do not think that this was a result of Hutchins's attitude. He must have thought that the subject was hopeless, yet, even if he had thought otherwise, I doubt that he could have stayed the decline. When the department—or at least Louis Wirth—would have appointed Karl Mannheim after his dismissal by the Nazis, Hutchins discouraged it. It is difficult to imagine what might have been the result of Mannheim's transplantation to Chicago in 1933 rather than to the London School of Economics.

Hutchins took a more active hand in furthering the attrition of the tradition established in political science by Charles Merriam. Although Merriam had been a supporter of Hutchins's appointment to the presidency and continued to support him in many important matters, and even though Hutchins seems to have liked Merriam personally, Hutchins disapproved thoroughly of Merriam's empirical conception of political science. The result was the departure from the University of two of Merriam's most prized young men.

Hutchins's most important positive accomplishment in connection with the department of political science was his support for the appointment of Leo Strauss from three proposed candidates—the other two were Alessandro d'Entreves and Alfred Cobban. This showed Hutchins at his best; the other two candidates were good scholars and they were strongly recommended by John Nef, with whom Hutchins was very friendly. Nonetheless, when I as executive secretary of the Committee on Social Thought put the case for Strauss before him in the summer of 1949, he force-fully agreed that Strauss was obviously the strongest candidate. (He also agreed during that summer to the appointment of Michael Polanyi to the Committee on Social Thought under similar conditions.) Strauss had much to recommend him to Hutchins. He was a very distinguished student of "great books"; he disliked the modern world and thought that it had gone astray as a result of its departure from the tenets of classical political philosophy; he was also a German; and in 1949 Hutchins was much more appreciative of German scholarship than he had been in the 1930s. Still, whatever the grounds, Hutchins inclined toward the right man both with respect to his outstanding intellectual merits and his partial congeniality with Hutchins's ideas of what a university should be. Through the appointment of Strauss, the University of Chicago developed into a major center for the study of the classical tradition of political philosophy. The appointment of Leo Strauss was an act in the same direction as his initiative in creating the Committee on Social Thought and his continued support of it. It was of a piece with his dislike of the specialization of research in science.

Hutchins's relations with the physical and biological sciences were paradoxical. For all sorts of reasons, he did not like these subjects. He disliked specialization as much as anything in the world of learning; he was also against science because it praised methodical empirical observation and seemed to deny the autonomy of rational speculative philosophy and its metaphysical foundations. I think too that, although Hutchins had no religious beliefs, he was opposed to modern science, which was alleged to have discredited the foundations of religious faith; I think that he also associated science with technology and the active pursuit of wealth, both of which he disliked, although ambivalently.

The scientists reciprocated Hutchins's views for a variety of their own reasons. They were dead set against Hutchins and his schemes. They were very much against his desire to concentrate the first two years of undergraduate study on obligatory survey courses. They wanted the undergraduates to move into their special or major subjects before reaching the third year; the chemists were especially disturbed by Hutchins's disapproval of specialized studies in the first two years of the students' careers in the University. They and the other scientists were alarmed by his belief in the necessity of a foundation of knowledge in metaphysics, much in the way in which Gideonse, Wirth, and Knight were. But, in my recollection, the only scientist who joined in public the attack on Hutchins and his friends was Anton Carlson. The scientists provided much of the opposition to Hutchins's programs; they did so quietly and for good reasons and poor ones. They, too, were affected by the Thomist penumbra which Adler contributed to the image of Hutchins at the University of Chicago.

The scientists were not brawlers. They stayed out of the public eye and looked after their own affairs. Certain departments declined in the 1930s, and the University of Chicago ceased to be preeminent in various fields in which it had led in the preceding decades. Nonetheless, many distinguished appointments were made in the 1930s in the division of the physical sciences, and they did not have to be forced on Hutchins. On the contrary, he was usually very forthcoming: Subrahmanyan Chandrasekhar in astrophysics, Saunders MacLane and Marshall Stone in mathematics, and others were appointed before or just after the war. After the Second World War, the appointments of Antoni Zygmund, André Weil, Enrico Fermi, James Franck, and Harold Urey maintained in some fields, and restored in others, the reputation of the University of Chicago.

Much of the recovery of the position of the University of Chicago after 1945 came about through the presence on the campus during the war of the Metallurgy Project, as the work on atomic research was officially called. Urey, Fermi, and Franck came to Chicago that way. For the last six or seven years of Hutchins's administration, the University of Chicago returned to its old eminence in certain of the natural sciences. This was another of the numerous paradoxes of Hutchins's career. Those branches of learning with which he was least congenial prospered most; the paradox was accentuated in the physical sciences because the renewed eminence of the University in those fields came about through the Metallurgy Project. Hutchins had been for a short time associated with the America First Committee before the entry of the United States into the Second World War. Yet his University prospered in the fields he liked least through its share in the production of a decisive weapon for use in a war which he had opposed.

There was also irony in the changes in the division of the humanities at the University of Chicago during Hutchins's time there. I do not know what his attitude toward or knowledge of these subjects was while he was at Yale. Indeed, I gathered from Mr. Ashmore's account that, as a student at Oberlin and at Yale, Hutchins seems to have had no great intellectual interests in any academic subject, although he gained the highest marks. (Law seems to have been the only field of study that aroused his interest.) After he came to Chicago, the humanities appeared to be the first candidate for his affections. There was such an affinity between them and the program of the study of "great books" to which he was devoted. Nevertheless, it did not at all turn out that way. He allowed the humanities division to decay at Chicago, without attempting to replace it by another type of division pursuing humanistic studies in a manner closer to his heart.

The department of classics should have thrived under Hutchins's jurisdiction, but it did not. Classical studies have for many decades had a hard time in the United States because Latin and Greek have retreated so steadily from the secondary schools and also because classical scholars have stuck so fast to the traditional philological mode. Nonetheless, when Hutchins settled into the presidency of Chicago and began to espouse the superiority of the ancients to the moderns, it would have been reasonable to predict that he would treat the department of classics with special indulgence. He did not. He was indifferent to it. Werner Jaeger came to the department for a short stay but then went on to Harvard. For a time in the 1930s, as a result of the Nazi dismissal of Jewish university teachers, the world was flooded with outstanding classical scholars. Hutchins, as far as I know, had no desire to take advantage of these misfortunes on behalf of the classics department. Even at the beginning of the German exodus, when I was new at the University, I was struck by the failure of the University of Chicago to draw on the supply of accomplished scholars whom the Nazis had made available to the universities of the Western world. The Oriental Institute, which had already had very close connections with Germany from the very beginning of James Breasted's career, was, I think, the only part of the University of Chicago that sought to retrieve what benefits were available from the catastrophe which befell the learned world of Germany. It benefited greatly from the appointment of such Jewish refugee scholars as Leo Oppenheim and Benno Landsberger.

The departments of modern languages suffered like most of the other humanistic subjects. Of course, it is difficult in the United States for a department of Germanic languages and literature to be as good as an outstanding department in a German university or for a department of French or Italian to match the work of an outstanding group in a French or Italian university. But the fact remains that those departments at Chicago declined from their earlier American eminence and showed no signs of revival until Hutchins's brief Germanophile phase towards and after the end of the war. The French department, when I came to the University, was one of the most respected in the country, but by the time of Hutchins's departure, it had sunk to second rank. Oriental studies other than the study of the ancient Middle East lay inert; modern European history was the same.

The English department with Manley and Rickert, Sherburn and Crane had been an outstanding center of meticulous editorial, historical, and bibliographical scholarship—what in Germany had been called *Philologie*—and it continued with slight diminution in these parts of the field as its attention shifted toward a theory of criticism based on the study of Aristotle. The "Chicago critics" became one of the few points of eminence in the humanities division. This did not seem to me to be a very fruitful development but it was nevertheless considered a very respectable intellectual achievement. It was the only one in the division of the humanities which had some affinity with Hutchins's own preferences; it was to a large extent the result of the influence of Richard McKeon who had been brought to Chicago through Adler's intercession.

The department of philosophy had not been to Hutchins's taste when he came to Chicago, although its outlook would have been consistent with that of his few years at the Yale Law School. Perhaps his experience in attempting unsuccessfully to change it in the direction sought by Mortimer Adler was the cause of his later reluctance to become engaged in conflicts with the well-established departments of the University. Yet this policy was inconsistently followed. On rare occasions, he took an active hand in an appointment, as in the case of Leo Strauss; sometimes but not often he blocked an appointment or promotion on which he felt strongly, though more often he did not interfere when a proposal for the appointment of a mediocrity came before him. But even this pattern was not consistently adhered to. The philosophical outlook of Rudolf Carnap must have been as abhorrent to him as anything in the intellectual world of the twentieth century. Yet the appointment of Carnap to the department toward which Hutchins originally had the most covetous intentions requires explanation. Perhaps the explanation lies in his usually exigent sense of quality. He might well have seen that Carnap was the most distinguished philosopher of his kind, even though the kind was distasteful to him. His appreciation of Frank Knight was perhaps like this; he admired Knight's passionate intellectual honesty and great acuity and he was not deterred from this by Knight's often abusive public treatment of Hutchins's own views and policies. I think that he also had a genuine affection for Knight who, though often trying to many who knew him, was a most endearing, as well as a curmudgeonly sagacious man and an intellect both searching and profound.

The one part of the University of Chicago Hutchins must have taken unqualified satisfaction in was the Law School. It dealt with the one field of academic life with which he had substantial experience and where his intellectual discrimination did not encounter any resistance from his espousal of "principles." He came to the Law School when it was already very good, and when he left it, it was in the first rank of law schools in the country. He felt at ease with the Law School and he had strong admirers there. His appointment of Edward Levi as dean at an early age, against resistance from some trustees because Levi was Jewish, was perhaps the most notable appointment he made during his presidency. Levi later became provost and then president of the University, and under his care the University of Chicago regained much of the ground it had lost over three decades.

Hutchins left important marks on the University of Chicago, and he generated an atmosphere of intellectual passion in the University which was unique in my experience of universities in the United States and elsewhere. Some of this intellectual excitement came from the stimulus of the conflicts within the University. A spirit of divisiveness was fostered; it was exhilarating to its participants and, because it seemed to involve "principles" and was nominally about education, it made a better impression on its participants than it deserved while it misled outside observers. Frank Knight, the sadly cynical idealist, once formulated an adaptation of Gresham's law about money which he called "Knight's law." "Knight's law" asserted that "bad talk drives out good talk." "Knight's law" certainly was in operation at the University of Chicago in the more than twenty years of Hutchins's presidency. The divisions within the teaching staff and to some extent in the student body were partly divisions about serious educational matters, particularly about the amount of liberal education and the amount of specialized education that ought to be contained in the undergraduate curriculum. This was a genuine issue. It was overlaid and obscured by the spurious issues of Aristotelian and Thomistic philosophy versus secularism, "intellectualism" versus pragmatism, and "great books" versus textbooks. Before long the spurious issues crowded out the genuine issues.

Whoever has written about the University of Chicago during the era of Robert Hutchins's presidency—toward the end his title was changed to chancellor—was impressed by the intensity of the intellectual tone there. Since all this was about the superiority of the ancients to the moderns, it was taken to be ipso facto intellectual, but much of it was unjustifiable anger and sheer animal spirits. Nonetheless, the University of Chicago was actually a place of great seriousness and animation, and much of this serious animation was about the interpretation of Greek plays, Aristotle's *Ethics*, Plato's *Republic*, and similar works. All undergraduates had to study classical texts in English translation, of course; many, though, were stimulated to learn Greek, and there were many teachers with genuine intellectual zeal about what they were doing. They read deeply and widely; most of them wrote very little and spent much time in discussion with students and one another. In many students, the outcome was genuine reverence for philosophical discourse and learning, and to this day many look back to those years as the best of their lives. This was an important part of Hutchins's achievement.

As far as the intensity of the intellectual experience is concerned, it must be said that the University of Chicago practically from its beginning in the 1890s had conducted its affairs with a serious—some would say grim, others gloomy—conviction of the supreme importance of scientific and scholarly learning. Most of the teachers were deeply devoted to teaching and most of the students, both undergraduate and graduate, were devoted to learning. Those who recall the University of Chicago of the 1920s, or who like me came upon traces of it in the 1930s, testify to the vigor and gravity with which ideas were pondered there. They were, however, ideas which arose out of or in connection with scientific and scholarly research; and "idle speculation" was not well looked upon. The new excitation brought about by the presence of Robert Hutchins was something different: in its subject matter, its rhetoric, its intentions.

Of course, the teachers of the University of Chicago continued to be passionately interested in their research, and they continued to discuss as they had discussed. The novelty of the discussions which followed on the installation of Hutchins was that the disputes were mainly about the right organization of higher education, about the best syllabus, and to some extent, about a relatively small number of great authors. The discussion of the ideas of Plato and Aristotle was often about their ideas, but it was also often carried on as a challenge to the ancien régime of the University of Chicago; and it was taken to be such by those who thought they were being challenged. It was at least in part the thrill of combat and not just the stirring experience of ideas. Much of the public combat was made up of deformation and simplifications of serious ideas—both the "Hutchins-party" and its antagonists were very productive of such substitutes for honest thought.

Hutchins's scouts, Adler and the publicist Milton Mayer, aggravated the situation. The former did so by his schematic, ostensibly rigorous, syllogistic mode of presentation, which proceeded with apparent logical necessity from postulates that were alien to the outlook and idiom of his interlocutors and above all by his dogmatic and often angry tone of voice; Milton Mayer, an ignorant and sentimental zealot who combined cynicism and naïveté, put off the opponents of Hutchins by his fluent flippancy. The other side was no better. Frank Knight, who was the most distinguished of Hutchins's opponents by his own intellectual attainments and by his earnestness, was a querulous, cranky debater who would fasten on a point and not let it go; he was, moreover, often injurious to those with whom he disagreed and was equally quick to take offense. In fact, one of the most impressive things about Robert Hutchins was his amused and patient affection for Frank Knight.

As the years passed, a spirit of acrimony developed within the University of Chicago, which went from bad to worse. Sentiments hardened. It came to a deadlock when, during the war, Hutchins attempted to institute constitutionally a plebiscitary device that would have given him the powers of the great university presidents of the period before 1914—before the growth of departmental autonomy and of the more widespread participation by the teaching staff in university government that has now become quite common. Hutchins's proposal was defeated in the university senate—consisting then only of full professors—by a large majority. The matter stood at a stalemate until a trustee, the wise lawyer Laird Bell, put forward a scheme which was then accepted by the board of trustees and from which neither Hutchins nor the committee of the senate demurred.

Mr. Ashmore tells of the generally forgotten episode of Hutchins's proposal to abolish ranks in the faculties of the University and to introduce the "4-E contract" whereby salaries would be increased and all earnings of teachers from services outside the University would be turned over to the University. Nothing came of these efforts to make the University into a community, solidary and equal, of learned men and women, wholly concentrated on the pursuit and transmission of truth. The proposal did nothing more than stir up a small commotion. It was really no more than an incidental and awkward manifestation of Hutchins's desire to create an intellectual community, pervaded by mutual understanding and ruled by an undistracted search for truth through dialogue.

The extraordinary intensity of discussion at the University of Chicago belied the accusations directed against Hutchins by some of his adversaries within the University and by some of his critics outside it. One of the most common charges was that his philosophical outlook implied a single correct answer to every question and that if he had his way he would establish a reigning and compulsory dogma, based on Aristotelian metaphysics. Nothing could have been further from the truth. His critics were vituperative, but with rare exception he never did anything to obstruct their academic careers within the University of Chicago.

Hutchins not only accepted criticism from the members of the faculty without recrimination, he also supported them when they ran into heavy weather outside the University as a consequence of their rightly or wrongly attributed support for Communist causes. One fellow traveler whom I knew quite well, Frederick L. Schuman, then an assistant professor of political science, was subjected to inquiry by an investigative committee of the state legislature of Illinois. Schuman was incontestably a fellow traveler. He told me that, when he received a summons to appear before the committee, he was invited by Hutchins to visit him in his office. Hutchins told him that when he appeared before the inquisitors, he should not deny what he had said but should emphasize that he had said it according to his best judgment, on the basis of his studies of the subject and after due reflection, and that if he did so he could count with certainty on the support of Hutchins, the chairman of his department, and the University board of trustees. I do not think that there were many—if indeed any—other university presidents in the United States who, in the decades when legislators and publicists were harassing Communists and fellow travelers and decent persons wrongly accused of subversive intentions, came to the support of their teaching staff in this admirably courageous way.

It was under Robert Hutchins, too, that black scholars were

appointed to the University of Chicago; I think here particularly of Alison Davis and Abram Harris. This was long before affirmative action was conceived.

When Hutchins resigned in 1952 there was a sense of bereavement in the University of Chicago. For more than two decades his handsome presence, his wit, his national reputation had filled the University and preoccupied its minds more than was good for any institution. Now that he was gone, the place seemed empty. With his departure came also the awareness that the University of Chicago was no longer what it had been. After all the delight of debate about genuine and spurious issues, the members of the University of Chicago became aware that its preeminence had subsided. Other universities had got ahead of it. Harvard and the University of California at Berkeley, the University of Michigan and Stanford University had moved up in the years after the end of the Second World War. The University of Chicago ceased to be intellectually as attractive as it had been. Other universities were in a better position. Some had more money, others were located in more pleasant places, others had more social prestige. Outstanding figures of the University of Chicago accepted appointments elsewhere, the retirement or death of outstanding teachers was followed by the appointment of less outstanding ones.

Whereas, before the war, the University of Chicago had been on the same level as Harvard and the University of California at Berkeley, the situation had changed. Harvard was very much richer, it was in a more pleasant place, and it also had more prestige. It also began to appoint members of the "new class" of outstanding Jewish academics, which it had probably been less ready to accept before the outbreak of the Second World War; the University of California at Berkeley had been an outstanding university for a long time, and, as a state university in an expanding and prosperous state close to the brilliant city of San Francisco and enjoying a far more attractive natural environment than Chicago, also pressed forward. As a result of this ascent of this handful of other universities, the University of Chicago which, with, for a time, Johns Hopkins University and for a shorter time, Clark University, had shown the way to the country, yielded its position as

a foremost institution of scientific and scholarly education and research.

This decline occurred during Hutchins's administration and
he was not unaware of it. Ashmore quotes an address to the annual
dinner given by the trustees to the teaching staff in which Hutchins spoke of the need to restore the departments to "their pre-
depression distinction." He said this as early as 1935. The process
continued throughout the 1930s and 1940s. To what extent
Hutchins was responsible for this general decline is difficult
to say.

Mr. Ashmore brings out very clearly the strong Calvinist
strain in Hutchins. The idealistic hopeful Protestantism of his
forebears, their austerity and piety, lived on in Hutchins throughout his life. He was a pious agnostic; he had ceased to be a Christian when he was a young man, but the moral strain of his ancestral Christianity never left him. He believed in natural law
without a deity; he believed natural law could be grasped
through reason.

Hutchins was above all a man of principles. He believed that
the acquisition of fundamental principles was the right end of university education and research. He did not think that scientific
research could attain such principles; he did not think that traditional humanistic research could attain them. Erudition did not
satisfy him, scientific truth did not satisfy him. He was convinced
that these principles could be found in metaphysics. This is what
he learned from Mortimer Adler. He believed that, through "dialogue," clarity could be attained and persuasion achieved. Methodical research, historical research, the scholarly editing of texts, the
writing of biographies, sociological studies, ethnology—all these
activities of the natural and social sciences and of the humanistic
disciplines were not activities which greatly interested Hutchins.
Of course, he never directly said this, because that would have
entailed the abolition of universities of the type which had developed from the German university of the nineteenth century.
Nonetheless, I think that this is what he really thought about science and learning.

Hutchins did not disapprove of all scholars and scientists.
He admired R. H. Tawney, but it was the social philosopher in

Tawney rather than the historian he admired. He liked John Nef, but not so much the learned historian of the British coal industry and of the relations between government and industry in France and England in the sixteenth and seventeenth centuries as the aspiring reformer of historical writing who sought to foster the ideas of love and beauty through historical work. He liked many more scholars and scientists than he intellectually approved of. He liked brilliant persons, profound persons, clever persons, fluent persons, learned persons, persons of eminence, and persons who spoke rapidly and, if they happened to be scholars or scientists, that was all right too.

No wonder, then, that despite the brilliance of the Hutchins era in Chicago, the University of Chicago slipped somewhat during this period. That it did not do so more is evidence of the deep vitality of a great institution and of the fact that Hutchins was a better man and a more faithful servant of his institution than his principles would have led him to be.

Hutchins had little reverence for the traditions of institutions; he also had even less sense for the setting of institutions. This was another reason why the University of Chicago slipped in the time of his presidency. The local setting of the University of Chicago was changing throughout the 1930s and 1940s, but Hutchins did not wish to try to cope with the situation.

When I first came to Hyde Park, the district in Chicago where the University is located, in the first half of the 1930s, it was a very seemly district, not at all very pleasing to the eye but sober and well kept. Most of the residential buildings were dismally ugly, but they were well looked after. The districts immediately to the south were respectable lower-middle-class and working-class residential areas. Likewise to the north, where there were several large buildings, some like tenements, in which bohemian graduate students lived. To the east, between the campus and Jackson Park, there was an area of respectable apartment buildings and single-family residences. German Jews, many of them refugees from the Nazis, some of earlier arrival, were settled there. On the west, there was beautiful Washington Park, which separated the university area from the "Black Belt," as it was then called. Toward the end of the 1930s, signs of deterioration began to appear just at the corners of 55th Street, where there were continuous rows of small shops on both sides of the street for more than a mile: grocery shops, delicatessens, butcher shops, bakeries, upholsterers, small restaurants, dry goods shops, ladies' dress shops. There was an inexpensive cinema which played the excellent films of the 1930s. Above the shops were poorer residences. The decay began to show itself at first toward the east and west ends of 55th Street where there were intersections of trolleycar lines. I recall noticing in the "spot-maps," which were so cultivated by Chicago sociologists of that generation, that the spots representing the residences of those charged by the police with delinquent and criminal actions were becoming dense at each end of 55th Street. When I once mentioned this to Louis Wirth, he replied angrily that I was a Fascist. By that he meant that I was criticizing the Negroes and the poor. Of course, that was preposterous. It was clear then that the deterioration of the district was beginning.

When I came back in the middle of the 1940s to the University after an absence of several years, I saw that the deterioration had gone much further. Except for those residences, very close to the center of the campus, into which Japanese-American families, released from detention camps, had moved, gardens had gone to weeds, houses were unpainted, there were obvious signs of dilapidation encircling the immediate area of the University.

Not that Hutchins either fostered this delapidation or could have avoided it or turned it back. But I had the distinct impression that he was indifferent to it. Each summer, on my return from London, I used to call on him to give him my unsolicited assessment of the state of the University. He was always very kind; I suppose that my observations must have amused him. He used to listen to me with his remarkably sweet smile. On the occasion of my visit in the summer of 1949, I said to him that the University was in danger because the physical deterioration and social disorder of an already not very beautiful district, along with the competition from Harvard and California, were causing some of our best teachers to leave and making it more difficult to persuade outstandingly promising younger teachers to accept appointments at the University. With characteristically charming and witty condescension, he replied, "You are wrong. Don't you know that the greatness of the University of Chicago has always rested on the fact that Chicago is so boring that our professors do not have anything else to do except to work?" It may be that he felt differently, but I never had any indication that he thought that there was anything in what I said.

I have also heard it said that the University of Chicago was in poor financial condition in the last years of Hutchins's presidency, and that this was a result of his failure to win the support of the wealthy. I cannot give any opinion about this except to say that the position of the University of Chicago among the leading private universities of the country has always been difficult because of the economic origins and professional destinations of its students. We have not traditionally had students who come from wealthy families, and our graduates normally enter the learned professions and academic life rather than business. We have a very faithful and appreciative alumni who contribute generously to the University, but for the most part they do not include very wealthy persons. I do not know whether Hutchins could have done better than he did in this realm.

After he left the University of Chicago, Robert Hutchins seemed to be a prince in exile. I am not sure that it wasn't that way from the very beginning. I think that at first he was glad to get the burden of the University off his shoulders, and he was happy, as an associate director of the Ford Foundation, to be in a position to act generously in support of civil liberties and public education. As always, he was forthright, trenchant, and courageous. But the fidelity to friends and his courage in resolutely refusing to dissemble his beliefs, which had done harm to his position at the University of Chicago, and then at the Fund for the Republic, and finally at the Center for the Study of Democratic Institutions, afflicted him at the Ford Foundation, too. Mr. Ashmore offers a detailed and impartial account of these years. It is an account of a giant among pygmies, most of whom he himself had chosen.

Robert Hutchins sometimes impressed one as a man of extraordinary shrewdness in estimating the qualities of individual human beings. His judgments were always succinct, sharply for-

mulated, and seemed to touch on some very significant characteristics. He had an exceptional sense of intellectual quality. Yet in
his own life that is where he seemed sometimes to go furthest
astray and did himself the most damage. Putting aside for the moment the perhaps fatal step that he took in his early years at the
University of Chicago in allowing Mortimer Adler to appear to
present his views, and leaving aside, too, any question of Mortimer Adler's merits as a philosopher, I have no doubt that it did
great damage to Robert Hutchins's effectiveness as president to
have Mortimer Adler so closely associated with him. Hutchins's
loyalty to Adler might be evidence of the virtue of fidelity; it certainly bespeaks courage in the face of harsh criticism. Nonetheless, the association was so close, at least in the minds of so many
members of the University, that Hutchins's attitude was taken to
be identical with what Adler said. Adler was so rude to those who
disagreed with him and he always seemed so angry and so deroga-
tory toward so many individuals and activities in the University
that the antagonism which he aroused was extended to Hutchins
and damaged him badly.

This account of Robert Hutchins's career at the University
of Chicago does not sufficiently evoke the effect of his strikingly
lofty visage, his sovereign bearing, and the economy of his spoken
and written expression. It scarcely indicates his courtesy and his
cool affections, or his sardonic and disarming self-depreciation.
These were all qualities he had in wonderful abundance. There is
much about Robert Hutchins that I do not know. Although he was
also one of the most pleasing men to be with whom I can recall, I
was never intimate with him. Even those who were closer to him
than I came up against his impenetrable reserve. It could not have
been otherwise, given the puritanism and moral rigorism which
he had inherited from his ancestors. Mr. Ashmore's story of
Hutchins's life reveals this unmistakably.

Yet somehow things did not work out as Robert Hutchins
wished, and as those who loved and admired him wished. No good
accomplishments endure forever and most careers end up in an-
nulment. In Hutchins's case, the failure was more than was necessary in view of his great merits. And not all of the failure is simply
to be attributed to the accidents of external fortune. They grew

from two flaws, one a flaw of intellect, the other a flaw of judgment. The flaw of intellect was that he believed that the truths which should guide mankind are capable of general and exact formulation. Hutchins was a man of principle; he believed that principles could be promulgated and that once learned they could serve as direct and unambiguous guides to conduct. He had no patience for the principles which lie unarticulated and embodied in the traditions of institutions and individual experience. He believed that principles could be discovered by ratiocination, that they must be clear and simple, and that clarity and simplicity were sufficient for the guidance of individuals and their societies through the rough course of human existence. This itself was contradictory to the tinge of cynicism in his sardonic world-weariness and in his own often remarkable artfulness as an administrator.

Was this a result of a utopian idealism? Whatever it was, it led Hutchins to keep bad company—the bad company of false idealists, doctrinaires, formulaic reformers, intellectual mediocrities, and intellectual bullies on whose behalf he used his failing physical strength in the last decade of his life to save the Center for the Study of Democratic Institutions in Santa Barbara. This combination of excessively clear ideals, an excessive confidence in ratiocination, an irrepressible honesty, and an unquestioning loyalty to those undeserving of it undid him. But not entirely. For all his flaws, Robert Hutchins was one of the greatest university presidents of the present century. He was a good citizen and a patriot who cared for the well-being of the human race. He was a man of honor and he tried to live up to his convictions, which he never hid.

This is how the career of this glittering, entirely extraordinary man appears to me and that is why I am so sad in contemplating it.

six

LEOPOLD LABEDZ

LEOPOLD LABEDZ, who died in March of last year, was the editor of *Survey: A Journal of East and West Studies.* He was a great editor and an incomparable repository of information about the world of Communism. He was also a man of indomitable courage with a wonderful sense of humor, who aroused the affections of many persons.

Leopold Labedz was about five feet, eight inches in height. He was as bald as a monk. His cheeks were pink without being florid; his broad brow was equally pink. He had bright blue eyes. His torso had the shape of a rugby football. His wrists and ankles were slender and trim. His shirt was always white and freshly laundered; his suit well pressed; his shoes perfectly shined. Wherever he went, he carried a heavy, inevitably overstuffed black briefcase, not at all shabby but a little the worse for always being jammed full of cuttings, books, papers, and manuscripts. He walked rapidly in rather short steps. He had a marvelously sweet grin, slightly mischievous, slightly embarrassed; as he grew older, the smile saddened.

Leopold was a brave, learned, tenacious, selfless, headstrong, witty, affectionate, excitable person, frequently indignant, sometimes aggrieved but, invariably, quickly reconciled and quickly, although not always, forgetting his grievances. He enjoyed being in restaurants until closing time. I am told that, when young, he was a good dancer and bridge player. He was extremely gregarious. It was almost as if, at all times, he had to be busily engaged in conversation or listening to the conversations of others, even the conversations of those who were not his interlocutors. He enjoyed the company of his close friends, he enjoyed almost as much the company of new and old acquaintances. He enjoyed talking and he enjoyed hearing others talk—if they had something worthwhile to say. He enjoyed especially talking with and listening to Eastern Europeans newly arrived in London.

He frequently returned to his house in East Finchley at about midnight and then sat up until about three or four o'clock in the morning, reading Central and Eastern European newspapers and periodicals. He must also have read many books in numerous languages in these early morning hours.

His house appeared to be rather tidy; newspapers were in neat piles; large, strong black plastic trash bags, which were filled to the top with newspaper cuttings, offprints, journals, etc., stood in a wide well-disciplined row about the wall of his drawing room. They gave a cold, funereal, but not disorderly tone to an otherwise conventionally furnished room that was also fairly full of upholstered furniture. There was nothing dusty or disheveled about the negotiable parts of the house.

Leopold was a zealous user of the Xerox machine. I often received copies of articles from very out-of-the-way journals, often articles of some years back, which he had mentioned in conversation and of which I had not been aware. His office at Ilford House, 133 Oxford Street, where he usually arrived, perfectly groomed, cheeks shining, at about 3:00 P.M. and remained until about 8:30 P.M., also gave a relatively orderly impression. Periodicals, although many were piled on the floor and on tables and chairs, seemed to have had well-ordered places belonging to them on the shelves that covered all the walls up to the ceiling.

I think that at both of his seats, he was much helped—at the office, by the faithful and talented young women, often rather learned, who were his assistants, and at home by a legendary Polish woman whom I never saw, who looked after him efficiently, but perhaps with incessant scolding, about which he sometimes complained. The "Polish nanny" was of great help to him in raising his daughter.

Conversation in Leopold's home often required the support of some cutting or offprint. A search in one or another of the black plastic bags sometimes produced the desired item; at other times, the search ended in failure and a sad smile of resignation. I thought that it was remarkable that these searches were successful as often as they were, given the fact that the interior of the bags seemed to have been as chaotic as their exteriors were orderly. It was evidence of his memory that he was ever able to retrieve anything from those bags. At least one room on the ground floor of the house in East Finchley was so crammed, apparently with old newspapers, journals, and books, that he strictly forbade me ever to open its door, lest a cascade of papers pour out onto the floor beyond its threshold.

He was fastidious in his taste for food, as he was in dress, but more oddly so. He was, except for *pommes frites*, an almost unqualifiedly consistent enemy of vegetables. There was nothing ethical or principled about his aversion to vegetables. He would occasionally eat carrots if they had been cooked with a sufficiently large amount of sugar. Sometimes, when he ordered a beefsteak or an escallop in a restaurant, it might be served with a few flecks of parsley. These were, if not too numerous, painstakingly removed by Leopold with the care of a police inspector sifting dust at the scene of an explosion. Salads were of course very strictly refused. Tomatoes in the form of *salsa di pomodoro*, and in that form only, were accepted. In some of the best restaurants in Paris, where I sometimes used to dine with him, he ate only *entrecôte* and *pommes frites*.

Until the great change in his life caused by illness, he seldom had a meal at home. On rare—very rare—occasions he roasted a chicken; even more rarely he cooked some very sweetened carrots. As a beverage, he almost always drank a Diet Coke. I think that Diet Cokes replaced Cokes when he learned that he had diabetes. He never drank wine or spirits during the time I knew him.

II

The Leopold Labedz I have described here was the Leopold Labedz whom I first met in 1953 at the flat of Jane Degras. Jane Degras was a fiery, meticulous little woman who had once been a member of the Marx-Engels Institute in Moscow, working on the Marx-Engels *Gesamtausgabe;* after she became anti-Communist as a result of her life in the Soviet Union, she was a member of the Soviet section of the Royal Institute of International Affairs (Chatham House) in St. James's Square and, more important, editorial assistant on *Survey* and the scourge of Leopold Labedz. In a way that combined affection and acrimony, Jane Degras was one of the sources of the relative regularity with which *Survey* appeared.

I saw Leopold frequently throughout the 1960s and 1970s. *Minerva,* the journal I have edited since 1961, began its life in Ilford House on the fourth floor, about fifty feet from Leopold's office. After we moved to Macmillans' near Temple Bar, I continued to see him frequently; in those days I went to London nearly every week and I often called on him in his office and on him and Melvin Lasky, in the evenings, when they were together in Lasky's room at *Encounter.* On some occasions he came to dine with me in Cambridge, once bringing Svetlana Stalin with him. He visited me a number of times in Chicago, staying at my flat for several days on each visit. There was always a great deal to talk about. He was a model of sweetness and courtesy when I had other guests, but when they left, usually around midnight, he would tell me for hours of his life from 1939 to 1942. His accounts were vivid and enthralling and so densely recounted that I could never interrupt him successfully to ask him to clarify certain points. It is on the basis of those accounts that the next part of my portrait of Leopold Labedz is based. Since I never was able to persuade him to write his autobiography, my account of his life is an impoverished and vague summary of the extraordinarily enchanting and horrifying things he told me in those early morning hours.

III

Leopold Labedz would have been a man of great civil courage, great learning, and penetrating understanding of international politics, as well as a charming, witty, selfless friend, whatever his earlier life had been. It was his nature to be that way. The sequence of cataclysmic and amusing—amusing only in retrospect—experiences that preceded his arrival in England in 1947 served as the rich stock on which a powerful intelligence and a precise memory could draw in their irrepressible exercise. He practically never referred to these experiences in his writings and he seldom dwelt on them in his conversations. Yet, when I seized the opportunity to encourage him, wonderful stories emerged. But only after midnight.

Readers of Leopold Labedz's writings will recall his two articles on Isaac Deutscher, a "critical" but faithful devotee of Stalin and a prominent spokesman of the critical pro-Stalinist and pro-Communist section of British intellectual opinion for a long succession of years after the Second World War. Leopold wrote about Deutscher in two articles, the second of which was delayed in publication by long consultations with libel lawyers. When Leopold wrote on any subject, he exhausted the sources. In one part of the long essay, which I read in manuscript, he referred to some poetry written by Deutscher in a short-lived Polish highbrow literary periodical of the second half of the 1930s. I asked him how he was able to obtain a copy of those poems in London. He said that he had not read them in London; he had read them in the Tashkent public library sometime in 1942. I asked him how he came to read them there, of all places. He told me.

But let me first reconstruct the main outline of Leopold Labedz's history before he came to London. He was born in Simbirsk—which was also the birthplace of Lenin and Kerensky—on January 22, 1920. His father was a physician in Warsaw, apparently of some eminence and success; his mother, who died when he was very small, was also a physician. Leopold studied in the Kreczmara Gymnasium with Leopold Tyrmand, the Polish émigré writer (Richard Pipes, professor of Russian history at Harvard, studied there four years afterward). Leopold matriculated at the University of Warsaw in 1937; I never learned anything about that period except for his reminiscence of the attacks on Jewish students at the University by anti-Semitic students. I think that he himself fought back. He did not make a point of saying explicitly that he had not "taken it lying down," but that is what I inferred.

In the late summer or autumn of 1938, Leopold went to Paris to study at the Sorbonne. He apparently studied medicine there but found time to read many French novels, to see many French films, and to hear Edith Piaf sing. He was already interested in the social sciences, and he read a bit of political philosophy. He seems to have had no plans for a career. (He never did.) It appears that he spent a lot of time in cafés, reading books and periodicals, not becoming closely attached to any one individual or group but generally happy to be in Paris, despite his certainty that war was going to break out. Just before it did he returned to Poland, seemingly for the summer vacation. Within the first weeks of the Soviet invasion of Eastern Poland, Leopold's father, who had probably been in the Polish military medical service, was taken by the Soviet army to act as chief physician of a relatively modern hospital in Eastern Poland. The hospital was reserved for patients who were very high-ranking officials of the Communist party of the Soviet Union who were in Poland to plan and carry out damaging acts against Poland. Leopold somehow gained an appointment as librarian of the hospital. His father's standing as chief physician apparently gave him immunity from the depredations of the Soviet NKVD. He himself had light duties.

True to himself, Leopold Labedz read books from the hospital library. He became especially friendly with one Russian, Aleksei Kapler, who had been a filmmaker but, more important, a speechwriter for Stalin. Kapler had fallen somewhat out of grace—by no means completely, because he was still a privileged Party member. Just what he was doing in Poland at that time is unclear. He was well enough to go for long walks with Leopold, then about twenty-one years old and fluent in Russian. Kapler unburdened his heart to Leopold in the course of long, almost daily, walks in the forest. He told Leopold a great deal about "life at the top." That was Leopold's first contact with the inside of the Kremlin. No scholar working on Soviet affairs, however knowing, ever had such a source of information about what went on so close to Stalin.

Once it became apparent that the Germans intended to move eastward in mid-1941, the hospital moved; it moved again and fairly often, and Leopold's father and Leopold moved with it. Conditions of life in the Soviet Union had begun to deteriorate severely as the German army advanced. Somehow Leopold became separated from his father.

There was apparently a period between Leopold's separation from his father and his joining the Polish forces when he was on his own. (I could never get a coherent account of this period from him or from his friends.) Even after he joined the Polish army early in 1942, he seems to have been on his own much of the time. The military unit to which he was assigned must have also moved repeatedly; it apparently had no regular roll call. The disaggregated body must have retained sufficient organization to provide some sort of meals even if only irregularly, but they were meals that Leopold could not eat since they contained no meat, but only vegetables. In the ensuing months, he became a scarecrow, falling in weight to about one hundred pounds. The Polish soldiers, and Leopold certainly, were kept to no discipline. They wandered about; if they saw a breadline, they joined it. Otherwise, they prowled about like living ghosts, eyes staring out of their heads, lice-infested, looking for crusts and scraps of discarded food.

Leopold had one advantage over his fellow soldiers. For them, a library was a place to sit down, a relatively warm and relatively clean place. For Leopold, a library was a place to read books. Leopold had discovered the Tashkent public library in his aimless, bedraggled wanderings, looking for food, hoping to find a place to rest. Seeing the library, a single dim light in a dusty lifeless scene, he went in. However disorderly it might have been within, it was a nearly divine order compared with the outside. Leopold began to order all sorts of books to be brought to him. After a time, the clerks refused to bring any more books for him. Where books were concerned, Leopold was even more ravenous than he was for meat. He was not one to accept refusals.

Weak though he was, Leopold could raise his voice. He demanded to see the head of the library. After some squabbling, he was ushered into that person's presence. The director was an oldish man, probably in his sixties, bent, thin, unsympathetic, his coldness of mien emphasized by his pince-nez. He was obviously a man who did not want any commotion around him. All else might be disregarded but not commotion. And here was Leopold, a creator of commotion. The librarian appeared to be a traditional Tsarist, and then Communist *tchinovnik*. The librarian weakened to the extent of asking Leopold why he wished to read so many books. Leopold told him what little there was to tell about his academic career. When Leopold mentioned his studies at the Sorbonne, the old librarian broke down. He too had studied in Paris before the First World War. He began to reminisce: it had been the happiest time of his life; he recalled streets and cafés and bookshops. He began to sob. Russia, when he returned, went to war; then came the succession of the revolution, the civil war, famines, epidemics, trials—it was all too much for him. He could not stand the turmoil, so he withdrew to what he thought would be the peace and quiet of the librarianship in Tashkent. But there was no escape from the cruel, dusty, broken treadmill of Soviet society. Recollections of Paris had brought before his mind reminders of a now-impossible happiness.

His recollections and sentiments about his time in Paris and his Parisian friends, which were separated from Leopold's own experiences by about sixteen years, aroused and animated what little was left of fellow feeling in his desiccated soul. Pulling himself together and resuming his position of authority, he told Leopold: "You will be free to read any books, periodicals, or papers in the library except *Pravda* or *Izvestia* from 1918 to 1920. Please do not ask for my permission to read those papers. It will be worth my life if I give you permission to see them. So, please do not ask me to allow you to do so." That is how Leopold came to read the works of Isaac Deutscher, the poetical apologist for Stalin, in the Tashkent public library.

This was only one incident among hundreds. Leopold was not a yarn spinner. He was not a person to speak about himself melodramatically. He spoke about himself only if led to it. But he had a great talent, helped by meticulous memory, for physical, physiognomic, and verbal details. Even in stories of which he was the central figure—which were those I was interested in—his interlocutors got as much or more attention and consideration than he. Had he been able to write it, Leopold might have left one of the best autobiographies of the century.

IV

When the war in Europe was over, Leopold knew that he would not go back to Poland. He knew too much about Communism and the Soviet Union to return to the certainty of a totalitarian society in Poland. He decided to accept the alternative of resettlement in Great Britain, offered by the Foreign Office to Polish soldiers who had fought under the British flag. Leopold did not rush to England, where he never had been. He spoke English very haltingly; indeed, he never lost his strong Polish accent when speaking or certain charming stylistic irregularities when writing.

After the war, Leopold spent some time at the University of Bologna. Some of his friends say that he studied medicine there. Other friends say that he studied law. Again, reading books was his main activity. He apparently did attend some lectures in political philosophy and jurisprudence, but I doubt whether he had professional ambitions. One piece of evidence that he studied law was the extraordinarily detailed and precise knowledge of Cesare Beccaria's *Dei delitti e delle pene* that he once adduced in an argument with Professor Leon Radzinowicz. The famous historian of criminal law was checkmated by Labedz's mastery of the professor's own bailiwick. I doubt whether he ever intended to become either a physician or a lawyer. Nor did he really think seriously of an academic career. For him, reading books was the highest good; it was never a means to some other end.

He arrived in London at the end of 1946, and in April of that year Leopold became attached to the Polish Resettlement Corps. He therefore remained officially in the Polish army until April 1949. At the beginning of the 1950s, he became a student at the London School of Economics as a candidate for the degree of bachelor of science in economics with sociology as his special subject. He soon established a reputation for his wide knowledge, his delivery of endless disquisitions in tutorials, his very active partici-

pation in class discussions. He was always very respectful of
his teachers, never overbearing towards his fellow students, who
knew far less than he did. In his finals, he answered only one question, writing at great length; he did not write anything on the
other questions. This perplexed his examiners. Some of them
wished to give him a failing grade, and it was only the active intervention of Mrs. Jean Floud that gained him a II,2—in the second
class of the second class.

It is not known whether he ever registered as a graduate student, but he spent much time at the LSE in seminars and he became known for his exceptional erudition and his amiable disposition. Leopold was a regular participant for many years in Leonard
Schapiro's famous seminar on Soviet studies at the School. He was
a regular attendant for about ten years, but I do not think that he
was registered as a student after he received the bachelor's degree.
It is from that seminar that his fame in London grew.

Whatever Leopold's status at the School, he was surely very
much at home there. He knew all the main teachers, senior and
junior; he studied all the books taught at the School in political
science and sociology. Naturally, he read all the literature on the
Soviet Union. He had a good, later well-remembered, knowledge
of Pareto's *Trattato*, Weber's *Wirtschaft und Gesellschaft*, and the
other classics of modern social science; they do not seem to have
deeply entered into his thought; they seemed more like acquisitions that he preserved and occasionally invoked but did not use.

Leopold was not interested in forming theories; his interest
lay in gaining a clearer and more specific understanding of the
Communist system. He had an intimate, very detailed knowledge
of the history of Bolshevism and of the Soviet Union. His knowledge of the satellite Communist countries and of Communist parties in India and China, Italy, the United States, and elsewhere
throughout the world was also very thorough, but he did not study
these countries in the way in which he studied the Soviet Union.
Nevertheless, he knew almost everything there was to be known
about all of these Communist countries as well as about the Communist parties, socialist parties, and leftist intellectuals in Western Europe and the United States.

When China and the Soviet Union dissolved their alliance,

Leopold—who had written very penetratingly from the very beginning on the separation between Communist China and the Soviet Union—became a favorite of certain officials, particularly the military attaché, of the Chinese embassy in London. He twice visited the People's Republic of China on the invitation of the Chinese Foreign Ministry. His overriding interest was in Communism in Europe.

Yet, with all the universally acknowledged thoroughness of Leopold's knowledge of the Communist regime in the Soviet Union and its satellites in Europe, it is difficult to say that he studied the Soviet Union in any conventional sense. It is difficult to imagine Leopold Labedz, sitting at a desk for hours and hours, in a library or at home, day after day. He always seemed to be in movement. When he was in his office at Ilford House, he was on the telephone much of the time. When the telephone calls were over and often while they were going on, he was engaged in conversation with visiting Poles, Czechs, and Eastern Europeans, or sometimes American academic students of the Soviet Union. Then, at about 8:30 P.M. he would rise and say that he had to be off. I think that he very seldom went home from his office. Instead, he frequently went directly to the *Encounter* office for a long jaw with its editor, Melvin Lasky; on other evenings he would go to a restaurant or a café to meet someone who knew a lot about Communism or from whom he could learn of that person's firsthand experience of Communism. Nevertheless, he did write long letters, sometimes by hand; he did read manuscripts and correspond with authors. He was also very familiar with books on contemporary politics and recent history in English, French, German, and Italian. So he must from time to time have sat quietly alone for prolonged periods. That must have been at intervals between periods of reading *Pravda, Tribuna Ludu, Rudy Pravo,* etc., between midnight, when he returned home to East Finchley, and 3:00 or 4:00 A.M., when he went to bed in a bedroom piled deeply with books.

The explanation of how he joined this busy, externally directed life to his highly differentiated and specific stock of knowledge must lie in the fantastic speed with which he read and his no less fantastic retentiveness. To this should be added his insatiable drive to absorb the content of any printed surface. Print at any angle drew him as by a magnet. When he came into a room to see a person seated at a paper- or book-littered desk, he read all that was open—upside down!

When Leopold and *Survey* took possession of each other, his range of reading narrowed from the breadth of all the years that preceded. He did not read so many novels. When he was younger— perhaps as a schoolboy in Poland, as a student in Paris, and as the collector of a private library when he was in the Polish forces in Italy—he read novels, philosophy, and, of course, history. (I think that he did not read books in religion; he had no religious sympathy.) His reading of novels must at one time have been as zealous as his reading of books on Communism was later. He was the only person I ever met—he himself, when I mentioned the book to him, observed the same from his side—who remembered *Silbermann* by Jacques de Lacretelle, a very modest novel written in the 1920s about a Jewish boy in a French school. But when the world became more serious, he read the writings of novelists only if they were in some way connected with politics and if their authors were—like Arthur Koestler, Manes Sperber, and Ignazio Silone— his friends or were fellow travelers on the other side.

This busyness of movement, reading, and talking was one feature of Leopold's life in London, interrupted by quite frequent short journeys to Paris, Berlin, Rome, Stockholm. The talk and movement were addressed to several concentric circles of individuals. At the very center were Walter Laqueur, Melvin Lasky, and Max Hayward, with the latter two becoming increasingly preponderant after 1965. Then there was a wider circle consisting of Lionel Bloch, David Floyd, and Marion Bieber. There was another circle, perhaps less frequently seen, less intimate but perhaps more esteemed than the others; Hugh Seton-Watson stood out among these. Beyond these circles were countless persons of all nationalities from whom he gained information, exchanged jokes, and pleased by his own amiability and intelligence. No one ever spoke ill of Leopold, not even Jane Degras, who admitted his virtues but who denounced him vehemently for his disregard of printers' deadlines.

V

I do not know what Leopold lived on between 1953 and the early 1960s, when he began to draw some income from the Congress for Cultural Freedom. It is possible that his father, now established in medical practice in London, supported him. I have the impression that in *Survey*'s first issues, when it was little more than a four-page newsletter about cultural developments in the Soviet Union after the death of Stalin, it was largely the creation of Walter Laqueur, who throughout his life has shown an exceptional ability to conceive and to carry out original projects in an orderly manner. At that stage, Leopold was Walter's assistant. When *Survey* became a thick, exceptionally informative quarterly on Communist affairs, Leopold, on Walter Laqueur's recommendation, became his co-editor.

I think that they did not always get on well together. Walter, who was a methodical and punctual worker, able to lay out a plan and to carry it out in an efficient, even if deceptively effortless, manner, was vexed by Leopold's unpunctuality and unwillingness to allow any manuscript to leave his hands.

Eventually the problem was resolved by Walter Laqueur's acceptance of more and more responsibilities. In addition to his unceasing production of solid scholarly books on important contemporary themes, he became director of the Wiener Library—the great private library of books and journals about Nazi Germany, Jews, and contemporary European history—as well as the editor of the *Journal of Contemporary History*. It was inevitable that he should reduce his obligations to *Survey*. Leopold then came into his own as the sole editor.

It was the beginning of the greatest period of Leopold's life. Although *Survey* was never an elegantly edited magazine—it was not a work of typographical beauty—it was a masterly editorial achievement. Leopold's universal knowledge of Communism in theory and practice, past and present, and his firsthand knowledge of the entire cosmos of scholarly work bearing on Communism, and of all those who did that work, gave him superb qualifications for the editorial role. The growing fame of *Survey*, and Leopold's acknowledged mastery of his subject, his personal charm and transparent integrity, as well as his genuinely friendly disposition, made available to him a reservoir of authors such as few journals could command. His contact with Eastern Europeans also made available to him articles and documents, the publication of which added to the great merit of *Survey.*

In Great Britain, the Foreign Office and the Ministry of Defense did not indicate any awareness of Leopold's existence, or, if they did, he and they communicated so secretly that one never heard of it. The situation was different in the United States. The United States Department of State was as indifferent to Leopold as was its British opposite number. But in Washington, thanks to his friendship with Richard Perle, at that time an adviser to the late Senator Henry Jackson, and with other influential persons, his knowledge and counsel were much appreciated. Senator Henry Jackson had Leopold testify before the Senate Foreign Affairs Committee; his testimony was spectacular. (He appeared together with Robert Conquest and Bernard Lewis.) He became a good friend and confidant of General Edward Rowny, who was a very important figure in the United States Disarmament Agency, and he continued to see and to be appreciated by—and to appreciate equally—Richard Perle when he was Assistant Secretary of Defense.

In the late 1960s, and through the 1970s and into the early 1980s, *Survey* was at its height and so was Leopold. A brilliant article by Bernard Levin in *The Times* (London) on Leopold was only one among other public testimonials to the achievement of *Survey.* Levin referred to him as, in appearance, an "Eastern European Mr Pickwick"; it was a happy notion and Leopold was pleased by it.

Leopold was an outstanding raconteur. His capacity for mimicry and re-enactment, his sense for details, were at a high point in his anecdotes. He was especially good in anecdotes about the boorishness and stupidity of the police—the militia—in Communist Poland. He was a treasure-house of the questions and answers of Radio Erevan, a mythical broadcasting station in Armenia. But he was not limited to these. Amusing stories like those of the interview between the shades of Brezhnev and Tsar Nicholas II in the next world, or of the visit of General Jaruzelski to Lenin's tomb to seek Lenin's guidance about how to deal with Solidarnòcs, appeared in a steady flow. Where they came from, I do not know; Leopold had such a large supply that he never repeated himself. And they were never part of a self-exhibition. They were an additional reason why his company gave so much pleasure.

VI

When the Soviet novelist M. A. Sholokhov was to be awarded the Nobel Prize for Literature for 1965, Leopold, despite very severe illness, traveled to Stockholm with Mark Bonham-Carter, and, in collaboration with David Carver of International PEN, he organized a huge manifestation on behalf of Yuli Daniel and Andrei Sinyavsky, the two Russian dissident writers who had been arrested in the Soviet Union. It received much attention in the press and surely helped to restrain many Western intellectuals from following their traditional inclination to swallow the Soviet line.

On another occasion, when the Helsinki group met to discuss the "third basket," Leopold was there. He represented no one officially, and he was excluded from the meetings. But he could attend the press conferences. The Soviet delegate was pleased to declare very aggressively that the Soviet Union adhered in every respect and in all details to the Helsinki agreement. This was Leopold's opportunity. He took the floor, addressing the Soviet spokesman very insistently. He asked why the Soviet Union, if it conforms so completely to the agreement, refuses to allow into the country harmless French and German magazines—and he rattled off the names of a number of them that were similar to *Ladies' Home Journal* and *Good Housekeeping.* The Soviet spokesman denied that they were refused entrance. He became heated; Leopold, knowing he had the upper hand, remained calm. He went on asking about other obscure and harmless journals. Then he asked, "And why do you ban *Mécanique populaire*?" (A French equivalent of *Popular Mechanics.*) The Soviet representative became loudly abusive. Leopold calmly held up for the gathering to see the official Soviet list of publications that were denied entry to the Soviet Union. He made it clear that his queries came from that list. His adversary was very disconcerted.

How did Leopold come to have that list? It was given him by a friendly Polish, nominally Communist, official, who had been provided with the list to guide Polish Communist censors. Leopold often got such documents. He got them because he was a presence in Eastern Europe, although he was not allowed to set foot there. Decent Poles, Czechs, Hungarians, who served the Communist regimes half-heartedly, knew that they had an ally in Leopold.

He also had time for smaller matters. Once a colleague of mine in Cambridge told me of a young Austrian woman, who, when she was an employee in the cultural section of the Austrian embassy in Moscow, had fallen in love with a young Russian. They wished to marry and to take up residence in Austria. But this could not be done because the Soviet government would not allow him to leave unless they were married and it would not allow her to return to Moscow as she had to do in order to marry her fiancé. (She had gone back to Austria on leave and, before her departure, had been given a visa to return by the Soviet authorities, who had then refused to honor their own visa.)

I told Leopold about the case and arranged for the young woman to visit him. A short time later, Leopold called a press conference. Such was his reputation that, when he called a press conference, the leading correspondents of the British and Continental press in London came, knowing that they would learn something to their advantage. The case was laid before them; they wrote about it in their respective papers, and before very long the Soviet embassy in Vienna informed the young woman that her visa had been re-validated and that she was free to return to the Soviet Union to marry her fiancé.

But not everything went Leopold's way even at the height of his glories. There were times when the financial straits of *Survey* were very narrow. This depressed Leopold. Nevertheless, the journal survived various financial crises, thanks to the recurrent support of various American foundations, most notably the Heritage Foundation. The financial straits were made slightly more bearable by the fact that Leopold was never one to follow his own financial matters with a zealous eye. I doubt whether he ever really knew the facts of the financial situation of *Survey*, any more than he knew about his own finances. These were things that he preferred not to think about. I had heard that he did not always deposit his salary checks; he certainly knew very little about his income-tax liabilities.

There were undoubtedly moments of anxiety about financial matters, but these were things about which Leopold was never straightforward with others or perhaps even himself. To offset these more or less private anxieties were his obvious pleasure in the development of his daughter Natalie into a charming and indeed beautiful young woman and her choice of a career of caring for and restoring works of art, as well as her marriage to an admirable young astrophysicist, who was always tender and solicitous to Leopold in his hard times.

In a sense Leopold, apart from his care for Natalie, had no private life. I have the impression that his intellectual friends and close acquaintances were persons who were engaged in the great collective task of trying to improve the weak civility of the intellectuals of Western countries and to overcome their reluctance to accept a more truthful understanding of the dangers of Communism to liberal democratic society. All of Leopold's friends were located within the boundaries of this common intention. He also had Polish friends. There was no overlap of these two circles. His personal affections and loyalties lay within those boundaries.

VII

Leopold was never one to care for his health. He could not have combined care for his own health with his agitated dashing about, his failure to eat regularly or properly, his frenetic studies, and his sometimes desperately improvised, because inevitably belated, editorial work. Of course, I do not know whether a more orderly life and better nutrition would have forestalled the coming and the progress of Leopold's diabetes.

I knew that Leopold suffered from circulatory disorders, but he was the very opposite of a hypochondriac and he did not complain. Even towards the very end of his life in the middle of March, just about a week before he died, when I asked him how he felt, he said, "Not too bad," with an air of melancholy and cheerfulness. He never dwelt, at least in speaking with me, on his physical difficulties, even after both his legs were amputated. Before the gangrene set in on the toes of his right foot, he only very rarely complained about the pains in his legs. Once in Geneva in 1985, and once in Chicago several years later, he asked me to stop while we were walking until the pain in his legs passed. He might have been under medical care in those years, but it was practically impossible to find out from him whether this was so.

On one occasion, about twenty years earlier, when he was driving me from Konstanz to the airport, he momentarily lost control of the car; it swerved, and he brought it to an abrupt halt on the side of the road. He must have had a slight stroke or heart attack. He rested for about five minutes. When I insisted that we should not continue but should take a taxi back to Konstanz, he would not hear of it. In later years, he insistently denied that such an incident had ever occurred.

The obstinacy with which Leopold resisted vegetables was no less strong than his reluctance to seek medical advice and assistance. His consent to the first amputation was given only after long arguments with physicians and friends during which his condition grew worse and the necessary magnitude of the amputation increased.

Likewise, he was very obstinate about the course of physiotherapy that might have enabled him, after his first amputation, to walk with an artificial leg. He, according to one of our common friends, misdirected the artificial limb that had been fitted for him, when it needed adjustment; the same person was convinced that Leopold would resist all efforts to teach him to walk with the artificial limb; and she was right. The question was rendered irrelevant when gangrene appeared in the toes of his other foot. Once he had to undergo a second amputation, the matter of walking on two artificial limbs was never raised.

Yet it must be said that Leopold adapted himself to his new circumstances with extraordinary fortitude; he did not complain about his misfortune. There was never any self-pity. To be legless was simply another hard fact of life to which he had to reconcile himself. He never uttered a word of complaint.

While he was in the hospital after the first amputation, another major catastrophe descended on him. As a result of broken water pipes, his house in East Finchley became flooded. His newspapers, journals, and books were severely damaged. Much had to be discarded. After he sustained that loss, no further trouble could have crushed him.

VIII

Leopold Labedz could not have lived in any other way than he did. He would have to have been a rather different sort of person, one less charming, less endearing, less exasperating, less merry, and less sad in order to meet the requirements of a more healthful regime or a more normal schedule of eating, sleeping, working. He would have been very unlike the Leopold Labedz his friends knew and loved, who impressed us with his unceasing flow of knowledge and his uncalculating selflessness and civil courage and who exasperated us by his obstinacy, and then by his distress, usually about small points.

But that is the way he was. The misfortunes that marked the last years of his life and that changed its external pattern—his rushing about, his endless readiness for conversation, his omnivorous appetite for more knowledge—shook him but they did not derail him.

The last few years of Leopold's life were very painful for him and for his friends. He lived in a nominally "sheltered flat" in a pleasant district in Ealing. It was a rather pleasant flat, very light and with a not unpleasant view of rooftops and trees. It was spacious enough. It had at least two good-sized rooms and a very adequate, thoroughly modern kitchen. The building had a "warden," and a woman "did for him" daily—as well as she could among the growing towers of Eastern European newspapers.

He seemed to be very satisfied with his arrangement in the "sheltered flat." He moved about in a wheelchair, bathed himself, and for much of his period of disablement, prepared his own meals in a microwave oven—mostly sausages, "chips," and pasta—and his inevitable Diet Cokes.

At first, characteristically, Leopold rebuffed the suggestion that he receive lunches and dinners from "meals on wheels." After a time, he began to refer with evident satisfaction to the service, although he had to resign himself to receiving cooked vegetables, which he had repeatedly asked to be withheld from the plate on which the meat dish that he had requested was delivered.

The flat soon became crowded with newspapers; in addition to two or three British newspapers and the *International Herald-Tribune*, he received about a half-dozen Eastern European dailies. There were not many books. But much worse than the piles of newspapers in which nothing sought could be found, and the absence of the many books that he mined with such speed, was what he felt to be his isolation.

Leopold would not go out of the flat by himself, although the doors and the lift permitted him to do so. He received fewer visitors than he wished because of the rather arduous journey from Central London to Ealing by underground and then the half-mile walk to his residence. Several of his Polish friends were very faithful to him and came fairly regularly. In the past few years, I myself found it increasingly difficult to travel to London from Cambridge, to walk long distances in the underground and up many flights of stairs at Ealing station. I spoke to him several times a week when I was in Cambridge; the calls usually were for about twenty minutes at a time. Often, when I telephoned, the line was busy. Leopold, in all his painful experience of isolation, was seldom out of the reach of someone else's voice.

On two occasions he traveled to Poland, where he was jubilantly received. On one occasion he even traveled to the United States. On several occasions, he traveled to Rusper in the Sussex countryside to visit his friend Melvin Lasky, but for most of the time, he stayed within the increasingly congested flat.

After *Survey* ceased publication, the flow of periodicals, American and Continental, which had been the line of life for him, was suspended. It was a crushing injury to him; it should never have been done. He received practically no new books. This was a terrible loss to one who used to peruse about twenty books a week. Then a kind friend arranged for the home delivery service of the Ealing public library to bring books to him and to collect them when he was finished. He was as happy as a lark. This offered the prospect of an approximation to his earlier life. Alas, he died only about a month after the delivery of books began.

Leopold had from time to time thought that he could continue to edit *Survey* once he recovered from his second amputation. For a variety of reasons, this proved to be impracticable. For one thing, the patrons who had supported the journal ceased to be willing to do so; it seems that the broken schedule was not acceptable to them. Furthermore, no preparations had been made for Labedz to continue his editorial work from his flat once the offices at Ilford House had been given up. He had no assistants since there was no money to pay them.

I am not sure how to assess the effect on Leopold of the breakdown of the Communist regimes in Eastern and Central Europe. He knew the truth about their failures and weakness better than anyone alive. Yet he did not expect them to abdicate as they did.

Several years before, he and I attended a large symposium in Geneva entitled "The Future of Communism." It was organized by Professor Alexander Stroumas, who insisted that only a short life awaited the Communist regimes before they collapsed. I was skeptical. Leopold was more than skeptical. He thought that the Communist rulers of those countries, although they believed not at all in Marxism or Communism, would not renounce their privileges and would not hesitate to use the powers of coercion at their disposal to hold what they had. Yet, it must be said in Leopold's favor that it was he who helped more than anyone else to make widely known Almarik's views as he put them forward in *Can the Soviet Union Survive 1984?*

Yet, when the abdication occurred, Leopold admitted to being surprised. His fascination continued unabated, but, unusually for him, he admitted that he was uncertain about exactly what was happening and what might happen next. His flexibility of mind in the face of these unwonted developments was very gratifying to me.

IX

Leopold Labedz lived most of his adult life in public—in seminars, colloquia, symposia, press conferences, and in discussions over lunch and dinner. He never spoke about himself but only about one aspect or another of the Cold War. He was a Cold Warrior—among intellectuals, one of the best—and he was not apologetic about it. He had been a severe critic of détente, which he correctly saw to be a one-sided affair. He was not one of those who thought that the Cold War was over and won. He thought that the denial of the existence of the Cold War was a naïve or cowardly act. He denounced those who promoted or refused to resist the growth or influence of the Communist idea and of Communism as practiced in Eastern Europe—in the Soviet Union and in the "peoples' democracies." With Raymond Aron, Ignazio Silone, Robert Conquest, Sidney Hook, Arthur Koestler, Melvin Lasky, and others of that circle, he was a hero of the Cold War, to whom we all owe a debt.

He had a private side, too, but he did not attend to it. He was not given to self-analysis, and if he even engaged in it, he never spoke to his friends—certainly not to me—about what he discovered. He seldom allowed anyone to see what he thought should be kept private. But he did have a private life. From 1989 onward—perhaps even from an earlier date—his life was a tale of acute suffering. Even in his best times from the 1960s to the 1980s, he concealed his grief or made little of it when it became patent to others.

Sometimes when I thought of Leopold, I thought of a small, delicate boy, brought up in a refined household, treated by his family with the utmost consideration and yet deeply sensitive, not only where things of the intellect were concerned but also in matters of sentiment. From 1939 onward, Leopold Labedz had a very hard life—not the kind of life to which he was brought up. Things were never as bad as they were from 1940 to 1942 when he entered Iran with the Polish army, but they were hard nonetheless. In some respects, the Italian campaign of the Second World War was the best part of his life. After that he was an exile who had to fend for himself. Although he was treated very generously by a small band of good friends—among them Michael Josselson, Melvin Lasky, Walter Laqueur, and Lionel Bloch—and received much esteem from the 1960s to the 1980s, there were always thorns in his soul. I do not know what could have eased his pain. But pain it certainly was.

Leopold Labedz's achievements of civil courage and lucid intelligence were brought off in the face of this pain. All the more reason, therefore, why I, for one, shall always think of him with profound gratitude.

seven

HAROLD LASKI

THE YEAR 1993 was the centenary of Harold Laski's birth. As was fitting, the London School of Economics, where he had been professor of government from 1925 until his death at the age of 57 in 1950, celebrated the occasion by a quiet commemorative meeting addressed by two protégés. The LSE also took note of the occasion by producing, in a magazine published for former students, a long article by Isaac Kramnick and Barry Sherman, the co-authors of a recent biography of Laski. It was right that the LSE should express its appreciation and bring before the present generation of its students the man who during his three decades as a teacher there did perhaps more than any other teacher to make the LSE known, admired, and beloved throughout the world.

In his lifetime, Harold had been much more than a teacher at the London School of Economics. More than any other academic of his time, he busied himself with party politics and he moved—in fact and in fiction—in the presence of the eminent. Even more than Bertrand Russell, he was the most prominent Anglo-American intellectual figure of his time. In certain important circles in the United States, he was as much at home as he was in Great Britain. He thought of himself as by right the universally acknowledged connoisseur in Britain of things American, and in the United States of things British. When he spoke it was with the proud presumption that he was at the pinnacle of the Anglo-American world. He was not only a renowned professor;

he was the hero of British socialist intellectuals and of American collectivistic liberals. In each country, he was granted greater attention by virtue of his eminence in the other.

In Laski's time, the union of British socialism and American liberalism was the last remaining link between the older social and intellectual alliance of Great Britain and the United States. The social alliance, marked by the marriages of British aristocrats with American heiresses, had ended sometime before. But the intellectual alliance, more actively cultivated in the United States than in Great Britain, went on much longer. It was still strong during the lifetime of Harold Laski. It was partly a product of Rhodes scholarships; it was also a product of the deficient self-confidence of American intellectual liberals who, with their socialistic and collectivistic sympathies, readily looked to Great Britain as the seat of their ideal. American universities in Laski's time had not attained the state of independence which has become so much clearer since his death. In Laski's day, that intellectual alliance was still real, and he was its most prominent embodiment.

All that has now gone, and with it has gone Harold Laski's prominence. All of his very numerous books are out of print. None of those books appears in the reading list for courses in his own department printed in the *Calendar* of the London School of Economics for 1993–94, except for his edition of a translation of a French book of the sixteenth century.

I

The Isaac Kramnick and Barry Sherman biography has recalled Laski to my mind and led me to reflect on the basis of his great reputation and on the grounds for his all but complete disappearance from the intellectual scene. Harold Laski has been in oblivion for at least a third of a century. In the preceding third of a century he was one of the best-known intellectuals in the world. His numerous books and articles—in popular newspapers, in learned reviews, and in superior journals of opinion—were received with appreciation for his scholarship, his public spirit, and his courageous enunciation of whatever needed to be said; but since then, at the latest since 1960, his name has been forgotten.

II

Laski's first circle in the United States was a small but select group; Justice Oliver Wendell Holmes, Jr., Justice Louis Brandeis, Professor Felix Frankfurter, and the young Walter Lippmann were at its center. They took Laski to their hearts as soon as he came to the United States in 1916. In addition to these really worthy figures, there was a wider circle of the readers of *The New Republic* and a small number of progressive academic social scientists, mainly economists and political scientists.

American anglophilia, which has diminished rather considerably in recent decades, had then been very strong for many years. One stream of that anglophilia comprised American monarchists, refined conservatives, devotees of tradition *tout court*, professors of English literature; all loved one Great Britain, the Great Britain of stately homes and marble halls, of the clubs of Pall Mall, of the salons of Bedford Square, of Oxford and Cambridge, of pomp and dignity, of amiable and witty eccentricity. That was their Great Britain. American democratic socialists, of whom there were very few, and collectivistic liberals, of whom there were many more, especially with the coming of the Great Depression, constituted the other stream of American anglophilia.

For this group, there was another Great Britain—the Great Britain of the Fabian Society, George Bernard Shaw, Sidney and Beatrice Webb and R. H. Tawney, the British Labour Party, *The New Statesman,* and the London School of Economics. Many younger and middle-aged Americans wished that the United States were more like Great Britain, a country of social conscience and refined tastes, a country where intellectuals were respected and played an influential role in politics. In these circles, Harold Laski was an idol.

The impression of Laski's brilliance was accentuated by his physical appearance. He was short and extremely thin; he had narrow shoulders joined by a thin neck to a very small head with black hair slicked down and divided in the middle by a wide white avenue of a part. He had a small black mustache. His bright black eyes, seen through thin, black-framed spectacles, gave him the appearance of an adolescent prodigy, which is certainly how he began. He soon moved from being an adolescent prodigy to an *enfant terrible.* Neither his intellectual style nor his physical appearance changed greatly throughout his life. Each accentuated the other.

For many, the London School of Economics, which had become a college of the University of London, epitomized this, the socialist side of England, from the early 1920s. It had no superior in the world as a center of teaching and research in the social sciences. Founded by the Webbs, Shaw, and H. G. Wells, the LSE seemed to be the heart of this other England. There were many outstanding scholars and teachers at the school in the 1920s and 1930s—Friedrich Hayek, Lionel Robbins, Bronislaw Malinowski, R. H. Tawney, Eileen Power, and Harold Laski among them. The first two were scarcely known at that time outside of academic economics. Malinowski was already famous as an original anthropologist and, though he was a Pole, he stood to the credit of Great Britain. Tawney's reputation as a socialist, a great writer, a sagacious economic historian, was just beginning to become known in the United States at a time when Laski had already become prominently and firmly established. Of this stellar faculty, Laski was the most prolific, the most fluent, the most popular teacher, and the one most before the public eye. In the United States he was much more known than any other British intellectual, and Americans had lots of opportunities to become aware of his presence. To mention the London School of Economics in those days was to evoke the name and image of Harold Laski.

The late Sir Arthur Lewis, who was a colleague of Laski and myself at the London School of Economics, once said to me: "However much we criticize the School, it must be remembered that it is the most important higher educational institution in Asia and Africa." He should have added that, at the height of Harold Laski's activities, it was also one of the most important higher educational institutions in the social sciences in North America. And that was largely because Harold Laski was a professor there.

The British in the 1920s did not take great interest in the United States. Lord Bryce, author of *The American Common-*

wealth, was an exceptional person of great intellectual distinction; he had moreover been British ambassador to the United States, about which he wrote with a detached intimacy and maturity of scholarship equalled only by Tocqueville. But Bryce never entered into American life as Laski did. Another British scholar, Denis Brogan, once a protégé of Laski, was very much at home in the United States and he wrote very well about it, probably with more intimacy and insight than Laski. But Brogan never formed such close ties with some of its leading figures as Laski did.

III

Harold Laski was born into a prosperous and pious Manchester Jewish family. His parents were the second generation of immigrants from Poland. Already as a boy, Laski attracted appreciative attention for his learning. He made a brilliant career first at the renowned Manchester Grammar School and then at New College, Oxford. After initially stumbling on the study of biology, he shifted to history and resumed his precocity. In 1914, he went to McGill University in Montreal; while he was there, he met Norman Hapgood, a journalist famous in his time, who called him to the attention of Felix Frankfurter. That was the beginning of Laski's American connection. He taught at Harvard University for four years where he made a dazzling impression. In 1920, he returned to England as a lecturer at the London School of Economics. After a few years he became Reader and in 1927 he became Professor of Political Science at the London School of Economics, where he remained until his death in 1950.

In 1956, Anthony Crosland described Laski's writings of the 1930s and the ideas they contained as being an echo from another world. But what Crosland heard in 1956 was an echo of an echo. Laski's writings in his own lifetime were echoes rather than the expression of a human voice. This might seem paradoxical, especially since Laski was a man of such apparently inexhaustible energy. Yet, at the same time, he gave an impression of a lack of intellectual vitality. His words and his works were molded into precast forms.

Harold Laski was one of the most fluent speakers and writers of his generation, when eloquence was still regarded as a talent to be nourished and cultivated. Winston Churchill was one of those orators whose carefully molded rhetoric gave an impression of being not an already available ornament but rather a genuine expression of his own way of looking at the world. However mannered and archaic Churchill's manner of speech, one had the impression that they expressed a genuine substance. In Harold Laski's case, the ornamentation seemed at best, to me, more prominent than the substance. It is not that Laski said things about the world which he did not believe. He was not a hypocrite, but the art of espousal and the figure presented seemed to count far more with him than the truth of what he said.

Laski seems to have become different when he ceased to be a pluralist in the middle of the 1920s, when he became a British socialist and a member of the Labour Party, which he remained for the rest of his life. This would seem to testify to consistency and firmness of conviction. Yet his books repeated earlier books without being affected by or passing through his convictions. They were not guided by the facts of the world about which he wrote or any persistently seeking, deeply experienced insight into them. They were guided rather by the clichés provided by his previous declarations on the particular phenomenon: the rigidity of capitalistic society, the conflict of classes, the obligations of a socialist government. True, the content changed with changing circumstances; his arguments as a member of the leading circle of the Socialist league in favor of a "broad anti-Fascist front" were not the same phrases as he used at the time of the formation of the national government in 1932.

It is not that Laski lacked convictions in the sense of stable beliefs. He certainly had them. It is not that his was not an intelligence capable of reasoning and observation. Although he was perfectly capable of reasoning and observation, he did not draw on those capacities but instead repeated with appropriate variation things which he had said earlier—echoes, in other words, of echoes.

Perhaps I can illustrate my view by recounting what a sagacious old Bengali journalist once said in response to my question about whether he wrote and thought more easily in English or in

Bengali. "In English, of course," he replied, "because in English we do not have to think at all. We have all the phrases ready-made for us." Harold Laski had all his phrases ready-made for him; some of them he had made up himself when he was young, others he took from current opinion and the late Victorian and Edwardian style of his precocious boyhood.

It was a delight to hear him. His speeches were performances. Like his spoken style, Laski's written style had its model in Macauley and the stylists of the great age of modern eloquence. His sentences were long and complex, his metaphors were elaborate, sometimes even cumbersome. American and British academics and the educated public in both countries cannot nowadays sustain such studied effort of elegance and dignity of style. In an age in which academic writing is filled with slang and jargon, Laski's style was the very opposite.

IV

Harold Laski was often the subject of anti-Semitic remarks. His critics in business, journalism, and politics often included in their account of his moral and political defects the fact that he was a "Jew." Even within his own Labour Party his critics did not hesitate to point out or to imply that his political errors were connected with his being Jewish.

Of course, Laski was Jewish; he never attempted to conceal it. But for most of his life, at least in his public statements, he did not avow himself to be Jewish and, except for visits to his parents, he maintained no connections with the Jewish communities in London or Manchester. (His brother Neville, by contrast, was a very prominent leader of British Jewry.) When young, he disregarded the efforts of his parents to dissuade him from marrying his nominally Anglican fiancée, who was, like himself, a rationalist. He became reconciled—not very happily—with his parents only after his wife became a convert to Judaism; he himself disapproved of her conversion. The reconciliation with his parents did not lead him into any closer relations with the Jewish community.

From his boyhood, Laski had no sympathy with the efforts of Jews to continue traditional beliefs and practices in a world very alien to them. He believed that the Jews should become completely assimilated in their environing society. He thought their traditional beliefs irrational and superstitious, their traditional practices barbaric. When he was fifteen, he wrote a small book, still unpublished, called *The Chosen People*. It was a denial of the Jewish path of separation and an argument for assimilation. (Less than a half dozen years later, when he had become a "pluralist" of some eminence, he did not modify his rejection of a separate life for the Jews.) He did not make these arguments on the grounds that British civilization was superior to Jewish civilization—he was never a British nationalist. In fact, there is not even any evidence of strong patriotic beliefs on Laski's part about the value of British society.

Harold Laski was a rather superficial scientific rationalist. He was indeed for a year president of the Rationalist Press Association. He came closer to Jewry—but not to Judaism—only after the formation of the National Socialist government in Germany. Well before that, when he was at Harvard, he was brought into contact with Zionists and Zionist affairs by Felix Frankfurter. With Frankfurter, Brandeis tried to interest Laski in Zionism, but nothing came of it. Nevertheless, when in the late 1920s the Arabs began to attack Jews in Palestine, Frankfurter's efforts to draw Laski into Zionist affairs were more successful. Laski became an active and fruitful interlocutor, pressing the British case and urging the American Zionists to be more moderate in their actions and demands. In 1945, however, he announced that he had become a Zionist, renounced his old belief in assimilation, but reaffirmed his condemnation of the Jewish religion.

Laski had already been in contact with Zionism in his paternal home. His father was a Zionist, and Chaim Weizmann, who was for many years an outstanding industrial chemist and a teacher at the University of Manchester, often visited the Laski household. The senior Laski and Weizmann disagreed about whether Palestine or East Africa was the proper place for the Jewish state-to-be then in formation.

During the agitation in 1929 between the American Zionists and the Labour government, Laski said that he was not a Zionist but a Jew and therefore opposed a policy which sacrificed "Jewish interests" to the Arab persecutors of the Jews. In these negotiations, Laski did really play an active part.

In 1943, Laski laid great emphasis on his being a Jew. He tried, unsuccessfully, to persuade the Labour Party conference to denounce the murders of Jews by the Nazis. He referred to himself as a "Jew in the fullest sense of the word." Later in the year, he said to Moshe Sharett, his former pupil and future foreign minister of Israel, that "I am Jewish. I am part of my people."

Probably Laski's most successful public action was his intervention in 1946, at the request of the British consul in Turin, when more than a thousand Jewish refugees had boarded a ship at La Spezia to go to Palestine. The British government had requested the Italian government to prevent the departure of the ship, since the passengers had no immigration certificates from the British to enter Palestine. The passengers began a hunger strike. In response to a fervent plea by Laski, far from his usual Marxist clichés, he persuaded the Jews to postpone the strike until he had had time to confer with the foreign secretary and persuade him to issue the certificates. They were issued in two installments. It was a heroic achievement.

I have dwelt at length on Laski's reentry into Jewish life because it shows both his virtues and his defects. The persecution of the Jews by the Nazis and the reluctance of the British government to allow those who escaped from death at the hands of the Germans aroused what were perhaps Laski's best qualities—his compassion and fellow-feeling. These qualities had often been manifested to his pupils and to the workingmen who attended his adult-education classes over many years. They probably came into play in his relationship with his close friends—of whom he seems to have had very few in Great Britain, apparently none so close as his friendship with Felix Frankfurter in its best years.

Laski's chief defect was intellectual and very significant. Laski was intellectually incapable of appreciating primordial things such as ethnicity and nationality and patriotism. When he was a pluralist in his early years, he referred often to the Church because the relation of church and state was the main subject dealt with by J. N. Figgis, from which his own pluralistic inspiration immediately came. Laski had no real understanding of what the claims of the Church rested on; he was religiously atonal and blind. Had he been a little less so, he might have avoided the assertion made in at least one of his later writings that socialism was a replacement of Christianity. Laski's rationalism was simply a response to the world of a very superficial intelligence.

Even when he avowed being Jewish and became a Zionist, at least as far as British policy on immigration into Palestine was concerned, the profound changes in his conception of what he was and of the reanimated ties of affinity with Jewry did not arouse in him any reflection about the nature of national, ethnic, and religious communities.

V

Much the same is just as true for Laski's political theories. He was quick and he was often impressive in his formulations but they signified very little. When he was a pluralist he did not ponder deeply on the implications and particularly the presuppositions of pluralism. And then, of a sudden, he ceased to be a pluralist. He ceased, he once said, because he had read Morris Cohen's brief essay on collective ghosts. From Cohen's tentatively phrased doubt, Laski, who was committed by his earlier writings to believe that corporate bodies are distinctive and irreducible entities, simply ceased to regard himself as a pluralist. Such, certainly, is not the decision of a person who has thought profoundly.

When Laski left pluralism he went to nearly the diametrically opposite. He became a Fabian socialist who believed in the superiority of strong central government. Why to Fabian socialism? One explanation is that it was espoused by the Webbs, who were certainly very weighty witnesses on behalf of anything they took an interest in. The Webbs took an interest in the new LSE lecturer and brought him into their company. Sidney and Beatrice Webb together were like a juggernaut and Laski threw himself before it. The Webbs were wedded to the idea of national efficiency, national health, etc.—the sort of ideas that had made Laski into a precociously brilliant eugenist when he was a schoolboy and which had induced him to study biology in his first period at Oxford. (His wife, Frida, was a eugenist at that time and she, while apparently never disagreeing with Laski, and being always un-swervingly loyal and loving to him, also had a very strong influence on him.)

Returning to England reanimated the beliefs about "national efficiency" that Laski had before he became a pluralist. It must also be said that, although there was a strong current of pluralism in England at the time, it was nowhere as strong as the powerful influence of the Webbs together and the charming and persuasive Beatrice Webb on her own—she did all the talking for the two of them—who brought Laski into the Fabian circle. Laski continued to see the Webbs, even after he had found the company of such public figures as R. B. Haldane and Ramsey MacDonald, with whom he used to lunch and to dine and about whom he then boasted. The transition to centralized socialism for Laski was very easy.

From Fabian socialism, it was easy for Laski to become the great admirer of the achievements of the Soviet Union, with the reservation, which he never withdrew, about its suppression of civil and intellectual liberties. His becoming what he called a Marxist was really no fundamental change. He did not espouse any of the preposterous bric-a-brac of Marxists such as the four stages of human society, the theory of dialectical and historical materialism, and the rest of it. He simply cottoned onto the imagery of class struggle and of the revolutionary overthrow of the capitalistic order of society. Of course, this brought him to the point where he began to appear to be a fellow-traveller—although he thought he was being no more than a really consistent and uncompromising socialist. He did not become an exponent of the "third force," though he did, after the Second World War, try to effect the unity of the socialist parties of the European continent. He was already unyielding in his denunciation of American imperialism, and he believed that the difficulties engendered within the Soviet Union were only defensive measures to protect itself from the expansive policies of American imperialism.

Of course, these developments in Laski's political beliefs brought him into conflict with his friend Felix Frankfurter. He gravitated thereupon towards a section of American opinion the level of which was far below that on which he had moved during his earlier, Harvard years. Holmes and Brandeis were dead; Lippmann had become what Laski thought was a reactionary in conservative guise. (In fact, Lippmann had become a genuine individualistic constitutional liberal.) Laski was too far gone in the collectivistic direction; for him the touchstone of a sound economic outlook was a thoroughgoing socialism-cum-civil liberties.

There were innumerable collectivistic liberals, inside and outside the universities and colleges, who adored Laski and gathered in large numbers to hear him. Of his new friends in the United States, Max Lerner was the most eminent. Whatever Max Lerner's merits, he was certainly not in the intellectual class of Brandeis, Frankfurter, Roscoe Pound, Oliver Wendell Holmes, Jr., or Walter Lippmann. Although much was made of Laski in the United States after the Second World War, his admirers were thrilled by his distinctive variant of fellow-travelling, his repeated expressions of disapproval of American policy towards the Soviet Union, and his belief that the American government wished to rule the world for the profit of American capitalists.

Laski enjoyed company, especially admiring company, and he had plenty of that on his visits to the United States in the 1930s and again after the war. But they were not the kinds of persons whom he preferred; he preferred the company of the great, the influential, the well-connected. After the death of Franklin Delano Roosevelt, and the attenuation of his friendship with Frankfurter, he never had that again.

VI

I cannot readily think of any academic intellectual of the present century in the English-speaking world who continued in his academic post, who taught his classes regularly and saw his students at length and in large numbers, and who at the same time was so much engaged in activities outside the university as Harold Laski. There was scarcely any kind of political activity—except being a head of government, cabinet member, or a member of Parliament—in which Laski did not engage. He was very active in the Labour Party, repeatedly trying to organize groups within the party to press the leadership and the government to move more decisively towards socialism. He was also active in such subsidiary organizations as the Socialist League—a radical faction of the Labour Party, more sympathetic with the Communist Party of Great Britain and its strategems than the majority of the Labour Party. He was one of the organizers of the National Council of Civil Liberties, participated in its various manifestations, speaking and writing on its behalf. From 1931 onward, he attended most of the annual conferences of the Labour Party; for seven years he was a member of the party's National Executive Committee and for one year was its deputy chairman, and for another—the year of the general election of 1945—he was chairman of the National Executive Committee and thus bore great responsibilities for the conduct of the campaign.

Although the Socialist League was a failure because it was too friendly with the Communist Party, the Left Book Club that Laski founded together with the publisher Victor Gollancz, his contemporary at Balliol and a kindred spirit in the 1930s, and John Strachey, who was still very close to the Communist Party through most of the decade, was another story. If the term fellow-travelling had any meaning in Great Britain during this period and for some years later, it was to be found in the Left Book Club and the *Left Book News*, a monthly magazine which was sent to Book Club subscribers. I do not know that Laski spent much time in the affairs of the Left Book Club, but he did not have to because he could get through a heavy budget of work in a short time. In his capacity as co-editor of an obviously fellow-travelling enterprise, he did not cease to exercise his discriminatory powers, mixing expression of approval of the Soviet Union with criticism of it and of the Communist Party of Great Britain. Nevertheless, he never dissociated himself from it and from fellow-travelling generally.

Laski engaged in countless other activities: the foundation of *Tribune* which was the organ of the radical, to some extent fellow-travelling, members of the Parliamentary Labour Party; the foundation of *The Realist*, a shortlived intellectual—rationalist—quarterly, and of *The Political Quarterly*, a rather serious and well-edited organ for the intellectuals of the Labour Party. Early in this period, he also served as president of the Rationalist Press Association and contributed to its publications. Much earlier, he had been active in the feminist movement—probably largely under his wife's influence. For many years, he also lectured before classes of the Workers Educational Association.

These activities would have filled the days of any normal mortal. Not so for Harold Laski. None of them were allowed to dominate his schedule. His main activities remained those of Professor of Political Science at the London School of Economics. He said that he spent seven hours each day every week at the school and it is likely that this was as near the truth as he usually came. Between 1922 and 1925, he also taught politics at Magdalen College, Cambridge, two days each week. Throughout the Second World War, when the London School of Economics was evacuated to Cambridge, he spent several days a week in Cambridge, lecturing and seeing students. But it was from his teaching at the LSE that the bulk of his income was earned. (His journalistic activities paid very meagerly.) And it was from his professorship that his standing was obtained.

Had Laski not been a professor but only a freelance writer, intimately and intensively engaged in radical political activities, he would not have attracted the attention that he did. I think, too, that he was very proud of being a professor. It has been said that even before he entered upon his professorship, he entered his name in the London telephone directory as "Professor H. J. Laski." There is every reason to think that he did not shirk his duties as the professor. I never heard of his missing a lecture, except when he was ill or travelling abroad. His lectures were, I have been told by his students, from both before and after the Second World War, never anything but elegant; they appeared to his students perfect in composition and form. He always had time for his students. No less important, he took to heart his responsibilities as professor; in those days, the professor—there was very seldom more than one professor to a department—was head of the department. It would be difficult for an American or even a British academic of the present generation to imagine the conditions of secretarial austerity under which university teachers, including heads of departments, worked at that time. According to Laski's own statement in defense of his extraordinarily profuse journalistic activity, it provided him with £200 per year from which he paid for his own secretary. Despite this, he attended to the business of his department very responsibly.

How did Laski do it all? My hypothesis is that it was done at the expense of serious intellectual work and hard thought on his manuscripts. I think that, in the last decades of his life, he ceased to study any subject intensively. Since he remembered so much (although not as much as he thought he remembered) and spoke and wrote so voluminously, the time for this extraordinary range of activities must have been gained at the expense of his intellectual activities: at the expense, that is, of thought and study.

VII

When I first came into personal contact with Harold Laski at the London School of Economics, the students continued to speak of him with great affection and reverence. Nor did I hear any criticism from his colleagues; this might have been a result of discretion rather than approval. I never heard R. H. Tawney say anything explicitly in criticism of him; Tawney, who looked and spoke like an untidy angel who had learned English from the Authorized Version and who had a very cutting tongue, never used it against Laski. The economists of the LSE did not take him seriously, but they rather liked him.

Maybe I heard no criticism because he had ceased to be taken seriously. I do recall that his reputation as a fabulist was very widespread. This was before the publication of his correspondence with Oliver Wendell Holmes, Jr., and the establishment of his reputation as an embroiderer of the truth, not to say a creator of harmless untruths. His very recounting of any experience that he said he had was immediately discounted. No one ever said: "Harold told me . . ." with the expectation that the retelling of the story told by Laski would be taken at its face value. It was known that, despite his *soi-disant* Marxist egalitarianism, one of Laski's greatest pleasures was to be in the company of the great and the mighty and that his very greatest pleasure was to say that he had been in their company. Beatrice Webb in her diaries refers not infrequently to his tales, which were harmless and amusing but which she did not take to be the truth. Oliver Wendell Holmes, Jr., was an early witness to Laski's unsteady relations with the truth whenever he told about some experiences of his own. By the 1930s, his irrepressible need to elaborate and to fabricate came to be accepted by everyone who had any dealings with him.

Let me give an example of Laski's irrepressible penchant for fabrication. Once I mentioned in a lecture the memoirs of Alexander Herzen. One of my students became interested and began to read *My Past and Thoughts*. One day, she was asked by Laski—she was also his pupil—what she was reading. She told him. He asked her whether she knew that our library, the library of the London School of Economics, had a set of Herzen's journal *Kolokol* that had been annotated by Lenin. I was interested in this. I was a member of the acquisitions committee of the library and we had to decide on whether the library should purchase expensive and out-of-the-way works.

I recalled that, some time before, we had been offered and had purchased a substantial run of *Kolokol*. The secretary of the committee, a dear little man named Eduard Rosenbaum, often spoke to me about some of the more interesting purchases before they were brought before the committee, but he had never mentioned anything distinctive about our newly acquired *Kolokol*. When I next saw him in the Senior Common Room, I asked him if there was anything singular about our *Kolokol*. He said he would examine it and let me know. A few days later, he told me that he had done so. Was there anything especially interesting about it? "Nothing especially interesting," he said, "except that the pages were entirely uncut and each volume bore the rubberstamp of the Russian Consulate in Brussels. The pages were entirely clean."

I am pretty sure that Laski could not read Russian script and no less sure that he was unacquainted with Lenin's written hand. The fabrication had a point of departure in reality—namely, our acquisition of the *Kolokol*. It was also entirely disinterested. Perhaps one might say that it was a minor work of perverse art, a work of art for art's sake.

The creation of these tales was not regarded as a vice; Laski was never called a liar. It was regarded rather as a foible, even an endearing foible. In fact, nearly everyone liked Harold Laski; it might be too much to say that he was loved by everyone except his wife and daughter and his older friends in the United States, but he was liked by great numbers of persons of many countries and nationalities.

Along with being an impressive fabricator, he was also a great snob. Democrat and egalitarian though he was, he found it necessary to be known as an intimate of the most eminent persons, lords of the realm, cabinet ministers living and dead, American presidents and senators and judges of the highest benches. It is quite likely that there was something truthful in those assertions of intimacy with the great on Laski's part, but it became less so with the passing of the years.

On the whole, his snobbery was well interwoven with his general benevolence, especially towards younger persons and a small number of older persons such as Mrs. Webb. The former, who were less critical about his disposition to neglect the truth, not only felt the genuine affection which he seems to have had for them but they also felt elevated by his company and by the company—perhaps only fictitious company—which he said he kept. Students not only felt his affection for them; they, from their side, had great affection for him.

VIII

No one known to me has ever raised a question about the possibility of a relationship between Laski's fabrication of stories and his work as a scholar. I do not mean that his fictional capacities were also at work in his scholarly work—which was largely done in his youthful years. His numerous books of later years were not works of scholarship; they had a strong political bent and they were radical political clichés rather than works which claimed to be scholarly. His *Rise of European Liberalism* was a memory of much reading several decades earlier formulated in very vague Marxist clichés. His Marxism entailed ideas about society which were certainly lacking in veracity. It is possible that Laski was the victim not only of an impulse to create fictitious anecdotes but also a related disposition to believe untrue propositions about society.

The shadowy line between truth and falsity in the social sciences is not always easy to observe and it is difficult to be bound by it precisely because it is so shadowy. That is why the rules of scholarly research are a necessary discipline over the disposition to disregard that line. Harold Laski found it too easy to believe what it was more agreeable to him to believe. The more confident he allowed himself to be about his exceptional gifts of memory and fluency, the more cloudy or attenuated his grasp of the world around him became.

Whereas the stories which he created about himself fell into a pattern, with a freshness and even originality about them, Laski's accounts of the state of British and American societies were as unrealistic as his anecdotes, but without the charm. They were increasingly reiterative and blurred. His Marxist analyses were of the sort that one encountered in any doctrinaire socialist journal. They were not even of the ingenious sort that clever but dishonest persons contrive in order to put a good face on Marxism. They were simple repetitions, in more elaborate style, of the propositions that whatever the government does is intended to strengthen the position of the capitalistic class, that the class struggle will be unceasing until class-society is abolished, that only socialism can remedy the injustices of capitalism, and that only a genuinely socialistic government, determined to abolish capitalism and to establish a genuinely socialistic regime, could do what is necessary. From the 1930s onward, he began to add that if a socialist government, elected by the working classes, was prevented by the obstruction of the property-owning classes and their middle-class allies from carrying out a comprehensive socialistic policy, it might be necessary to overcome their resistance by revolutionary action.

Laski, it should be said, grew very enamored of the word "revolution." Sometimes he used it to describe the process of a complete change of society from capitalism to socialism. The word "revolution" in this sense was scarcely different from its use in the term "the industrial revolution" or "the scientific revolution." But he also liked to use the term to refer to some vague image of a violent overthrow of the existing government to establish a socialistic society.

This brought him into great difficulties. When he used the

term in the violent sense, he was careless in not making clear—if that is what he really meant—that he did not desire a revolution but was only predicting the high probability of one if the socialist electorate and the socialist government were frustrated by the obstructive tactics of the property owners and their allies.

If only Laski had the common sense and self-restraint to say that a revolution would be regrettable if it occurred. But, no, his thought was too slovenly for that. He probably enjoyed the notion of a revolution. He enjoyed it because, though a person of a very proper and orderly mode of life, he enjoyed the thought of conflagrations and bloodshed, of the rushing about the streets of armed workingmen, of barricades and fusillades of the soldiers against "unarmed workers." (When he was an undergraduate, he did set off some sort of explosive in a village railway station in support of the feminist cause.) I think that he was thrilled to think of the possibility of such events in Great Britain. He also seems to have enjoyed saying things *pour épater le bourgeois*. This would be consistent with his declaration that he was a "Marxist" when all he did was espouse only a small part of the Marxist doctrine, and then only to reaffirm a belief which he had long held.

Whatever the explanation for Laski's turn towards revolution, it very probably did not emerge from serious study and thought. Anger was not part of Laski's moral constitution. I do not know of any one who ever said that he saw Laski in the state of anger. Nevertheless, he became friendly to the idea of revolution from the rhetoric of the radical left with whom he was critically sympathetic. Laski had always had a desire to please and to cut a figure. The espousal of revolution, however qualified, permitted him to do both.

IX

Laski's unserious Marxism took its revenge on him. Winston Churchill took advantage of Laski's ambiguous views about revolution and made it a central issue of the Tory campaign in the general election of 1945. After the immense victory of the Labour Party that year, Laski thought he would revenge himself on those publishers who had reproduced and affirmed Churchill's argument

about his espousal of revolution. He therefore instituted a libel
suit against a provincial paper that had reported a political meeting at which Laski spoke. He probably intended that, once victori-
ous in this minor suit, he would take action against the prosperous gutter press of London, which had repeated the charges
against him.

This was the greatest misfortune of Harold Laski's career.
His adversary engaged the services of the leading libel lawyer of
the country, Sir Patrick Hastings. Seizing the initiative and following a procedure of contemptuous insult and considerable skill in
the dubious practices of sharp-witted lawyers, Hastings humiliated Laski and hamstrung him from the very beginning. Laski
seems to have been on the verge of making the distinction of a
prediction of revolution and an incitation to revolution, but he
was kept off balance by Hastings's unceasing ridicule and contempt. Laski had always been proud of his gift of repartee, but
Hastings never permitted him to bring it into play. Hastings's bad-
gering and plain rudeness rattled him; he could not say what he
should have said years before, which was that he was not really
serious about revolution. The jury found for the defendant and
Laski had to meet the legal costs of the defense.

This was a crushing blow to Laski. He was degraded and defeated and was placed under a financial burden that would have
required him to sell his beloved library of sixteenth- and seven-
teenth-century books and pamphlets about which he had so often
boasted. Fortunately for him, friends and admirers came to his
rescue and that was averted. But his poor showing in the inter-
change with Hastings coincided with the pursuit by the Labour
government of a policy entirely contrary to what Laski wanted.
Laski hated Ernest Bevin's determination to support the American
policy of containment of the Soviet Union.

X

The demoralizing blow of the decision against him in the action
for libel, the rather far-reaching and very wounding disregard of
him after the first few months of the Labour government, the ac-
cumulating strain of his crushingly overloaded schedule of public

activities, all reduced Laski's vitality—still extraordinary by normal standards. It also had an enfeebling effect on the intellectual capacity on which he had been drawing for many years without renewal. He still faithfully observed his duties as a teacher; I doubt whether he fell short in his administrative responsibilities at the LSE or in his solicitude for his pupils. Nevertheless, the intellectual level of his writings declined.

Some of the decline in Laski's intellectual powers is attributable to some of his extraordinary gifts. This sounds paradoxical but it is not. The very traits of speed in reading, speed in writing, an extraordinarily retentive memory, and a fine turn for phrases that made him into such an outstanding scholar in his very early years, turned his head. Possession of these gifts flattered him into thinking that they were sufficient for intellectual work at the highest level. He had too much confidence in them, and they proved insufficient.

One of the reasons for the deterioration of Laski's scholarship was his excessive self-confidence. He did have a very exceptional memory, one both capacious and precise. But such a memory has to be continually nourished with new substance. His great fluency in speech and writing, no less exceptional than the retentiveness of his memory, was a notable gift but he was misled by it in a way different from the way in which his superb memory misled him. The memory misled him by inducing him to think that it was perfect. This fluency in collaboration with his memory misled him into thinking that ease in speaking and writing is tantamount to being right and truthful.

One summer, in the second half of the 1940s, he was visiting professor at Roosevelt University in Chicago. Roosevelt had been the YMCA College before the war, but with the flood of demobilized soldiers its governors decided to make it into an undergraduate institution. Its change of name to the deceased president's indicated its political viewpoint. It was natural for its governing body to think of Harold Laski for a visiting professorship. While he was in Chicago, he lived not very far from the University of Chicago, but he vowed that he would not visit the University because of his disdain for then President Robert Maynard Hutchins. He was invited by the students who edited *The University of Chicago*

Law Review to allow them to publish a contribution by him. He was pleased to do so and that summer, with characteristic speed, he wrote an article on "Morris Cohen's Approach to Legal Philosophy." The members of the staffs of the law reviews are students, and they take their editorial responsibilities conscientiously. Every contribution is gone over with a fine-tooth comb, every quotation, citation, and footnote is checked and re-checked for accuracy.

It so happened that that summer I, too, had contributed an article to the *Law Review* and one of the editors came to my room at the University to go over my article. He had formerly been an undergraduate student of mine and was quite friendly with me. After we finished going over my article, which had very few footnotes, we discussed his experiences as an editor of the *Law Review.* He told me that he had just finished editing Professor Laski's essay on Morris Cohen. He said it had been very demanding because nearly every footnote was wrong in some respect. Instead of giving a date of publication as 1908, Laski gave it as 1909; instead of citing the year of a volume in which some journal article had appeared as 1910, it was 1911. It was the same with page references; they were nearly all wrong but they were only slightly wrong.

Now, it should be remembered that Laski wrote the entire article, references and all, without using the library of the University of Chicago Law School. He lived about a mile and a half from the law school library. I saw him on quite a number of occasions that summer, but I never saw him on the campus. In fact, practically no one at the University knew that he was in Chicago. The long and short of it is that his paper on Morris Cohen was a tour de force, all of it drawn from memory and, though replete with errors, all of them minor errors.

XI

Against these deficiencies of character—vices without sin, moral defects without immorality—it is necessary to place Laski's virtues. His greatest virtue, aside from domestic affections and fidelity, was his ready sympathy and generosity. This, as I have suggested, was most notable in his relations with his students. The young men and women students of the London School of Economics were a very decent lot. They did not have the sense of effortless superiority of a Balliol man. They were probably mainly of lower-middle-class origin, or from the only moderately successful professional classes. After the war, some of the demobilized soldiers, sailors, and airmen studying there were of working-class origin. The young ladies were of a somewhat more genteel social origin than the young men. They were all perhaps a little bit uncertain of themselves.

The physical features of the London School of Economics were scarcely endearing to young hearts. It was a higgledy-piggledy collection of miscellaneous buildings of which, for a long time after the war, only two had been built expressly for the school. There was nothing elegant about any of them. The Webbs were all for efficiency in everything and so the LSE was not allowed to exchange a little efficiency for a little beauty.

Laski was to the LSE students a great figure but much more than that. With all his fame, which he usually embellished, with all his prodigious learning, the flaws of which the students could not detect, Laski was the one towering figure on the faculty whom the students could appreciate. Despite the mists of ambiguity and embroidering, there was much that was real in both his fame and his learning. But what was extraordinary was his ability to make the students feel at ease in his presence. I think that he had a genuine liking for them. His capacity to arouse affection and to show affection was the most visible and least fabricated thing about him.

Laski had a largehearted generosity. Friedrich von Hayek told me some years ago that when he was beginning to work on an edition of the letters of John Stuart Mill (later renounced when the University of Toronto Press began its great edition of Mill's works and correspondence) he tried to compile a list of Mill's letters. On a number of occasions, he discovered Mill letters in auctioneers' catalogues, and when he inquired of the auctioneers about who had purchased them, he was told that it had been Professor Laski. When Hayek applied to Laski to obtain copies of the letters, Laski no longer possessed them; sometimes he could not recall what had happened to them. On later occasions, Professor

Hayek accidentally met teachers in small American colleges who possessed Mill letters. When Laski visited such colleges to deliver lectures and found that they were interested in Mill, he would ask whether they would like to have a letter by Mill. On being told that they would indeed, he would whip a letter of Mill out of a case or envelope and present it. Professor Hayek said this had happened in several cases. The story is both plausible and characteristic.

XII

How can one sum up a life such as Laski's, brief though it was, when it combined so many different kinds of activities? He was a university teacher and scholar and he was an intellectual in politics. I do not recall any academic intellectual who was so thoroughly engaged in politics in the nineteenth and twentieth centuries. Max Weber, though intensely attentive to politics, was really drawn into political activity only in the last six years of his life. Except that he never stood for Parliament and hence was never a cabinet member, Laski did everything that a professional politician does. And he did this in addition to his publicistic work, and while performing his academic duties.

If Harold Laski left a monument it was not a monument of learned works written by himself and his protégés. His monument was the intangible spirit of intellectual exhilaration which helped to make the London School of Economics what it was. He did it not only by knowing so much more than his students—not in itself a great or uncommon achievement—and by delivering what he knew so meticulously, but by his personal attention to them individually and by his affection for them.

Charles Furth, who was Laski's publisher at Allen and Unwin, once said to me: "Harold Laski—the largest heart in London." Let that stand as Harold Laski's epitaph.

eight

KARL MANNHEIM

I FIRST ENCOUNTERED THE NAME OF KARL MANNHEIM in the late 1920s in the course of browsing through the journal of my intellectual promised land, the *Archiv für Sozialwissenschaft und Sozialpolitik,* edited for much of its existence by Max Weber, with the collaboration of Werner Sombart, Joseph Schumpeter, and others. It was the organ of the promised land which I yearned for but could not enter. My German was not good enough for that, but the resounding German nouns made me certain that that was where intellectual redemption was to be obtained. What promises were contained in such titles as *"Das Problem einer Soziologie des Wissens"* ("The Problem of a Sociology of Knowledge"), *"Das konservative Denken"* ("Conservative Thought"), *"Der Historismus,"* ("Historicism"), *"Über das Wesen und die Bedeutung des wirtschaftlichen Erfolgsstrebens"* ("Concerning the Nature and the Significance of Striving for Economic Success"), and so on. I knew vaguely what the nouns meant; I could occasionally decipher a whole sentence but not readily. At home in the evenings, I was trying to read Max Weber's posthumous *Wirtschaftsgeschichte (Economic History)* and the first volume of Sombart's *Der moderne Kapitalismus.* I read them word for word, looking up most words in the Muret Saunders dictionary, which I had bought a little while earlier for $2.50 from the bookseller George Allen's parents and which I still possess after seventy-five years, the worn-out relic of my repeatedly looking up the same words over and over again.

I was ignorant but not so ignorant as to think that Karl Mannheim, despite the melodramatic intellectual grandeur of his titles, took intellectual precedence over Weber and Sombart. It was while I was still an undergraduate that Mannheim's *Ideologie und Utopie* appeared, and I was dimly aware of the great commotion which it set going in Germany. (I learned about this from Mannheim's essay in *"Wissenssoziologie"* in Vierkandt's *Handwörterbuch der Soziologie*.)

In the spring of 1931, Karl Mannheim was a terra incognita to me. Mannheim did not enter into my thoughts for most of the next year, 1931–32, which I spent in New York as a student in a social work agency. That year was spent in delighted discovery of the scintillating insights of Georg Simmel, helpless pondering on Dilthey's *Einleitung* (*Introduction*), and in the salt-mine-like labor in reading word for word Weber's *Das antike Judentum* (*Ancient Judaism*), which caused me to have to look up almost every word. Gradually things improved. I was able to read much of Rilke's *Die Aufzeichnungen des Malte Laurids Brigge* (*The Notebooks of Malte Laurids Brigge*) in German with some reasonable understanding.

After my year as a student-trainee in social work in New York, I was persuaded by my good friend Sidney Sufrin to go to the University of Chicago. He enticed me by his accounts of the economist Frank Knight's somber and unremitting search for truth. I was also attracted, on my own, by Robert Park and the Chicago school of urban sociology. So I went to Chicago in September 1932. There, shortly after my arrival, I presented myself to Louis Wirth. I had already known of Wirth through his article on Tönnies of about 1927 and by his bibliography on urban sociology appended to *The City,* edited by Park and Ernest Burgess, which showed a considerable familiarity with the German literature on cities.

Wirth told me that he had just returned from a year in Germany—it was 1932, the last year in which such a thing was still possible for a civilized man. He asked me whether I had ever heard of Karl Mannheim. I confessed, with a mixture of embarrassment and pride, that I had indeed heard a lot about him, adding that he was an author with whom I had to become very familiar, though up to then I had read nothing written by him. Wirth told me that he had become acquainted with Mannheim in Frankfurt and had many conversations with him. He was obviously taken by Mannheim, particularly by Mannheim's assertion of his interest in learning about American sociology. Indeed, that was already evident in Mannheim's inaugural lecture at Frankfurt on *"Die Gegenwartsaufgaben der Soziologie"* ("The Present-Day Tasks of Sociology") in which he referred to the American sociologist W. I. Thomas's *The Polish Peasant.* Mannheim clearly desired an appreciative audience in the United States. This desire must itself have been to a large extent a precipitate of Wirth's visit. I think that before Wirth's visit, Mannheim never mentioned the United States or any American social scientist in any of his writings.

That winter, while I was still a social worker, I finally read *Ideologie und Utopie.* I was swept off my intellectual underpinnings by its daringly grandiose ambition. I was not entirely persuaded by the idea of the dependence of the attainment of objectivity in social science by the intellectual interchanges of a heterogeneous intelligentsia, free from "class interests." In the spring of that year, I read Mannheim's essay *"Wissenssoziologie"* in Vierkandt's *Handwörterbuch.* After the melodramatic terms of *Ideologie und Utopie,* it was a comedown. I was furthermore troubled—though fascinated nevertheless—by his furtive suggestions about the penetration of the processes of the genesis of a proposition into its validity. I was not persuaded, but my skepticism was rather faint in comparison with the impression the essay made on me. I had not yet read Max Weber's methodological writings, which would have been a prophylactic against such views.

I had not yet gone deeply enough into Max Weber's substantive propositions, only into his earth- and epoch-embracing categories in the first chapter of *Wirtschaft und Gesellschaft* (*Economy and Society*). But Mannheim had startling interpretations of historical events. His set of correlations between "conceptions of time" and political attitudes seemed very exciting, although it did appear, even then, to be slightly slapdash in its lack of factual par-

ticulars. I found its classification of types of time not quite satisfying.

I have failed to say that one of my reasons for my fascination
with Mannheim was the fact that he dealt with intellectuals, a
subject I was keenly interested in. I had spent several undergraduate years studying French (and English) literature of the eighteenth
and nineteenth centuries. Flaubert was at the center of my interest. I took it as my task to understand why Flaubert hated his
country and his fellow countrymen as passionately as he did. The
French poets of the latter part of the nineteenth century turned
their backs on their country. It was becoming the same in Great
Britain, with Wilde, Shaw, Wells, et al; and in the United States,
we had not only the self-exile of our greatest writer, Henry James,
and the withdrawal from mainstream life of Herman Melville but
also, later, the flood of intellectual exiles to Paris in the 1920s.

I thought that Mannheim could help me to understand this,
though he never made any reference to such things in his writings.
He was probably ignorant of them. Still, I thought I would gain
help in these matters from a writer who wrote so confidently
about intellectuals as the linchpins of society. Nonetheless, with
all my under-confident hesitations, in the winter of 1932–33 I became an exhilarated devotee of Mannheim.

In the spring of 1933, leaving the Goodman Theater after a
large demonstrative meeting of social workers, I saw Louis Wirth,
whose wife was one of Chicago's leading social workers. He
greeted me with an amicable acknowledgment of my existence;
during the winter term, I had attended his 8:00 A.M. class on the
history of German sociology several mornings each week. (I do
not believe that the course dealt with any of the epoch-spanning
views of Mannheim, Weber, Simmel, etc.) It was based mostly on
the three little volumes of *Soziologische Lesestücke,* edited by
Franz Oppenheimer and Gottfried Salomon. Wirth used to read
the crucial passages in the original German. I was the only student
in the class who more or less knew German. I had, moreover, the
texts in front of me. Wirth commented on the passages, often very
thoughtfully. He did not allude to Mannheim in that course.

That evening at the Goodman Theater, Wirth told me that
he would like me to call on him when it was convenient for me. I

made it convenient for myself with a minimum of delay. When we met, he told me briefly that he had received funds—rather exiguous funds—to support the employment of a research assistant for a year on a project designated as "the presuppositions of modern German sociology." The salary was to be $86.11 per month. I was at the time earning $125.00 per month as a family caseworker for the Cook County Bureau of Public Welfare. It was, I should emphasize, a fascinating post from which I have benefited for the rest of my life. Nevertheless, I did not hesitate for a moment. I told Wirth that I gladly and gratefully accepted his invitation to be his assistant. I felt myself elevated into the intellectual empyrean.

II

Wirth's project was not well thought out. It seems to have been inspired by Mannheim's discussion of the "*Standortsgebundenheit des Wissens*" ("Situational Dependence of Knowledge"), Spranger's lecture before the Akademie der Wissenschaften in Berlin about "the so-called presuppositionlessness of science" and, rather remotely, Max Weber's two essays on "*Wertfreiheit*" and "*Objektivität*." It was apparently also influenced by Cooley's "Nature of Social Knowledge" and some of Robert Park's writings and ruminations. One of its main issues was whether sociology was a science of the mind or a natural science, whether it was or could be a genuine empirical science or a science of the mind, whether it was a normative or an ideographic science. It presented no list of definite topics on which I should work or any list of books which I should read.

Once I began to work on the project, I repeatedly applied to Wirth to obtain clarification about his intention and clearer instruction for my own proceeding. It was all in vain; Wirth was always so busy and, when we did find time to speak, he could only tell me once more that he was interested in "the presuppositions" of social science. Nevertheless, I did not sit by waiting for more stringent instruction. I began in earnest to study Max Weber's writings. As might be expected, I studied the *Gesammelte Aufsätze zur Wissenschaftslehre* (*Collected Essays on Methodology*) until their pips squeaked. I also read Rickert, some Dilthey, whose works, despite my fantasies about what they contained, I found fairly impenetrable, Eduard Spranger, Erich Becher, Gustav Schmoller, Ferdinand Tönnies, Werner Sombart, Carl Menger, Ludwig Mises, Otto Bauer, Max Adler. I even read the horrible Horkheimer. I acquired an intimate knowledge of German social thought of the late-nineteenth and the early part of the twentieth centuries.

I read all the literature produced by the Germans in exile. I even read a little bit of the German social scientists who espoused—at least, at first—the Nazi cause. I refer here particularly to Hans Freyer, a writer from whom I learned a good deal despite his Nazi sympathies. I became a close friend of Alexander von Schelting, who had very different political views and had been the managing editor of the *Archiv* for most of its last decade; von Schelting was the most subtle and rigorous expositor of Max Weber's methodological writings.

In the course of all this, I naturally became friendly with the refugees from the Nazi regime. Hans Speier was perhaps the one to whom I was closest. My relationship with him dates from 1934, when I first wrote to him about his unpublished manuscript on *Die Angestellte in der deutschen Gesellschaft* ("The White-Collar Worker in German Society")—until he became so deeply enmeshed in the Rand Corporation in the 1960s that our paths separated. The fact that he had written his dissertation at Heidelberg under Mannheim's inspiration and supervision and his having been the emissary of the Graduate Faculty to Mannheim in Amsterdam in 1933 or 1934, to persuade him to come to the United States, brought us closer together. We were also separated by his rightly critical attitude towards Mannheim's commitment to the proposition of the *Standortsgebundenheit des Wissens* ("Situational Dependence of Knowledge"). I owe my discovery of the different behavior, the independent role of intellectual traditions and institutions, and the external (situational) determination of the content of thought to some of Speier's and my discussions about Mannheim's ultimately ambivalent and indecisive attitude.

All these personal associations and my becoming at home in the German academic world were a great benefit to me. But they were mostly peripheral to the "presuppositions of social sci-

ence" rather than at the heart of them. On the project proper—
whatever it could have been—I made little clearly ascertainable
progress. The project had, after all, not been conceived as a means
of educating me. It was supposed to produce material which was
to enable Louis Wirth, or Louis Wirth and me, to write a book. It
began to become evident that this was not going to happen. He
did get something. I wrote several long articles on other subjects
which bore his name alone or both of our names, which enhanced
his already high reputation for being a person who knew a lot
about many diverse things.

The main thing that Wirth got was the translation of *Ideologie und Utopie* and an incompletely salvaged introduction to the
English version of the book. That came about this way. Wirth told
me that Mannheim was very eager to have *Ideologie und Utopie*
translated into English. Wirth inquired very tentatively whether I
would be willing to do the translation. Of course, I agreed. It was
an honor to be thought so close to the pantheon and, furthermore,
I was eager to escape from the embarrassed confusion resulting
from the unfocused state of my work on the "presuppositions."

I began the translation in the spring of 1934 and had most of
a first draft ready by the end of the same term. Then I revised it
once myself. By the autumn of 1934, Wirth was in a lively correspondence with Mannheim, who was as fidgety, for no good reason, as a hen on a nest of woodpeckers. Much of the correspondence was, as I remember, fairly trivial, but it was evident that
Mannheim was very concerned that his book should strike the
right note in the United States. He wanted it to be interpreted as
integral to the American tradition of social thought. In this Wirth
encouraged him, repeatedly referring to John Dewey's *Human Nature and Conduct* as the American counterpart of *Ideologie und
Utopie.*

Part of Mannheim's fidgetiness might have been attributed
to his uncertainty about his status at the London School of Economics. Mannheim had first thought that his appointment was a
permanent one, when it was in fact an appointment for a short
time and was, I think, separately financed, outside the regular
budget of the School.

I should add that Mannheim was sensitive to the fact that

he was not a professor but only a "lecturer." Many German exiles suffered from sensitivities of rank in the relatively loosely stratified structure of Anglo-American universities. It was not solely that he did not enjoy the title of professor that he had enjoyed in Germany. There was a more substantial ground for his unhappiness at the LSE. Professor Morris Ginsberg, in accordance with the traditional right of the head of the department, delivered the course of introductory lectures, attendance at which was obligatory for all students. Mannheim had given the corresponding course in Frankfurt, which was immensely popular. He thought he was being deprived of this prerogative in London. At the LSE, his lectures were well and enthusiastically attended, above all by graduate students, Americans in particular.

I think also that Mannheim was attracted in a vague way by the possibility of making a career in the United States, as an alternative to his unsatisfactory situation in Great Britain. Leo Rosten was then an exceptional graduate student at Chicago, with a pretense to worldliness. Leo Rosten brought back golden tales of Mannheim's lectures, and he probably also, in his boastful way, suggested things to Mannheim about American social science that Mannheim wanted to hear.

In any case, Mannheim was frequently writing letters to Wirth about the translation that he had not yet seen and could not assess. First, the letters were only to Wirth, then he began to write to me, too, very deferentially, usually about very trivial points or none at all. Then one day, after the translation of the book was done, I received from Mannheim a long manuscript which he wished to have published as the introduction to *Ideologie und Utopie*. For me it was a thrilling composition of moral history, but I could not see how it could function as an introduction to a book which had as its central position a rather hesitant relativism and a desire to avoid the charges of relativism which his own assertions frequently justified. The introductory chapter—or essay—was a rather exciting piece of work, full of grandiose generalizations which in German had an especial resonance. In a tuned-down version, it is now available as the first chapter of *Ideology and Utopia*.

The revision of the translation was a very slow affair. Louis

Wirth and I reconsidered every word—I think the translation was as faithful to Mannheim's ideas as any translation could be, and it was, moreover, in good grammatical English, free of jargon and Germanisms. Another reason why it was so slow was that Wirth insisted on keeping open the door to his room in which we worked and which led into the corridor so that any passerby could come in to exchange a few words with him. Wirth was very popular, and his wisdom and his friendly words were cherished.

Nevertheless, we finally got it done. Then came the task of preparing the introduction. Wirth prepared a draft which was so embarrassing to me by its fatuity and inconsequence that I gave serious thought to telling him that I decided not to have my name attached as co-translator to the published version of the English text. I undertook instead to revise Wirth's introduction. I think that I got rid of the most humiliatingly fatuous parts, but not entirely. When Mannheim saw the text of the poor, although improved, introduction, he wrote to Wirth to praise it as *"ein abgerundetes Kunstwerk,"* or a perfectly formed work of art. That struck me as a pathetic confession of dependence on someone who could contribute to making his reputation in Anglo-American intellectual life and particularly in America.

In the mid-1930s, I—with the possible exception of Robert Merton and a handful of German refugees in the social sciences—was the only person who had read Mannheim's sociological writings of the 1920s. Whatever my hesitations about Mannheim's "epistemology," I threw myself with unquenchable exhilaration into his essays. I can now scarcely recall any of the specific propositions of those essays; such ideas as I do recall now seem to be largely truisms or impossibly vague. But at that time they were breathtaking observations.

So it was with Mannheim's *Mensch und Gesellschaft im Zeitalter des Umbaus (Man and Society in an Age of Reconstruction)*. I received a copy one morning and spent most of the rest of the day and deep into the night reading it in a state of great excitation. I am not sure that Wirth ever read it; if he did, he probably disapproved of it, even though he was a convert to the belief in the superiority of a planned society over an unplanned one. Without discussing the matter with Wirth, I informed Mannheim that I was ready to translate the book. It was small, and after my experience on the earlier book, I foresaw it as a speedy job.

This, though, was not enough for Mannheim—he wanted a large following and beyond that a larger public. He wanted to be a great intellectual figure on the level of Kant. One of the reviewers of *Ideology and Utopia* suggested that the intellectual achievement of that work placed the author on the level of Kant. I think that Mannheim yearned for such a standing. Yet, except in the minds of a few eminent senior academic and ecclesiastical figures in Great Britain, he did not have it. What he did have was a very distinguished connection through the Moot, a group of eminent men interested in religion and society whose members included T. S. Eliot, John Middleton Murry, John Oldham, Alexander David Lindsay, Edward Hallett Carr, and others. He was the only Central European refugee who participated in such a circle. He was very proud of that set of connections, but it was still not enough. He wanted ardently to gain acceptance in his new environment.

Indeed, after about 1935, Mannheim renounced his rich historical sociology to apply his intellectual powers to the practical problems of contemporary society. His attention turned increasingly to education, and gradually he came into close connection with the Institute of Education of the University of London under the direction of Sir Fred Clarke, an admirable man who took very warmly to Mannheim. In a way, this was a continuation and extension of Mannheim's deep concern about the crisis of modern society, which for him was epitomized in the rise and accession to power of the National Socialists in Germany. He greatly overestimated the strength of related tendencies in other Western countries. Like many Central European refugees in Western Europe and the United States, he underestimated no less the ramshackle obduracy of such countries as Great Britain, France, the Netherlands, and the United States, in their tenacious devotion to liberal democratic traditions.

Mannheim made strenuous attempts at adaptation to his new British and his anticipated American environment. I think that he yearned to become a figure with a prominent place in public opinion such as he had been already in intellectual circles in the last years of the Weimar period in Germany. He wanted to be a man of wide public influence. His popularity as a teacher at the London School of Economics, great though it was, was not sufficient for him. He was very popular at the School in the first years after his arrival. The students were greatly taken by his leaping imagination, his spirited observations about the complexity of social stratification, his wide-ranging historical references, and his studious personal consideration. He attracted a devoted following, none of whom ever produced any work along his lines. (Norbert Elias, the only sociologist who drew extensively on Mannheim's ideas, was not really his pupil; he had already been Mannheim's assistant at Frankfurt.)

Mannheim's *Man and Society in an Age of Reconstruction* appeared in 1935. It must have been written for the most part after he came to England; some of it might have been written in the intermediate and brief period he spent in the Netherlands. Most of this small book was devoted to the "age of planning," about which there was already much talk, under direct and indirect Soviet influence, in Great Britain and even more in the United States, the overflow of which seeped into Great Britain. Mannheim's response was to change his explanation of the crisis of Western societies from the loss of objectivity of moral and cognitive standards, which made mutual understanding and consensus almost impossible to attain, to a new explanation of the cause of the crisis as the failure to reconcile the policy of laissez-faire with the policy of a comprehensively planned society that yet left room for freedom.

My work on the translation of the new book produced a steady flow of letters from Mannheim. I sent him each chapter as it was put into reasonable and legible condition, and I added supplementary information and, above all, bibliographical references, particularly American bibliographical references. Meanwhile, he seems to have been hard at work in adapting the English-language edition to its anticipated Anglo-American—especially American—audience. The book appeared in this country in 1940, a thoroughly transformed work. It was about twice as long as the original text and was followed by an immense bibliography that contained items—many of them American—which he obviously had not read.

I contributed to a symposium organized around the book in *The Journal of Liberal Religion*. I tried to put the best face I could on my response to it, but evidently not quite successfully because Mannheim wrote to me in a slightly injured but still very friendly tone, saying that he hoped that we would soon be able to discuss our differences face-to-face. I was then making preparations for my journey to London, where I was to spend the next several years.

III

In the early autumn of 1942 I went to see Karl Mannheim in the flesh for the first time. I had telephoned him to inform him of my desire to see him, and he responded in a very welcoming way. I traveled to Golders Green by the underground and walked up the hill to Mannheim's house, which was between the Hampstead and the Golders Green tube stations. He occupied a small pretty little house in a close just backing on to Anna Pavlova's old house on the northern edge of the Heath.

Mannheim's servant admitted me and escorted me to his study. It was a moderate-sized room, lined with bookshelves from about three and a half feet to about seven feet from the floor. I glanced quickly at the books and recognized some of them by their bindings—Meinecke, Simmel, and others, and, above all, Max Weber's works. *Wirtschaft und Gesellschaft* (*Economy and Society*), bound into a single volume, seemed to have been assiduously studied to judge from the condition of the binding. On a large desk was a thick block of writing or drawing paper about twenty-four inches square. This was the paper on which Mannheim first sketched his ideas. The first appearance of an idea to Mannheim seems to have come with a "word" or a phrase. There were no sentences. Bit by bit, the scattered words and phrases, in no geometrically linear order, were transformed into sentences and paragraphs and then pages and chapters.

Sometimes in the midst of the scattered jottings and notations or in the margins of manuscripts, there would appear a charming drawing of an elephant, or a horse, or a dog. These little drawings were as fluently done as the final version of Mannheim's written manuscripts, which were done in a beautiful masterly German script such as was seldom seen in those days. German script had a few decades of elegance between the end of the hideous old script and present-day scratchings done with ball-point pens. Mannheim belonged to this epoch, not only in his script but in his general culture and his apprehensive solicitude about the fate of liberal European civilization.

Mannheim himself was a man of middle height—he was perhaps five feet, eight inches tall. He was broad-shouldered and stocky in general outline. His body looked stronger than his face indicated him to be. He had a pinkish, slightly tan complexion, soft-skinned but not puffy. He had a large bald dome, fringed with dark hair. His eyes smiled very affectionately, but he also appeared, as his first words to me indicated, rather uneasy. I had already noted this general demeanor of uneasiness in a photograph reproduced in one of his books published in the 1930s.

His first words, as I came into the room and shook hands, were, "What do they think of me in America?" That seemed to me a very odd question for a famous and distinguished scholar to ask of an utterly unknown and utterly undistinguished one. I did not tell him that, in fact, there was little thought about him in sociological circles in the United States, and what little there was, except for Wirth, was jealously unfriendly. Robert Lynd, for example—a mediocre, slightly leftist ex-clergyman—disliked Mannheim's insufficient sympathy with Marxism. Von Schelting's critical review of *Ideologie und Utopie* had been made scathing by the jealous, embittered Howard P. Becker, who was book-review editor of *The American Sociological Review*. Hans Speier's review in the *American Journal of Sociology* was more gentlemanly than the others and appreciative of Mannheim's many merits, but he did not conceal his disapproval of Mannheim's "epistemology."

I skirted around this query, speaking mostly of Louis Wirth's espousal of his cause. Then the conversation veered towards other topics—mostly about recent American sociological publications that might be congenial to Mannheim's efforts to turn his original German sociology of knowledge into an American social psychology in the style of John Dewey.

I saw Mannheim frequently over the next few years—at least

once a month. He was always very kind to me, but I think that he was a little daunted by me. He thought perhaps that I was too critical of his efforts to establish comprehensive social planning as the right object of liberal-democratic policy. I read the manuscript of the book on democracy that he had written on commission from the Royal Institute of International Affairs and criticized its vagueness and its optimism. He took this criticism—at least in my presence—extremely amiably: slightly amused, very kind, yet to be sure not altogether pleased. He said that it was too late to change the manuscript because it had already gone to the publishers, but the next time he wrote a book, he promised to take my criticisms very much to heart. He would heed them and correct himself; he made it seem as if he were a schoolboy and I was his teacher. He used repeatedly to seek my recommendations on the sociological literature he should read. He seems to have thought that I knew a great deal, much more than I in fact did.

Most of our conversation—in the years between my arrival in England in 1942 and my departure, and then on my return to take up the post at the London School of Economics that he had resigned to become professor of education at the Institute of Education of the University of London—did not deal with the deeper questions of sociology. I would have benefited immensely from such discussions. But much of our conversation was given to his complaints about his situation at the London School of Economics, where he was engaged in an unpleasant and unceasing discord with Morris Ginsberg, the professor of sociology and head of the department. Mannheim held Ginsberg responsible for whatever misfortunes he thought he suffered. They were largely, as far as I could make out, about matters of dignity. His failure to become professor of sociology was very painful for him. There was a powerfully rooted convention in British universities for there to be only one professor for each subject; at the London School of Economics, the department of economics was the only department to have more than one—it had both Lionel Robbins and Friedrich Hayek—but from this Mannheim obtained no consolation. He also suffered from what he thought was the contempt of Hayek and Nicholas Kaldor.

Karl Popper's arrival at the School in the autumn of 1946 was also felt by Mannheim to be an injury. It was just a short while after the publication of Popper's *The Open Society and Its Enemies*, which contained the first of the essays on "The Poverty of Historicism." Mannheim was wounded by these essays, because, though they scarcely referred to him explicitly, Popper clearly had him in mind as their target. Mannheim also thought—rightly—that Hayek's *Road to Serfdom* was directed against him.

As a result, Mannheim felt himself isolated at the LSE. Hayek and, by association, Robbins, and, by barely veiled intimations, Popper all seemed to be in cheerful collusion against him. Ginsberg's antagonism was not veiled. I do not think that they ever had any hard words, but the feeling that passed between them made it seem as if they had. So much did Mannheim bear the wounds of Ginsberg's utter and visible lack of sympathy that, when I arrived at Mannheim's home within an hour after learning of Mannheim's death, the first thing that Mrs. Mannheim said as she embraced me was, "Ginsberg killed him!"

In addition to all of this nerve-racking antagonism, Mannheim really was suffering from cardiac and pulmonary problems that aggravated each other. He led a hard life during the war. The London School of Economics had been evacuated to Cambridge throughout the war (the Ministry of Air had taken over its buildings in London). This meant that Mannheim, who would not consider a change of residence, spent about two nights each week at Westminster College, a Presbyterian theological college, which was not an integral part of the University. It must have been very cold and uncomfortable there—every place was cold in England during the winters of the war, and Mannheim found the journeys by rail between London and Cambridge difficult. They were in fact difficult for healthy younger persons like myself, who did not have to make the journey regularly. This burden was accompanied by another burden—namely, weekly journeys between Nottingham and London; the Institute of Education had, like the School of Economics, been required to give over its quarters to the Ministry of Information. As Mannheim's ties to the School of Economics were loosening because he felt so little at home there, they were becoming more tightly bound with Nottingham. But this had heavy physical costs.

Despite the severe strain on his health, Mannheim always found time to receive me. I never saw him outside his house except once when I heard him lecture at University College London. I was always given a fine dinner that, though sparse in quantity, was invariably delicious, being cooked by the devoted servant of the Mannheim's, Julia, a Hungarian woman who had been with the family for many years and who was deeply devoted to them. (In the end she inherited the house in which the family had lived.) There was always a bottle of fine wine at dinner, at a time when any kind of wine was difficult to obtain.

In addition to the excellent dinners, I was also indulged by the company Mannheim invited for my delectation. (I find it hard to think that he could have thought that I was equally as interesting to his guests.) The guests included Arthur Koestler; Arthur T. M. Wilson, colonel in the directorate of army psychiatry and one of the most brilliant men I ever met; and Edward Glover, who was at the forefront of psychoanalysis at the time. These guests were persons of exceptional talent and intelligence. Some of them became friends of mine for the rest of their lives, and many of them had a tremendous intellectual and professional influence on the subsequent course of my life.

In the early evening of January 7, 1947, I was in a taxi accompanying Michael Polanyi to King's Cross Station for his return journey to Manchester, where he was still professor of physical chemistry. Polanyi was a little older than Mannheim, but they were both members of the Galileo Society. They had known each other in Budapest. Although he was working in the Kaiser Wilhelm Institute for the study of man-made fibers, Polanyi was an intellectual highbrow, especially interested in social affairs. He was a liberal and a severe critic of social planning. He had very little sympathy with Mannheim—to the point of indifference— while Mannheim was very sensitive to "Michi's" lack of sympathy. When I said to Polanyi, as we were nearing the station, that Karl Mannheim had died, Polanyi made no reply at all. He was probably thinking of one of his philosophical conundrums and there was no clear category in his mind for Mannheim.

The emigration was an unmitigated catastrophe for Mannheim. He did not learn enough from his new environment as many refugees did, so that their transfer, however cruel, was not without some compensations. He learned no new techniques of research, as many scientists did; he did not come into rich traditions close enough to his own not to derail him. The tradition of Hobbes, Locke, Bentham, and John Stuart Mill was not close enough to Mannheim's own kind of liberalism to permit a moderately easy coming to rest in the new environment. There was no Anglo-American tradition of speculative historical sociology, no tradition of the history of ideas—despite many brilliant individual performances—to which he could attach himself. What Mannheim needed in England was the Warburg Institute, with its brilliant staff of European scholars, but at that time the Warburg Institute was undergoing the trauma of resettlement, and the removal of its marvelous library to London. Indeed, it was only by the time of Mannheim's death that Fritz Saxl, the director, was able to establish the Warburg Institute on a firm footing.

Mannheim had no like-minded refugee colleagues to sustain him. Only Adolf Löwe, a man of immense practical experience and capacities, was available to him, but he was in Manchester living on the tiny stipend of a fellowship at the University. The few Hungarian art historians—Arnold Hauser and Frederick Antal—were Marxists, and Mannheim did not feel at home with them, though as far as I know he was certainly on amicable terms with them.

So, despite his membership in the Moot, T. S. Eliot's profound appreciation of his intellectual and moral qualities, and other strong indications that he was not entirely alone, nothing assuaged Mannheim's anxiety about his status and his future. That was a great pity. He was a man of great intellectual and moral merit. He was a good person, capable of receiving and expressing affection, but he needed more than that. He had a genuine drive for truth and delight in intellectual activity. He said many things which are still worthy of meditation.

nine

ARNALDO DANTE MOMIGLIANO

I

Arnaldo Dante Momigliano was a very great scholar. Officially he was an ancient historian, a historian of Greece and Rome. He was, however, as much at home in Jewish history. He was, of course, a master at the highest level of political history but even more of the culture of all Mediterranean antiquity, especially its religions and historical writings. Administrative organization, military affairs, law, education—he read all the literature of all these subjects in all the languages in which such works appeared.

He was a teacher who demanded the utmost from his pupils and inspired the best of them to try to meet his standards. Those who were not the best were impressed by his intellectual greatness and his eagerness to help them. His colleagues everywhere were dazzled by his omniscient erudition and they loved him for his warmth of heart and his sometimes sardonic but never injurious sense of humor.

He was a person of extraordinary range and variety of intellectual interests, technical competence, and fearless originality. His bibliography lists about 750 papers, books, monographs, and book reviews, excluding innumerable translations into languages other than those in which they were originally written. He also wrote more than 400 articles, some quite long, for encyclopaedias. These were never publicistic articles: practically every one of them, as also his book reviews, was a work of the most rigorous scholarship with numerous footnotes most of which contained several bibliographical references, with full details about volumes, issue numbers, year of publication and pages. His memory was as capacious and precise as his interests were broad and deep but he never allowed anything of his to be published until all the references and quotations had been checked. He seldom had the services of an assistant.

He rarely set a task for himself which he did not carry out. There were few exceptions to this exercise of self-discipline; he did not publish his Sather Lectures on the history of classical historiography although they were fully written, and, as far as I know, he did not carry out his plans to write books on the history of liberty in the ancient world or on the political ideas of Tacitus or on the influence of antiquarian studies on the rise of sociology.

Except at meal-time conversations with friends, and conversations over cups of coffee with the members of his seminars after the seminars were over, he worked incessantly, avidly, and with pleasant excitement. He read with very great speed, retaining in his memory practically everything. He wrote rapidly, not only the texts of his lectures but very often the comments which he made after the presentation of a paper at his seminar. There was never a lull in his program of work.

He never claimed certainty when he was uncertain. He was, as he once said of Mommsen, capable of both the *ars nesciendi* and the *ars sciendi.* In his manner of exposition, he could convey in his writings his own experience of discovery. One could almost see him at work reading manuscripts at Leiden or in Florence. He had a knack for a telling observation: the growth of interest in Etruscan things as manifested in the opening in the Vatican of a separate room for Etruscan vases; the dormancy of the Greek tradition in Greek Italy shown in the turn of attention to the temples at Paestum, which although very prominently visible for more than a millennium, had been left unnoticed until the eighteenth century. He had great skill in portraiture—sometimes a full portrait, filled with vivid, sometimes amusing, often affectionate passages, sometimes no more than a sentence or a phrase—in which he expressed his affection and appreciation of a person who had left some mark on the growth of historical knowledge. With all this unequaled erudition, he was always level-headed. He was fascinated by theories and he liked the company of theorists but he seldom took their theories at face value.

In his physical appearance, Arnaldo Momigliano was the opposite of what was suggested by the precision and the thoroughness of his scholarship. The garments on his short broad frame were as ill-fitting as the control over his sources was exact. The knot of his necktie seldom came up to his collar, his trousers and jackets looked ample enough to clothe another person of similar dimensions. Different parts of his apparel were held together by large safety pins. Pens and pencils protruded from his breast pocket in the way that decorations mark the breast of a senior general of the Soviet armed forces. In the pockets of his trousers were two large key rings each holding about fifty keys. In his inside coat pockets, there were all sorts of things, crumpled bank notes of various national currencies, airline tickets folded and folded again, registration cards, and large numbers of letters, also folded many times; he always carried with him his passport and other precious documents in a special little bag. In one of his outside pockets there was always a thick commercial receipt book with each slip numbered and carbon papers for two copies of every entry. For Arnaldo Momigliano there was nothing commercial about these slips. They were the necessary bibliographical instruments of his titanic mastery of the literature of his many subjects in nearly every European language. Any room he occupied was soon turned into a chaos of manuscripts, off-prints, books, and letters in which he could almost at once find whatever he was seeking. This meticulousness in what really counted and haphazardness in what did not count made the sight of his flashing eyes, his benign smile, and ready laugh all the more precious. To see Momigliano in a bookshop inspecting new and old books, or to see him scurrying in a library, was a wonderful sight.

II

Arnaldo Momigliano's life as a scholar began in his home in Caraglio in the province of Cuneo. He was born on 5 September 1908 into a learned, liberal, and pious Piedmontese Jewish family, "in a house full of books: Italian books, Hebrew books, French books, Latin and Greek writers either in the original or in translation." He was tutored at home and also attended a village school; then he went to the University of Turin where he came under the teaching of Gaetano De Sanctis, one of the most eminent of the modern historians of antiquity. When De Sanctis was appointed to the professorship at Rome in 1929, Momigliano followed him. In 1931, he became *libero docente*; in 1933, he was appointed to an assistant professorship of Greek history at Rome to carry on the task of De Sanctis, who had resigned because he would not take the oath of allegiance to the Fascist regime. In 1936, he became professor of Roman history at the University of Turin. In 1938, he was dismissed from his post because he was Jewish and in 1939 he left Italy to take refuge in England. He settled in Oxford and remained there for eight years.

In Oxford he continued to work as he had in Italy. He and his wife and their small daughter—now an outstanding historian of Italian language and literature at University College London—lived in extremely straitened circumstances; he had no university or college appointment. Still, he worked unbrokenly with his accustomed assiduity and speed. Nevertheless, his list of publications grew more slowly during the first years in Oxford. These were the early years of the war; publication had become impossible in the continental organs of classical studies in which he had published earlier. Also, settling in a foreign country was very difficult, although he quickly became bilingual and developed a characteristic clear, subtle, and often witty English style of writing. He was warmly received and encouraged by the then Camden Professor of ancient history at Oxford, Hugh Last, who had taken an interest in his work long before they ever met, and he formed many long-lasting and happy friendships there, particularly with Mrs. Isobel Henderson and Dr. Beryl Smalley. In Oxford too he had the good fortune to associate with a number of great German classical scholars, mostly Jewish, who had been driven into exile; these included Eduard Fraenkel, Paul Maas, Felix Jacoby and Rudolf Pfeiffer.

After the war, he was invited by Benedetto Croce to become

the director of the institute for historical studies which Croce had founded in Naples from his own resources. Momigliano rejected this invitation as he did the invitation of the University of Turin which then proceeded to reappoint him to a supernumerary professorship. This decision not to return to Italy was not easy because at the time he had no proper livelihood.

In 1947, he was appointed to a lectureship in ancient history at the University of Bristol and in 1949 to the readership in the same subject. In 1951, he was elected to the professorship of ancient history at University College, London, the college of which George Grote (1794–1871), the liberal banker-historian of Greek thought, was one of the founders. Grote was one of the authors who had inspired Arnaldo Momigliano when he was a boy. Their coming together on Gower Street was a happy omen, correctly read. For twenty-four years, Arnaldo Momigliano was professor at University College.

Once more exile brought him benefits. Only a few hundred yards away from his room in University College was the Warburg Institute, where he had the free run of the marvelous library and the company of Fritz Saxl, Gertrud Bing and of many exiles from the continent who were engaged in transforming the history of ideas. His productivity recovered the momentum of his twenties. In 1955, a courageous Italian publisher, Giuseppe De Luca, undertook the publication of the first volume of his papers and reviews. *Contributo alla Storia degli Studi classici* was the first of the series of large volumes. In 1987, *Ottavo Contributo alla Storia degli Studi classici e del mondo antico* appeared; they are written in English, Italian, German and French; the writings in English became more preponderant with the years. The entire series comes to eleven volumes; at least one more is likely to appear. These large volumes contain only a fraction of Momigliano's writings. In 1971, he published *The Development of Greek Biography*, which had been delivered as the Carl Newell Jackson Classical Lectures at Harvard University, and, in 1977, *Alien Wisdom: The Limits of Hellenization*, which had been delivered as the Trevelyan Lectures at Cambridge University. "The Classical Foundations of Modern Historiography," delivered as the Sather Lectures at the University of California in 1962, is being prepared for publication. In addition to those works which appeared in book form, he also published three volumes of essays in English, *Studies in Historiography* (1966), *Essays in Ancient and Modern Historiography* (1977), and *On Pagans, Jews and Christians* (1987). Four volumes of his writings appeared in Italian in his last years. *Storiografia greca* (1982), *Sui Fondamenti della Storia antica* (1984), *Tra Storia a Storicismo* (1986), and *Storia e storiografia antica* (1987). A French collection, *Problèmes d'historiographie ancienne et moderne*, appeared in 1983.

When he reached the age of retirement in London, he became Alexander White Visiting Professor at the University of Chicago. He held this professorship until his death, except for one year when he was the Lurcy Visiting Professor at the same university. He spent the autumn and spring terms of each year in Chicago. From 1964, he was also supernumerary professor at the Scuola Normale Superiore of Pisa. At Chicago, Pisa, and the Warburg Institute, he continued to conduct seminars which were great intellectual events. At Pisa his seminars were on Eduard Meyer, Max Weber, Hermann Usener, Karl Otfried Müller, Ulrich von Wilamowitz-Moellendorff, and other great figures of classical learning. At Chicago he delivered every year to large audiences a series of four or five public lectures. They covered topics like: "Religion and Biography in the Roman Empire"; "Roman Imperialism and the Roman Empire"; "Some Problems of Roman Religion"; "New Paths of Classicism in the Nineteenth Century"; "Two Types of Universal History"; "Questions of Archaic Greek History"; and "The Origins of Rome." They were masterpieces in the exposition of the results of scholarly research and they were deeply appreciated every year by numerous students and colleagues of many different departments.

After his retirement from University College London, he became a member of All Souls College, Oxford, and spent parts of the winter and long vacation terms there. When this arrangement came to an end, he was elected into a visiting fellowship of Peterhouse, Cambridge and subsequently to an honorary fellowship at that college. He came there frequently for several days at a time. All the while, he continued to maintain his large flat in London which became more and more crowded by his immense library of books on all the subjects he worked on and in all the languages he used.

He was severely stricken in May 1987, only a short time after his last lecture. He seemed to be on the path to recovery during his stay in Chicago, first in the University of Chicago Hospital and then at the home of a colleague. He returned to London on 21 July and thereafter made little progress. He worried all the time about the danger that his intellectual powers and his ability to work would decline—although he still managed to do some work, reading, writing a book review and the preface to *Pagine ebraiche* (published posthumously), and correcting proofs while more or less confined to bed. There was a marked decline in the last week of August and he was admitted to the Central Middlesex Hospital where he died on September 1, 1987, a few days short of his seventy-ninth birthday.

III

Arnaldo Momigliano's professional career was marked by at least one abruptly coerced shift (from Italy to Great Britain), and numerous freely chosen cyclical shifts among at least three countries. His intellectual career, however, was very continuous and stable.

He began his career as a scholar with his mind focused simultaneously on the Greeks, the Romans, and the Jews. These three topics remained central to his work until the very end. In 1977 he wrote,

In a sense in my scholarly life, I have done nothing else but try to understand what I owe to the Jewish house in which I was brought up and to the Christian-Roman-Celtic village in which I was born. . . . If the relations between Greeks and Jews have loomed large in my research, it is partly because we Jews have become what we are by measuring ourselves against Greek wisdom. . . .

There were, however, some shifts in the balance in his diverse fields of interest. Although his major works were on Greek, Jewish, and Roman subjects—he began with Thucydides, Philip of Macedon, Claudius, and the Maccabees—the Jews occupied a less salient position in his interests after his first years and became more prominent in his last two decades. Furthermore, his attention was diminishingly given to political history and was given increasingly to religious subjects—not just Jewish religion but also Roman religion and the religions of the Roman Empire. Early Christianity and Christian ecclesiastical history also became more prominent in his historiographic studies.

Momigliano's interests were never amalgamated into an explicit, single program or plan to be realized over a long time. There were nevertheless certain major interests and attitudes which pervaded a great deal of his work. One such interest was the expansion and restrictions on the expansion of each of the four societies and civilizations which he studied. His interest in universal history was an interest not just in the way in which the ancients conceived of the sequence of empires; it was an interest in the ways and extent to which each of them thought of its predecessors and its neighbors. This was the theme of his writings on the Book of Daniel, on the response of the Jews to Alexander's empire and its successors, on Roman rule in Palestine, on the Greek settlements in Italy, on the Maccabees, on the Romans and the Trojans, on the Greeks and Persians, on the origins of Rome and its expansion in Italy, on the knowledge of Greek in Gaul, and, above all, on the subject of his most important book: *Alien Wisdom: The Limits of Hellenization*.

His second major interest was in historiography. His knowledge of the reemergence of the historiography of classical antiquity in the fourteenth and fifteenth centuries in Italy, and, a little later, in Northern Europe, was as thorough as his knowledge of the ancient works themselves. Moreover, he knew the sources on which they had drawn, the events to which they referred and interpretations of these events by earlier and subsequent historians. He was equally at home among French and Italian historians, librarians and antiquarians of the seventeenth and eighteenth centuries, with Dutch historians of the seventeenth century, with Gibbon, Vico and Grote, Italian and German classical historiography of the nineteenth century. It was however the German historians of the ancient world who were especially interesting to him. The cruelties which his family suffered at the hands of the Germans during the Second World War—eleven members of his family, including his parents, were murdered in German concentration camps—and his own exile did not cause any distortion of his powers of discriminating assessment of intellectual achievement.

For Momigliano, the writing of history was not just a tradition of beliefs about past events. It was a tradition of the search for and the establishment of true propositions about the events of the past. Historical research was about evidence—evidence of events which had occurred and which had left a precipitate in writing, in inscriptions, on coins, and in the materials and patterns discovered by archaeologists. The assessment of "tradition," whether oral or written, in the light of such evidence was the task of the historian. Momigliano's admiration for Herodotus and Thucydides derived in part from the self-consciousness of their use of evidence—in their cases, oral evidence or first-hand observations of events. His account of the reputation of Herodotus is an account of the evaluations of Herodotus's techniques of gathering and assessing evidence and the significance of those evaluations in the history of historiography. What interested him to a very large extent about Herodotus and Thucydides was their deliberate effort to write their works on the basis of evidence which they regarded as reliable. That is why Thucydides confined his historical writing to an account of events of which he had first-hand experience; Herodotus allowed himself to go somewhat further back in time through interviews with individuals who had experienced the events about which he, Herodotus, wished to know. Momigliano made a pronounced distinction between, on the one hand, the writing of history using other written histories as the main source, and, therewith, forgoing the discovery of any new facts, and, on the other hand, the writing of history on the basis of the study of sources more or less contemporaneously connected with the events, persons, etc., under study.

Momigliano repeatedly stressed the insufficiency but at the same time the indispensability of the study of literary evidence and the need to complement but not replace it by the study of archaeological, numismatic, epigraphic, and iconological sources. He did not disparage traditional classical philological scholarship which consisted in the improvement of written texts. On the contrary, he appreciated it very much but he also saw that literary evidence was not enough. Historical writing on the basis of the precipitates of actions and persons which are the object of such study is, of course, not the only kind of historical writing, but the discovery that such evidence must be taken into account in political and other kinds of chronological history was for Momigliano a turning point in the history of historiography. "Ancient History and the Antiquarian" which is one of the most famous of his papers (1950) on the history of historiography was a vindication of one major current of historical research in which the primacy of reliable evidence remained in the forefront, in contrast with "philosophical" and edifying history which used evidence uncritically and for purposes ulterior to the establishment of truth based on reliable evidence.

He regarded Gibbon as the agent of that turning point and this was one of the many reasons why he was so respectful towards him. By the nineteenth century, this transformation became so well established that, by the middle of the century and since then, it has been so much taken for granted that it is thought that it could never have been any different.

Momigliano applied his enormous learning and his great prestige to vindicate the antiquarians who had been for a very long time regarded as an inferior class of hewers of wood and drawers of water. It was because of this attribution of inferior dignity that Herodotus was so long held at arm's length. Momigliano was determined to right the balance, not simply to do justice to worthy and unjustly condemned scholars but to delineate more clearly the constitution of historical knowledge.

The central postulate of Momigliano's study of the history of historiography is that it is possible to attain the truth about events of the past. This too has long been taken for granted until relatively recently but it has ceased to be so and that caused Momigliano unceasing concern. The resurgence and pervasive influence of Marxism among academics in all countries and the frivolities of literary critics who no less widely deny the difference between fictional narratives and historical narratives both challenge the dignity of the human intellect. Momigliano would have none of that; it was to the vindication of historical research that he devoted his Lurcy Lecture at the University of Chicago on "Considerations on History in an Age of Ideologies" and several other papers of his last years, attempting to stay this flood of irrationality which blissfully or fanatically denied the place of evidence in the formation of historical knowledge.

There were several other themes in Momigliano's work. One had to do with his conviction that classical studies had to be extended by opening themselves to the viewpoints or theories of other branches of learning, above all of the social sciences and especially sociology and anthropology. Another had to do with religion. With regard to the first, he invoked the value of sociology for the study of ancient history more frequently in his later years than in the earlier ones. He wrote five papers in which Max Weber was the main object of discussion, and one on the ideas of Marcel Mauss about the person. But he himself did not adduce Max Weber's ideas in his own analyses. In the one essay devoted exclusively to Weber, i.e., on the Jews as a "pariah-people," he thought Max Weber was wrong. Nevertheless, Weber's work was frequently invoked as indicative of the kind of thing ancient historians should deal with. Sometimes other scholars were censured for having failed to consider Weber's views.

He regarded the research procedures of sociology in some respects as the fulfillment of the antiquarian program through its search for valid evidence gathered by direct observation, interviewing, and statistical analysis where the data were sufficient in quantity and quality. But he also encouraged interest in sociological analysis which could offer general categories and theories. Sociological classifications and general categories, like those of the introductory chapters of Weber's *Wirtschaft und Gesellschaft*, had an affinity—in Momigliano's mind—with Mommsen's *Römisches Strafrecht* which was presented through classification and general categories rather than chronologically.

Momigliano was so sympathetic to sociology, and especially to Max Weber's sociology, for another reason—namely, that it offered large perspectives. In Max Weber's case, it also proposed a picture of an entire economy in relation to the rest of society and, above all, it dealt with religious beliefs and institutions in their interconnections with social order, politics, and economy.

That last was a strong recommendation to Momigliano's approbation. He once said to me, obviously with whole hearted approval, that Weber was one of the few scholars who understood that religion was the foundation of society. Perhaps that is the reason why in the last period of his life he also took up Fustel de Coulange's *La Cité antique* once more.

He admired Mikhail Rostovtzeff as one of the very greatest of all ancient historians but he criticized him for not being "aware of the profound impact that the religious needs of man had upon his development." One of his criticisms of Marxist historians pointed to their "inability to recognize both the springs and the complexities of religious life." Momigliano refused to regard religious belief as an epiphenomenon. He thought that it had a genuine autonomy but not an autonomy so complete as to justify the division between sacred and profane history or between Biblical and ancient history. He denied their separateness both because the criteria of the validity of evidence were the same in both kinds of historical writing and also because there was such an intertwinement of the sacred and the profane in all phases of life that understanding was hampered by holding them separate from each other.

I am not certain about what Momigliano's religious views were. I have no doubt about his piety to his Jewish ancestors, or of the firmness and clarity of his image of himself as a Jew and as the heir to the traditions of Jewry. But whether he believed that truths of religion could be established and adhered to by a person who believed in evidence as he believed in it for the purposes of historical research is very doubtful.

There can be no doubt about his certainty that scrupulous adherence to the criteria of the validity of evidence in historical studies could lead to the assertion of reliably true propositions. He was perfectly ready to admit that the setting of the problems of investigation might be affected by the outlook of an age or generation or by current political conceptions or by religious attachments and beliefs, but there the jurisdiction of these external "factors" ended. Momigliano believed in the capacity of human beings to train and discipline their minds to the point where they are capable of discerning what is before them, to interpret it rationally

and to come to conclusions which can be confirmed or discon-
firmed by others—not merely agreed or disagreed with by others.
Freedom and moral independence were necessary for the historian
to discover the truth. It is difficult for the historian to seek the
truth in tyrannical regimes whose rulers depend on a particular
image of their past. For this, and other reasons, Momigliano was
a liberal. What he said of George Grote represented very well his
own position as an embodiment of the "all-redeeming virtue of
the liberal mind. He was determined to respect evidence from
whatever part it came; he recognized freedom of speech, tolerance,
and compromise as the conditions of civilization; he respected
sentiment, but admired reason."

IV

In the last quarter of a century of his life, Arnaldo Momigliano
became one of the best-known scholars in the world. His name
was not bruited about in the newspapers. He did not appear on
television. He never became fashionable through the denunciation of bourgeois society and the espousal of Communism; his
name did not circulate in the same milieux as those of Chomsky,
Habermas, Lévi-Strauss, Sartre, or Foucault. Nevertheless, he was
widely known and greatly appreciated by the educated public in
Europe and America. No great scholar of the present century except perhaps Huizinga or Croce or Scholem was so esteemed in so
many countries. All the more remarkable, he wrote no popular
book, if one excepts the school textbook which he wrote in the
1930s; he was not a commentator in the press on public events
like Raymond Aron, nor the author of a book of observations on
the contemporary scene, like Huizinga, nor like Croce, the creator
of a system of philosophy and the spiritual leader of the opposition
to a tyrant. His fame rested on the proliferating, tentacular reach
of his scholarship.

The misfortunes of exile paradoxically enhanced his fame by
bringing him out of Italy and into Great Britain. Being there and
writing in English gave him an audience which he would not have
had in Italy. Furthermore, being in Great Britain in the years after
the war enhanced his self-confidence; had he gone back to Italy,

the doubts he would have had to overcome about the condition of Italy would probably have had a depressing effect.

When Arnaldo Momigliano, at just about the age of thirty, came to Oxford, he was not very well known. His book on Claudius and his chapters in the *Cambridge Ancient History* had notified the Oxford ancient historians that they had acquired a colleague of exceptional talents. Although there was no post for him, British scholars became very aware of him. He moved as an equal in the highest intellectual circles made up of very eminent German refugee classicists and some great British scholars.

Arnaldo Momigliano was, already from his early years as a scholar, a member of that stratum of the intellectual world constituted by the greatest scholars of his own time and of past generations. Arnaldo Momigliano was not to be exceeded in his respect for his great elders, living and recently or long since dead, but he lived with them in the deferential and critical intimacy of equality; deference did not preclude disagreement. He lived in the intellectual company of Barthold Georg Niebuhr, Johannes Gustav Droysen, Hermann Usener, Theodor Mommsen, Eduard Meyer, Jacob Bernays, Mikhail Rostovtzeff, Arthur Darby Nock, and Norman Baynes; Shlomo Goitein, Gershom Scholem, and Elias Bickerman. Some of them he knew personally, others died before he reached maturity, others were long dead. They formed a gallery, a pantheon of the living and the recently and the long dead who nevertheless knew that they belonged to a single community on whose shoulders lay, when they were alive, a weighty responsibility to maintain and advance the tradition of knowledge of the ancient world. Arnaldo Momigliano belonged by right to this circle and it was acknowledged that he did. This is demonstrated in some measure by the vast number of honors he was accorded by the learned world.

He was visiting fellow of Peterhouse, Cambridge, then honorary fellow of that college and of University College, London, and he was an associate of All Souls College, Oxford. He was a visiting professor at Harvard on three occasions, at Yale, Johns Hopkins, Bryn Mawr, Michigan, the École normale supérieure, and the Collège de France.

He was a fellow of the British Academy and a member of the

Institut de France, the American Philosophical Society, the American Academy of Arts and Sciences, as well as of the Accademia dei Lincei, of the Arcadia, of the Koninglijke Nederlandse Akademie van Wetenschappen, the Accademia delle Scienze of Turin, the German Archaeological Institute in Rome, and the Israel Academy of Science and Humanities and of many other learned societies. He was invited to deliver the Trevelyan Lectures at Cambridge University, the Grinfield Lectures on the Septuagint at Oxford University, the Flexner Lectures at Bryn Mawr College, the Sather Lectures at the University of California at Berkeley, the Lurcy Lectures at the University of Chicago, and the Gauss Lectures at Princeton. He held honorary doctorates from the University of Chicago, the University of London, Cambridge University, Oxford University, the University of Leiden, the Hebrew University of Jerusalem and the University of Tel Aviv, the University of Bristol, Columbia University, Brandeis University, the Hebrew Union College, Yale University, the University of Edinburgh and the University of Marburg in the Federal Republic of Germany. He was an honorary Knight of the British Empire, the recipient of numerous prizes, among them the Kenyon Medal of the British Academy, the gold medal of the Italian Ministry of Education, the Premio Feltrinelli, the Premio Cantoni of the University of Florence, the Kaplun Prize of the Hebrew University of Jerusalem, and a prize fellowship of the MacArthur Foundation.

All these external honors, which gave him much pleasure, were only a very limited expression of the appreciation, deference, and affection which he received from his colleagues and pupils in many countries and many disciplines. He was one of the greatest scholars of his age, perhaps of any age.

ten

JOHN U. NEF

ROBERT PARK WAS THE FOUNDER of a dynasty which ran into three generations of teachers at the University of Chicago. I think that the Park dynasty is the longest in the history of the University. John Nef was the second of a dynasty of two generations but his dynasty began with the founding of the University. His father was the first professor of chemistry from 1892 to 1915. Nef was brought up in Chicago by his widowed father—a stern Swiss who was remembered by Nef as having pulled him by the hand through European museums when he was a small boy. As an adolescent, following his father's death, he became the ward of George Herbert Mead. His future wife, Elinor Castle, was already the ward of Mead. Thus, Nef was a child of the regiment, a child of the University of Chicago as few others have been. He went to the Laboratory Schools from the elementary grades through high school. Then, instead of going to the University of Chicago, he went to Harvard. He had a brief spell as a candidate at the Officers' Training School of the United States Army, returned to Harvard, then he went to Europe, having married "Uncle George's" other ward. A long period of a pleasant, leisurely life in France and then in the middle of the 1920s at about the age of twenty-five, he settled down to a strict regime of scholarship.

Although he seems to have been a Francophile, he chose for his research a British topic—namely, the coal industry. He worked steadily, at the British Museum and at the Public Record Office.

In 1928, he returned to the United States to obtain the doctorate from the Graduate School of the Brookings Institution. I do not know when he decided to inscribe himself at Brookings. I think that he once said that Brookings had no required period of residence and no required courses; it required only a dissertation and that he had already prepared from the data gathered by his research in London. With the doctorate, he gained an appointment as a teacher of economics at Swarthmore College near Philadelphia. That experience seemed to have made little impression on him—at least he never mentioned to me anything about his experiences either in Swarthmore or Philadelphia. Before that year was over, Chicago reasserted its claim on him. In 1929, he was appointed to the departments of history and economics at the University of Chicago.

This was the fulfillment of what he had begun in Europe through the 1920s. He established himself very comfortably on Dorchester Avenue in Hyde Park. Heavy mahogany furniture in the dining room, a large round (or oval) table and about a dozen mahogany chairs, upholstered furniture, a grand piano and a secretary in the drawing room, upholstered chairs in the sun-porch. A long corridor lined on one side with glass-shelved bookcases led to the rooms at the rear of the apartment bedrooms for himself, his wife and his widowed mother-in-law and his own study, a large rectangular room with bookcases up to the ceiling on three sides. On the walls of the dining room and the living room there were beautiful paintings—Dufy, Rouault, Chagall, Cézanne, Renoir and many others. There were as I recall drawings in the corridor on the wall which was not lined with the bookcases.

There he lived, very comfortably, very free from financial worries, carrying on a life of hospitality and scholarship.

In 1962 John Nef resigned from the University of Chicago and moved to Washington. I think that he was very lonely in Chicago in the decade which followed his wife's death. He might also have thought that the Committee on Social Thought was firmly enough established to survive, especially if he could keep in close contact with it, if the chairman of the Committee were a faithful and devoted colleague who would be perfectly in harmony to John Nef's conception of the Committee.

I think that the departure of Robert Hutchins left him in a state of defenselessness. I know that he tried to keep himself in good relations with Lawrence Kimpton, Hutchins's successor, but he must also have perceived the fundamental absence of sympathy—exactly the opposite of what he had from Hutchins.

My acquaintance with John Nef began in the autumn of 1932. At that time, I had some knowledge of economic history and a great interest in it. I had studied, before I came to Chicago, John Hobson's *Evolution of Modern Capitalism*, Richard Henry Tawney's *Religion and the Rise of Capitalism* and Max Weber's *General Economic History*, translated by Frank Knight, and Mikhail Rostovtseff's *Social and Economic History of the Roman Empire*. I had read Karl Bücher's *Industrial Evolution*, some of Sombart's *Moderner Kapitalismus* and much of Henry Sée. I never talked about these books with anyone else because no one I knew had read them.

I had never heard of John Nef but seeing his name in the time-table according to which he was offering a course in British Economic History—I think that it was called that—I decided to attend. It was held in room 107 of the Social Science Research Building which was still new and, unusual for this University, the chairs were uniform and intact. We sat around a large and impressive oval table. That gave a certain dignity to the room. The teacher came in, he smiled. He had sparkling dark eyes, a round face, it was as short as it was wide. Of course, in those days, all professors wore neckties. But John Nef was dressed with taste. Even in those days, when professors were not the ragged lot which they have since become, John Nef's refinement and taste stood out.

Then he began to write names on the blackboard. I do not remember them exactly but they included Ephraim Lipson, R. H. Tawney, George Unwin, Arnold Toynbee—the older one—John Hobson, Werner Sombart, N. S. B. Gras. I immediately felt at home. He wrote the name of Rostovtseff on the board. I had never encountered in person anyone else who knew his name. I thought that I had found a "secret sharer."

Then he began to lecture. I had never heard such an orderly systematic lecture. He was so obviously a master of his subject.

As the course continued, he did not lecture from a written text but from long galley proofs. They were the proofs of *The Rise of the British Coal Industry* which was just about to appear. He sometimes read some passages from his text; for the rest of the time, he spoke with coherent construction of a printed text, although he spoke freely and did not read.

There was something else that stirred me deeply. This was the writing one day on the blackboard of the name of T. S. Eliot. John Nef was an economic historian, obviously already destined, once the *Coal Industry* appeared and then the remarkable articles on industrial output in the *Economic History Review* and the *Journal of Political Economy*, to become one of the major figures of a field which I regarded as basic to anyone who aspired to understand society. But bringing in T. S. Eliot! That was an act of intellectual grace for me.

So it went throughout the term. He gave statistics of the coal trade, he gave statistics of population, the occupational distribution of the British people, he spoke with ease and with no less precision about the movements of population, the growth of London, the enclosures, the diet, the households of England in the seventeenth century. He dealt with the confiscation and sale of monastic lands. At the beginning of each class, he wrote the names of authors on the board, many I have never heard of before. He wrote the names of inventors and enterprisers. He wrote the most important statistics on the board from time to time.

Every lecture was a perfectly turned out piece. I had never sat in a class in which the teacher lectured on the results of his own research. I could see for the first time how new knowledge was formed. Of course, I knew that real scholars did not just decant their own books from other books but John Nef gave me the opportunity to see how new general conceptions are formed from multitudes and multitudes of small facts, extracted from records, such as port books, and company accounts. My heart used to beat a bit faster when he lectured, when he pointed to some connection which bound together what had previously been random fragments to me. I had never been in the presence of a teacher who was a great scholar.

John Nef introduced me to a new world. I had come to the

University of Chicago because I had read some of the writings of Robert Park and his pupils and of Frank Knight. Park was away in the Orient and Knight was a treasure which still awaited me. John Nef, of whom I had never heard before, represented to me a world of learning which I had previously thought was only to be found in German universities.

After that first course, I attended many of his other courses. He always had something new to tell. Sometimes I went up to him after the class to ask a question or simply to stand near him while he spoke to another student. Later in the decade, I gained enough courage to go up to his office. He was always very welcoming, smiled while he spoke and listened attentively to my probably jejune remarks.

Still later in the decade, he invited me to dine at his apartment on Dorchester Avenue. There I met Tawney for the first time. On other occasions, I met G. C. Coulton, the scolding historian of the monasteries, and Charles McIlwain, the great scholar who wrote the history of British constitutional government. The dinners were delicious, so were the wines. All was perfectly prepared and served. After the dinner, the ladies withdrew to the drawing room; the men remained behind. Cigars and port were offered.

On top of all this was the wonderful experience of dining in a room the walls of which were covered by beautiful pictures of the great French painters of the last decade of the nineteenth century and of the first decades of the present century. It was like dining in a miniature and concentrated gallery.

All through the 1930s there appeared a steady flow of Nef's remarkable articles in the *Economic History Review* and the *Journal of Political Economy*, deepening and broadening the picture which he had painted of the history of the British coal industry. The range was very broad, extending to the history of mining on the Continent. In those days, economic history was also the history of legal and social institutions. John Nef enriched all this by references to works of literature and art.

In 1940, there appeared that remarkable small book on *Government and Industry in England and France, 1540–1640*. This is a work which merits description as a classic.

I was away from the University for several years during the war. When I returned, the Committee on Social Thought was already in existence. It took up much of John Nef's thought and affection. He was full of optimism about it. It seemed to him to be a way of overcoming the parochialism of recent scholarship and of realizing his and Robert Hutchins's aspirations for changing the character of the learned world.

In the summer of 1946, he asked me to read the manuscript—it was more than a thousand pages of typescript—on *The Rise of Industrial Civilization*. It was on a grand scale. It was not just about industry; it was about art, literature, architecture, and religion as well as industrial technology and commercial organization. It had the makings of a great book. It is still unpublished; perhaps it was left unfinished. It is possible that he did not finish it because he had given his heart and soul to the Committee on Social Thought. That, together with his works of towering scholarship, his Wiles lectures in Belfast, and *War and Industrial Civilization* remain his monuments. They are the monuments of a man of uncommon distinction of spirit, a great citizen of the republic of learning. To the extent that I have myself become a citizen of that republic, I owe a large debt to John Nef.

eleven

LEO SZILARD

TOWARDS THE END of August 1945, I received a telephone call from Leo Szilard. He had heard that I had been at work on a scheme for the international control of atomic energy, and we must meet. Very shortly thereafter, he came to my room. He was short and plump; he had a large head, a high, broad, somewhat sloping brow, and small, fine, neatly curving features. His hair, dark and combed back, had a broad grey streak running almost from the center of his forehead, and surmounted a ruddy face. It was the face of a benign, sad, gentle, mischievous cherub. The whole formed a picture of unresting sensitivity and intelligence, immensely energetic and controlled, and yet with great ease and gentleness of manner. He had sparkling eyes, a beautiful melancholic twinkle of a smile, and spoke in a low musical voice, which had a slight touch of a sob in it. He came right to the point. He glanced briefly at my draft of a rather complicated and utopian scheme which involved a universal labour market for scientists, detailed inspection, comprehensive aerial photography of the United States and the Soviet Union (and any other country which might become relevant), and the dissolution of all secrecy. (I later learned that my scheme was of a child-like simplicity compared with that which Szilard had been developing.) All he said was that we were thinking along the same lines and that we must "remain in touch." He then departed. The next day he telephoned again to say that he had spoken with Mr. Robert Hutchins, then Chancellor of the University of Chicago, who said that he shared our views.

Szilard came to see me almost at once—he had to come to me because his rooms were inaccessible to me; he was still an employee of the Metallurgical Laboratory, which was the name for the Chicago part of the "Manhattan Project." But even if his rooms had been accessible, he would have come to me despite the heat, the distance, and his eminence, since that was the way he was. He was always ready to inconvenience himself for whatever important cause he had in mind at the moment. He never engaged in unimportant ones—and he never claimed the precedence of age or distinction, although he was always willing to grant them to others.

In those days, conferences and seminars were just beginning to be the thing. We decided with Mr. Hutchins's support that we must have a conference at the University of Chicago to discuss international control. In the days which followed, we met frequently to work out plans for the conference. We always met in the Social Science Research Building, and he always came on foot. From my window, I could see him approaching, roly-poly; he walked smoothly and rapidly, the swift and regular agitation of his legs contrasting with the serenity of his bearing.

He liked me to meet him at all hours and would often prevail upon me to go out walking with him. Sometimes we went to his room in the flat of Professor Paul Weiss. It was a large room with bookshelves to the ceiling. They were bare. He had no physical property other than his clothing. He pressed me to rack my brain to think of persons of my acquaintance who had "inventive minds" or who might have valuable political connections and whom we might invite to our discussion. By the time our conference was held, Szilard no longer had any immediate interest in continuing on the path which had originally brought us together.

Like our more optimistic associates of that time, I thought that if we began with something very specific, centered on the newborn bomb, we could then go on to more general disarmament. He insisted that we must start with a more comprehensive settlement of the outstanding differences between the U.S. and the U.S.S.R. Without that, no progress could be made towards disarmament or the control of nuclear weapons. He argued against my view, but he never seemed to be criticising; as always, he was suggesting something positive. His own views were often dazzlingly unrealistic, but they were never mere criticisms of what anyone else was doing: they were rationally, meticulously, and ingeniously elaborated efforts to find something superior. This was characteristic of his procedure. He was always quick to generate new ideas, he seldom embraced the ideas of others, and he would very often discard his own ideas for something new and of his own invention which he thought better. I was told that in the Metallurgical Laboratory, he exasperated and even affronted certain persons whom he had inspired with important ideas in which, by the time the inspired persons had brought them to fulfilment and reported with gratification their results to Szilard, he had lost all interest.

At our sessions, which ran over a week and which were filled with eminent scientists, high civil servants, distinguished economists and political scientists, Szilard took no great interest in what anyone else said. But when we were not in session, he spent much of the time exploring leads to Washington. His mind was already on the next stages of the campaign, the renewal on a larger scale of the political campaign which he had set in motion within the Project in the form of the "Committee on Social and Political Implications." That campaign had broken against the unsympathetic and unimaginative singlemindedness of Secretary of State Byrnes. Now that he was free, he would pass into that "open conspiracy," the promulgation of which had drawn him to H. G. Wells.

As soon as the conference was over, he went off to Washington with Dr. Edward Condon. I had given him a few introductions and suggested a few names; he soon used these up and went far beyond them. He was conducting a largely one-man battle, in touch with Professor Urey, Dr. Condon, and other of his scientific friends. On occasion, he met with the younger scientists, like John Simpson and David Hill, encouraging them, picking up a scrap of gossip from them, and not telling them much of what he was doing. Meanwhile, the May-Johnson Bill, which had been drafted within the War Department for the post-war organisation of nuclear research and development, moved into the forefront of public attention. Szilard bore down on it. He made the rounds in Washington, trying to arouse the concern of Senators and Congressmen, State Department officials, and the grave and foolish ladies who ran salons frequented by the higher officials. He testified before the Congressional Committee which was holding hearings on the May-Johnson Bill, and he spoke against it so persistently, so reasonably, so unyieldingly, that he bewildered and angered the Congressmen who interrogated him. Thought I heard from him frequently, I did not see him again until the end of October or early November, when we had another conference, this time in Rye, New York. To this conference we invited more journalists and legislators, and fewer scientists and academic social scientists. For Szilard, this conference was part of his search for collaborators for his campaign. He was exerting a tremendous effort in trying to marshal new allies while trying to keep any of the old ones from getting out of his hands. I remember going to his suite in the building where we were staying. He was simultaneously on two separate long-distance calls on telephones in two rooms, going back and forth, putting down the receiver in one room while he went to take up the conversation in the other. All the while, actual and potential collaborators sat about; they were not let in on the substance of the telephone conversations which were about the very issues being talked about in the rooms.

After this he again disappeared into Washington, and it was some time before we saw him again in Chicago. In the meantime, the "scientists' movement," the Federation of Atomic Scientists and then the Federation of American Scientists, got under way. The Emergency Committee came into existence. The *Bulletin of the Atomic Scientists* was founded by Hyman Goldsmith and Eugene Rabinowitch. Szilard occasionally surfaced—sometimes only by telephone—at meetings of one or another of these groups, gave lots of advice, complex, daring, fantastic, and popped out again. When he came back he brought news of the battle and of the great figures and the lesser organizations. He identified himself with none of them. He was a kindly, solicitous, detached, and lone "operator." His opinions were cherished by scientists. Szilard never gave his information with any air of reporting about the great to the small: the lords of creation had no more charm for him than an obscure and responsive research student. With the exception of Albert Einstein and James Franck, he seemed to treat everyone as an equal—although even with Franck, he permitted himself the liberty of mixing jokes with affection. He was polite, universally indulgent (except about the State Department), succinctly critical whenever he felt he ought to be. When the campaign against the May-Johnson Bill seemed to be assured of victory, he began to appear more frequently in Chicago. The MacMahon Bill—which was to guarantee civilian control of atomic energy and leave the way open for freedom of research and international co-operation—was in part his creation. Together with Byron Miller, a government lawyer, and Edward Levi, then Professor of Law at Chicago, Szilard devoted many hours to the drafting of the bill and on occasion showed great patience with details.

Once the domestic legislation was out of the way, he returned to international problems which had engaged him since before the war. They never again moved very far from the center of his attention. When he was not concerned with bringing about a *détente* between the United States and the Soviet Union, he thought about the new states of Asia and Africa. He had ideas about elections like those of Jayaprakash Narayan and Marshal Ayub Khan, and for a time he persisted in the attempt to persuade me to organise a long-term study group to deal with the problem of new states. By the time I succeeded with my colleagues in organizing something like that, he had moved the matter to one side of his mind. Before doing so, however, he did make a substantial contribution to the development of oral contraceptives, since he was convinced that only the slowing down of the rate of population growth in the new states would provide the conditions for their progress, and their peaceful assimilation into the world community. But throughout the late forties and the fifties, his mind was busily engaged on the problems aggravated by nuclear weapons. He was full of contrivances. The Pugwash meetings were the realization of his idea of meetings of Soviet and Western scientists which had been on his mind since 1945 and which he had put forward in the postscript of his "Letter to Stalin." (On one occasion when we discussed this, he insisted that if such a meeting were to come off, then the Russians must argue the American case, the Americans the Russian case.)

By the early fifties, he had again taken up scientific research. He was through with physics. He thought there was nothing interesting to do in nuclear physics; it was just a matter of getting larger and larger machines, but fundamentally the process of discovery was simply a repetition of what had been done before. He began to work in what is now called molecular biology.

I tried several times to get him to settle down academically, and since he was full of brilliant notions about many of the matters with which sociologists, political scientists, and economists were concerned, I persuaded my colleagues to bring him into our Division of the University. He was to be appointed to a professorship in the Social Sciences, so that he could devote his attention officially and academically to the political and social aspects of science. It fell through because with the same playfully serious ingenuity which he manifested in his schemes for the dispersal of the urban population or for the "trading of cities" and in his system for changing the Polish-German frontier and rendering Germany an integral part of a European community, he devised such complicated conditions regarding the ways in which the different Divisions would contribute to his salary that the arrangement became impossible. I think that the real reason for this obstruction lay in his anxiety that he would be tied down too much to the University and would be less able to move about the country—especially to New York—than he had been.

In New York he spent a lot of time in a delicatessen frequented by Central European refugees on upper Broadway, somewhere in the region now known as "the Upper West Side kibbutz." I occasionally met him there and he was very insistent that I should have certain Eastern and Central European delicacies, which he praised in the disinterested and precise way in which he spoke of everything.

In New York at that time he thought that he had found a patron for his political activities in a businessman who gave him a desk in his office. (It turned out to be fruitless.) He used to spend time with his aged father, a Hungarian engineer, with his nephew, whom he regarded with great affection, and with a lady, Dr. Ger-trud Weiss, who later became his wife. I do not have the impression that during this time he was very active in promoting his political causes. He was writing and thinking, and occasionally he would send in some startling article to the *Bulletin of the Atomic Scientists* or a story of the type which later appeared in his book *The Voice of the Dolphins.*

He would come back for long stretches of time to Chicago, where he lived ascetically, with peculiar self-indulgences such as meals of French-fried onion rings, a speciality of a horrible restaurant frequented by students. A great favourite for lunch was a glass of buttermilk into which he poured the entire contents of the sugar bowl, followed by sherbert. If one lunched with him, he might be silent for a long time and then come up with a scheme for improving the selection of librarians. At other times, he would be after me to leave the United States and go to live in Australia or New Zealand or perhaps a small island in the Pacific, in order to be away from the dangers of nuclear warfare. He himself, nevertheless, spent his time in the cities which according to his increasingly pessimistic expectations would be the first to be destroyed by nuclear weapons.

He could be seen walking the streets with Aaron Novick (his collaborator and protégé in molecular biological research and now Professor at the University of Oregon); or he might sit long at lunch discussing some improvement of the patent law, or some improvement in the monetary system, with professors of law or economics; or else he might be seen walking along 57th Street or going into one of the little snack bars there with a young scientist. Sometimes, one saw him sitting with the saintly James Franck in one of those disagreeable places.

In the course of the years, from Szilard and from his friends, I learned a little of his past. He had spent his youth in Budapest as a member of a youthful circle, many of the members of which later gained renown as scientists. He studied engineering at first. He once said to me, in explanation of the remarkably large number of outstanding Hungarian physicists of his generation, that it had been possible because "physics was not taught in Hungary."

Towards the end of the First World War, he served as a junior cavalry officer in the Hungarian Army, but saw no action. After the war, he went to Germany, where he worked closely with Einstein, and where he habilitated as a *Privatdoxent*. He interested himself in everyone's business—without intruding into their private affairs. If he visited someone else's laboratory, he might well end by offering a comprehensive plan for its rearrangement. He interested himself in everything. He was a member of a seminar for the study of economic theory, particularly mathematical economics. He read novels, too, although his taste was not very good—he told me that he liked Louis Bromfield best among contemporary novelists. I once lent him the Mr. Norris book, and gave him *Prater Violet*. He never said a word about them. Bohemia did not interest him. He only liked intellectual and political unconventionality. He was, naturally enough, a great admirer of H. G. Wells. In the second half of the twenties, he went to London and visited Wells to obtain the Central European rights to the publication of translations of his writings. Wells's imagination of the future, his prediction of the atomic bomb, his belief in the centrality of science, and his ideas about the open conspiracy all attracted Szilard. Like most Central Europeans of his generation, he became a great admirer of Great Britain. I got the impression that his liking for Britain was based on his belief that it was a country where intellectuals could talk to the great of the land as a matter of course, and could thereby influence their decisions.

In 1932, he concluded that Hitler would come to power, and as a careful reader of the financial pages, he advised his friends to transfer their funds abroad. He decided that something must be done to save German scientists and scholars after the expulsions which he saw were inevitable. He thought first of an "international university" and gave up the idea.

He went to Vienna just after the Reichstag fire. The first dismissals had already taken place. While walking in the street, he unexpectedly met an old Berlin acquaintance, Jacob Marschak, a man with an inventive mind, who later became famous as an econometrician at All Souls, Chicago, Yale, and California. Szilard told him that he thought that they must do something to provide for those scientists and scholars who would have to leave Germany. Together they visited Gottfried Kuhnwald, the old, hunch-backed Jewish adviser of the Christian Social Party. Kuhnwald was a mysterious and shrewd man, very Austrian, with sideburns like Franz Josef. He agreed at once that there would be a great expulsion. He said that when it happened, the French would pray for the victims, the British would organise their rescue, and the Americans would pay for it. Kuhnwald advised them to consult a certain German economist who was then in Vienna. They did so, and were told that Sir William Beveridge was also in Vienna in connection with his work on the history of prices. They were told, too, that Beveridge was staying in the Regina Hotel, where Szilard was also registered. Szilard immediately called on Beveridge and put the problem to him. Beveridge said that he had already heard of certain dismissals and had thought of appointing one of the dismissed economists to the London School of Economics. Szilard then suggested to Kuhnwald that he invite Beveridge to dine with him. Kuhnwald was reluctant to do so, because, he said, if one invited Englishmen to dinner they became "too conceited." He suggested that he invite him to tea as an alternative. So, Kuhnwald, Beveridge, and Szilard met for tea. Beveridge agreed that as soon as he got back to England and got through the most important things on his agenda, he would try to form a committee to find places for the academic victims of Nazism; and he suggested that Szilard should come to London and occasionally prod him. If he prodded him long enough and frequently enough, he would probably be able to do something. Very shortly after Beveridge's departure, Szilard went to London. Beveridge was at once ready, and with his customary decisiveness, he set about the details of raising funds. In a relatively short time, the Academic Assistance Council was established. Szilard took a great interest in its working: he came regularly to the office to help out, provided contacts in Germany for the General-Secretary and arranged for the recruitment of Miss Esther Simpson, who remained its secretary throughout its existence.[1]

1. Beveridge in his book made no reference to Szilard's role and Szilard himself, in his conversations with me, never claimed credit for it. He never received any assistance from it either, although there were times in the middle thirties when he was living on a very narrow margin. What I know

After the Nazis came to power, Szilard went to London, where for some time he spent many hours of meditation and calculation in the lobby of the Strand Palace Hotel, reflecting on scientific matters and on the affairs of the world. He came into contact with Professor Lindemann, who (whatever his later conduct in the affairs studied by Sir Charles Snow) was very helpful to him—as he was to other refugee scientists. Szilard worked at Bart's and at the Clarendon, under Lindemann's sponsorship, and an effort was made to find a fellowship for him at an Oxford college, but it fell through. It was in this period that the "Szilard-Chalmers effect" was discovered. When Szilard was staying at the Strand Palace Hotel, he would occasionally wander over to the London School of Economics and listen to Harold Laski's eloquence. He liked the critical attitude which socialists took towards the injustices of the world, but he did not believe in their recipes. They were neither elegant enough nor ingenious enough. The beauties of the market mechanism were more congenial to his mind.

He was convinced that war was going to come to Europe and he had told his friends that he would settle in America a year before the outbreak of war. In January, 1937—a little less than a year too early—he transplanted himself to the United States.[2] He appeared at the Physics Department at Columbia, and tried to recruit physicists there to his way of of thinking. The atomic bomb had been on his mind for a long time—his appreciation of H. G. Wells and Harold Nicolson was bound up with their prevision of nuclear weapons. Now he began to work with Enrico Fermi, Herbert Anderson, and Wallace Zinn on a series of experiments to prove the possibility of a chain reaction. From the summer of 1939 onwards, he knocked at many doors to alert the Government to the significance of nuclear fission. He worried lest the Nazis

---

about this I have learned from other persons. It was absolutely characteristic of Szilard to do a thing like this, to be so foresightful, so selfless, so inquisitive, so imaginative, so unsparing of his own energy and time, and so undemanding of benefit or acknowledgment for himself.

2. It was in 1937 that he told a friend about his ideas regarding the feasibility of the atomic bomb and in the same conversation he spoke of his ideas for preserving peaches in tins in such a way that they would retain the texture and taste of the fresh fruit.

might discover the possibility of the bomb and he decided that America must work on it lest the Nazis beat them to it—but he also hoped that all who worked on it might find it to be impossible.

Ever since 1939 he had been trying to get the main nuclear physicists outside Germany to agree *not* to publish the results of their research. As so often, his colleagues could not appreciate what he was after in proposing an action so contrary to the ethos of competitive publicity. He withheld his own papers on the possibility of maintaining a chain reaction in a system of graphite and uranium, but it took months of hard work to elicit an official request from the Government for him to do so. His mind moved incessantly, impelled by obsessive and prophetic anguish, and over a tremendous range. While working at his research, he worried about the possibility that the Germans might get control of the uranium supplies of the Congo. He thought of proceeding through Einstein, first to the Belgian Royal Family, and then to the State Department. He began to be convinced that a direct approach to the White House was necessary to gain support for the research. He was now working closely with his old friend, Professor Eugene Wigner, now a Nobel laureate. Through another old friend, a refugee economic journalist, he went to Dr. Alexander Sachs, a banker, who knew the President. A plan was worked out. Szilard wrote the letter, Einstein signed it, and in October 1939, Sachs read it to the President. In the memorandum accompanying the letter, Szilard reported that a chain reaction based on fusion by slow neutrons seemed almost a certainty and that if the chain reaction could be maintained by fast neutrons—which was less certain—very powerful bombs might be possible.

This was the beginning—but the Government moved very slowly and under the distrustful counsel of conventional minds, civilian and military. Szilard struggled constantly against complacency, respect for protocol, red tape, and indecision. He wrote a memorandum in September 1942, entitled *What's Wrong With Us*, blaming the failure to make an important decision on the late Arthur Compton's unwillingness to be involved in controversy and on the security restrictions imposed by the Army. The judicious authors of the official history of the Manhattan District Project say that for Szilard, "the new and unusual held no cause for hesitation." The work went on with disappointments and triumphs. From September 1942 onward, Szilard was insisting among his friends on the Project that they pay more attention to the political problems to which their work was bound to lead. In January 1944 he wrote to Dr. Vannevar Bush urging him to intensify the work on the bomb because unless nuclear weapons were used in the present war, the peoples of the world would not understand their cataclysmic power and so would not be willing to make the sacrifices required for international control. In March 1945, he wrote a long paper arguing that the vulnerability of the United States to nuclear attack rendered it necessary for them to seek international control. He argued that the United States Government should raise the matter with the Soviet leaders immediately after it had demonstrated the effectiveness of the bomb. He assumed no aggressive intentions on the part of the Soviet Government in the post-war situation but regarded a dangerous armaments race as inevitable if no system of international control were established.

Again he persuaded Einstein to present his views to the President, as he had done five-and-a-half years before, but this time there was no response. In May 1945, Szilard and Professor Bartky, the Chicago astronomer, went to the White House, but the President's secretary would not give them an audience with the President. Instead, he sent them, together with Professor Urey, to James Byrnes, who was about to become Secretary of State. Szilard handed Byrnes the memorandum he had sent to Roosevelt. The interview went badly; Byrnes had no understanding for Szilard's viewpoint or style of thought.

During this period, within the Metallurgical Laboratory an intense discussion, driven largely by Szilard but by no means entirely his creation, was going on. The Committee on Social and Political Implications was worriedly exploring the political aftermath of their work. Their worries had troubled the virtuous and conscientious Arthur Compton, who undertook to transmit their views to the Scientists' Panel of the Interim Committee. On June 11th, the Committee on Social and Political Implications completed its report. The main points were: the secret of constructing a bomb cannot be monopolized; an arms race will result; an arms race would be disadvantageous to the United States because of its urban concentrations of population and industry. The only possible solution, the report concluded, is international control and in order not to prejudice the possibility of establishing such control, the United States should avoid alienating world opinion. For this reason Japan should be warned and the power of the bomb should be demonstrated in an uninhabited area. (The use of the bomb against Japan if the warning failed was not precluded.)

Together with Arthur Compton, James Franck took the report to Washington in person. They could not see the Secretary of War but had instead to turn the report over to a very junior assistant.

Early in July, Szilard felt that the matter could not remain where it was. He drew up a petition to the President in which he stated that the country which set the precedent for using the bomb would have "to bear the responsibility of opening the door to an era of devastation on an unimaginable scale." It would weaken the position of the United States so much that any future arguments it might make for international control would be discounted. He asked the President to forbid the use of the atomic bomb unless the terms offered to Japan for surrender had been made public and Japan refused to accept them. Sixty-nine of his colleagues signed the petition and it was sent to Washington. It was without impact. The bomb was used. It was not long after this that he sought me out.

Leo Szilard was original and eccentric in nearly everything he did. He was original and eccentric in his Benthamite institutional contrivances, in his mode of life, in his political ideas and methods. Yet he never sought to cut a figure. Everything he did was the result of the direct confrontation of a particular situation by a powerful intelligence which shunned the commonplace, and by a warm and compassionate heart.

Leo Szilard was an affectionately solicitous and considerate busybody. He never gossiped maliciously. There was nothing vengeful about him. He was not rancorous against former Secretary Byrnes; he only felt that he was a narrow and ungenerous person, too small for the tasks which had fallen to him. He had no feelings of animosity against anyone—not even against General Leslie Groves. He had during the Manhattan Project often exasperated the General by his unceasing flood of original ideas, his interest in post-war political problems, his ownership of a number of patents for processes connected with the bomb, his criticism of the rigidity of the Army's security procedure, and by just being his own lively, playful, unbureaucratic self. But he never spoke angrily about Groves; on the contrary, he always spoke of the General with courtesy, but also without attempting to hide his view of the poor quality of his intelligence and imagination. He once showed me with characteristically sad amusement a copy of an unpublished interview which a *Fortune* correspondent had had with Groves, in which the General said that one of the causes of Szilard's difficult character was the fact that "he never played baseball as a youth"— in contrast with Oppenheimer, who had played tennis and therefore had (it seemed to Groves at that time) developed a more reasonable and co-operative character. Szilard's amusement was not just about General Groves but about himself, too, and the odd situation in which two such persons had to get on with each other.

There was no malice in Leo Szilard; there was some feeling of guilt about the bomb. Once, after Edward Teller had succeeded in his efforts to gain support for the construction of the hydrogen bomb, Szilard said in a sighing aside, "Now Teller will know what it is to feel guilty." This was the only time that Szilard ever expressed to me any feeling of guilt for his role in the production of the atomic bomb. Yet, repeatedly in the fantasies which he published in the *Bulletin of the Atomic Scientists* and *The Voice of the Dolphins,* one sensed that he wished that he could undo what he had done and that he could withdraw from the world which he had done so much to fashion. I had the impression, too, that this was one of the reasons why he would have nothing more to do with nuclear physics.

Michael Polanyi has said that before Einstein and Max Planck, German science had been the scene of frightful acrimony among its great figures, and this acrimony seeped downward into the lower strata of university life. These two noble geniuses changed the moral atmosphere of German science. Leo Szilard was one of the products of this new atmosphere. Although many people who came into contact with his many-sided and incessantly active mind and his gently pungent personality were exasperated by his unwillingness to be tied down to administration, by the swift flow of his imagination and by his perpetual and perhaps even slightly perverse capacity to see beyond nearly everything which anyone else or he himself had said and to think up something more subtle or more ingenious, I think that there would be universal acknowledgment among all who knew him that he was entirely free of evil spirit, of any concern at all for self-advancement, and of any pleasure in the discomfiture of others (with the possible and intermittent exception of the State Department).

He was a restless, homeless spirit. He owned no property, very few books. He had no "stake in the country" in the ordinary sense. Hotel lobbies, cafés, Jewish delicatessens, poor restaurants, and city pavements were the setting for the discussions which were his main form of communication—he said the age of books had passed. He told me some years ago in justifying his refusal to follow a regular academic career that he regarded himself as a "knight errant," who wanted to be free to go wherever important ideas in science or in the effort to protect the human race would take him. That was the way in which he had tried to live and the way in which he wished to spend his remaining years. Fortunately, the generous flexibility of the University of Chicago, the affection of his friends, and the modesty of his own needs enabled him to do so.

In his last years, together with his friend Eugene Wigner, he was awarded the *Atoms for Peace* Prize. A steady flow of manuscripts of an increasingly lucid eloquence, the activities of the "Conference of Scientists on World Affairs" (Pugwash) and his own open conspiracy which he called "The Council for a Livable World"—conducted, fittingly enough, from the Dupont-Plaza Hotel in Washington—and a renewal of his activity in molecular biology took the energy which was almost undiminished by his illness. He sought out Khrushchev in Moscow to learn his views and to expound to him his own view of the nature of a comprehensive settlement of the conflicts between the United States and the Soviet Union—and he tried to convey the results of this long conversation to President Kennedy. The genuine anguish which prompted all this action never left him, but it never clouded the rationality of his argument. After his entry into the status of Professor Emeritus at the University of Chicago, he took up an appointment at the Salk Institute in La Jolla, California, where he was full of schemes for new research. The establishment (in close association with Victor Weiskopf) of the European Molecular Biology Organisation was one of the last of his many institutional inventions.

His response to the nearly fatal cancer which he withstood with typical unwillingness to allow anyone or anything to dominate him—he decided on and supervised with success his own radiation therapy—was of a piece with the rest of his life. One almost felt that his resourceful contrariness and his unwillingness ever to accept defeat and to sink away into apathy would enable him ultimately to withstand death itself.

These are some of the impressions left on me by this extraordinarily sweet and calmly desperate genius.